THE ULTIMATE BOOK OF
BEERS

THE ULTIMATE BOOK OF
BEERS

WITH OVER 400 ALES, LAGERS, STOUTS &
CRAFT BEERS FROM AROUND THE WORLD

Mark Kelly &
Stuart Derrick

Bath · New York · Cologne · Melbourne · Delhi
Hong Kong · Shenzhen · Singapore · Amsterdam

This edition published by
Parragon Books Ltd in 2014

Parragon Books Ltd
Chartist House
15–17 Trim Street
Bath BA1 1HA, UK
www.parragon.com

Written by Mark Kelly
Feature text by Stuart Derrick
Designed by five-twentyfive.com
Project manager Tarda Davison-Aitkins
Production by Henry Sparrow

ISBN 978-1-4723-7077-8

Printed in China

Mark Kelly began writing about beer in the
north-east of England in 2012. He currently
lives in south-west London and works for craft
beer retail outlet and wholesale distributor,
The Beer Boutique – drinking and selling
beer for a living. He also writes a beer blog at
marksoutofbeer.blogspot.co.uk

Stuart Derrick is a journalist, writer and
editor with more than 20 years' experience
writing for books, magazines, newspapers
and organizations that need sparkling
copy. He has written on subjects as diverse
as travel, parenthood, corporate finance,
marketing, motivation and broadcasting. His
work has appeared in a range of publications
including *The Sunday Times*, *Mail on Sunday*,
the *Guardian*, *Campaign*, *Marketing* and
Growing Business.

INTRODUCTION

BEERS BY REGION

18 THE AMERICAS

60 EUROPE

SINGHA

TAKE FOUR GOOD THINGS

Beer is a simple product made primarily of just four ingredients: malted barley, hops, water and yeast. It is the interplay of these elements, combined with the skill of the brewer, that can create a multitude of different flavours, aromas and types of beer.

MALT

Barley is the cereal grain that is commonly used in brewing. To create malt, barley is soaked in water until it begins to sprout, converting its starch reserves into sugars. This process is then halted by drying the grain in a kiln, providing a source of sugar and soluble starch for fermentation. The temperature of the kiln produces many different types of malt – such as pale, caramel or crystal, dark and roasted malts – which are used to create specific beers. Malt contributes to the flavour, colour and mouthfeel of a beer.

While barley is the traditional grain for brewing, brewers may also use wheat, oats, rye or other grains. Large commercial breweries sometimes use rice or corn to reduce their costs.

HOPS

Prior to the 15th century, most ale was flavoured with a mixture of herbs, spices and berries, such as bog myrtle, yarrow, heather, juniper or caraway. There is evidence that Benedictine monks were using hops in brewing by the early 9th century, although their use did not become widespread in Europe until some centuries later.

Hops are the female flowers from the hop plant and there are more than 50 recognized varieties. In brewing, hops add a bitterness that balances the sweetness that remains in beer after the fermentation process ends. Some varieties are primarily used for their aroma. Hops also act as a preservative in the beer: unhopped beer goes off very quickly. Different hop varieties can be added at different stages of the brewing process, which influences the aroma, flavour and style of the beer. Popular varieties include Fuggles, Goldings, Cascade and Saaz.

WATER

Beer is more than 95 per cent water, so it is little surprise that water quality has historically been an important determinant of where brewers locate. The flavour of a beer is strongly influenced by its water. Areas such as Burton upon Trent in the UK and Plzen in the Czech Republic became great brewing capitals because the composition of their water was suited to particular types of beer – English bitter and pilsner lager in these examples. Nowadays, chemical analysis and tinkering allows brewers to replicate the type of water needed for a particular beer, and many famous beers are now brewed in completely different areas to where they originated.

YEAST

These single-cell organisms are the catalysts that make the whole magical process of beer-making work. In consuming the sugar released from the malt, they produce alcohol and carbon dioxide during fermentation. Yeast occurs naturally in the environment, but specific yeasts are cultured for particular beers.

Although malt and hops are the main flavour components in beer, the strain of yeast also imparts its own flavour, prized by brewers. The recently revived Truman's beers in London were created using the cryogenically stored original yeast.

Ale production uses top-fermenting yeast, which rises to the top of the fermentation vessel and works at warm temperatures. Lager yeast is bottom fermenting and works more slowly, at lower temperatures, to produce lager's distinctive clean taste.

Belgian lambic beers use wild yeasts in a process of spontaneous fermentation. Champagne yeast can be used in beer production, particularly for secondary fermentation of high-strength brews.

BEER – 9,000 YEARS IN THE MAKING

Today, around a billion of us worldwide drink more than 133 billion litres of beer a year, but beer has been with us a very long time. In fact, it is one of the oldest processed foodstuffs.

Historians and archaeologists have found evidence of beer being produced and drunk as far back as the Neolithic period. Early Mesopotamian civilizations recorded their enjoyment of beer, and around 5,000 years ago, the ancient Egyptians lauded beer in their hieroglyphs, giving it wonderful names such as 'Joybringer' and 'Heavenly'.

It is thought that the first beers were produced by accident, perhaps by bread falling into a vat of soaking grain. This germinated and fed airborne yeasts to produce alcohol. This early beer bore little resemblance to the crystal clear brews we sup today. It was more like an alcoholic soup and could be very strong at around 10% ABV. Ancient engravings show it being drunk through tubes to filter out the solids. A smooth drink it was not.

Throughout history, beer was often considered as safer to drink than water, because the brewing process involves boiling the water. Even children drank a weak 'small beer'.

In the Middle Ages, brewing was largely a home-based activity undertaken by women or 'ale wives'. They would indicate that there was a brew ready by putting an ale wand outside their house. As beer was drunk with every meal, there was a ready market locally.

Monks were also important early brewers, producing beer for their community and the people who lived locally, selling it to support their orders. As this brewing was on a larger scale, monks helped develop more rigorous processes for brewing, advancing knowledge and improving quality along the way. Today Trappist communities in Belgium, Austria and the Netherlands produce distinctive beers such as Chimay, Orval and Westmalle.

Early beer was flavoured with a mixture of herbs, known as a gruit, but over several centuries hops began to be cultivated for use in beer. For a time, hopped 'beer' and unhopped 'ale' existed side by side, but by the 15th century hops were the flavouring agent of choice throughout much of Europe.

The Industrial Revolution helped transform brewing from a cottage industry to big business. As millions of people moved to cities, often to work in hot, sweaty factories, demand for beer boomed. Large-scale urban breweries developed to serve this market, helped by advances in manufacture and transportation.

Throughout the 17th and 18th centuries, industrial advances helped improve the quality of beer further. Coked coal allowed cleaner, more controllable malt kilns to produce lighter malt that could be used in paler ales. Industrial glass production replaced ceramic drinking cups with transparent vessels, allowing drinkers to see the quality of their beer, and encouraging brewers to improve it.

In 1840 Anton Dreher isolated the lager yeast – *Saccharomyces pastorianus* – and brewed the first Vienna lager. In 1842 Josef Groll brewed the first pilsner lager, a clear golden beer in Pilsen, Bohemia. It was a style that soon swept

around the world, not least to the US, where European brewers brought their skills to serve this huge new market.

Throughout the 20th century, beer production became more commercial as improvements in transportation and storage allowed brewers to sell beer far from its place of origin. This helped create massive global brands such as Heineken, Carlsberg and Budweiser.

In recent years, these have been complemented by something of a return to the smaller-scale roots of many brewers with the birth and growth of microbreweries and the ongoing craft brewing revolution.

This is just the latest turn in the story of beer, a tale that continues to evolve.

HOW BEER IS BREWED

Whether it's a massive global beer brand like Carlsberg, or a craft ale 'curated' in somebody's garage, the process for brewing beer has not changed in its essentials for hundreds of years.

MALTING

The brewing process starts with barley, although other grains, including wheat, rye or rice, can be used. The barley is soaked and allowed to begin germinating for several days, with the grains being turned occasionally.

When a small leaf, or acrospire, is almost the length of the grain, the process is halted by heating and drying. This 'kilning' process is usually undertaken by hot air being blown through the malt. The length of time and the temperature of malting help determine the type of malt produced. Lighter malts, for paler beers, are malted for a shorter time, while dark malts receive longer in the kiln, at a higher temperature.

THE MASH

Next, the malt is cracked by being run through a malt mill. This eases the release of the sugars, which are converted from starch in the malt as it is mixed with hot water. This process, called mashing, takes place in a vessel known as the mash tun. The liquid is then drained off and recirculated through the grains to ensure that all of the sugars have been captured. This is known as lautering and sparging.

BOILING

This liquid goes into a brew kettle for 'the boil'. Hops are added throughout the boiling stage to give bitterness, aroma and flavour. The liquid is now known as wort and goes through a filtering process to remove any solids.

The wort is then cooled quickly using pipes filled with cold water. This is to get the wort to a temperature at which yeast can be added before atmospheric yeast can contaminate the liquid. The beer is now ready to ferment and is transferred to a fermenting tank.

FERMENTATION

Time is the next key ingredient. Each type of beer requires a specific period of fermentation during which the yeast can get to work. The yeast feeds on the sugary mixture, producing alcohol and carbon dioxide. Each brewer has its own strain of yeast, which helps to create the particular flavour of the beer.

There are two main types of yeast in brewing. Top-fermenting yeast is used to create ales. This yeast typically operates at temperatures of between 10°C and 25°C. The yeast rises to the top of the fermentation tank and is skimmed off. Bottom-fermenting yeast is used to produce lager. It operates at lower temperatures of 7°C to 15°C, so the fermentation process takes longer.

FILTERING AND CONDITIONING

When the yeast has almost completely devoured the sugars in the fermenting beer, it is ready to be conditioned. The beer may be filtered to enhance its clarity and stabilize its flavour. Not all beer is filtered: for example, wheat beers are often cloudy and some new craft beers present 'haziness' as a mark of authenticity.

Ales may be cask- or bottle-conditioned, which means that an additional, secondary fermentation takes place. A little extra yeast and sugar or wort may be added to aid this stage. This creates a natural carbonation in the beer. Cask-conditioned ales are served without additional carbonation.

For lagers to mature, the lagering process involves storing the beer at near freezing temperatures for anything from one to six months. Towards the end of the process the beer is filtered to create the crystal clarity drinkers prize. The beer is then bottled or kegged and is ready to serve.

WHAT ARE YOU DRINKING?

Just as it is said that the Inuit have hundreds of words for different types of snow, there are many different names for the beverages known collectively as beer.

Beer experts often struggle to assign a beer to a particular style as there is no universally agreed method of categorizing them. What the experts do agree on is that there are an awful lot of different styles. These are just some of the beer styles you may come across.

LAGER

The most common beer in the world is clear, golden lager. To 'lager' means to store in German, and relates to the long period of maturation at low temperatures that lagers traditionally undergo. Although lager sometimes seems a fairly homogenous product, there are many different varieties, notably in Germany, where you might enjoy a light 'helles', a dark *dunkel* or a strong 'bock' lager.

PORTER

This dark beer originated in 18th-century London, where it was a favourite drink of manual labourers, such as market porters. Made with dark malt, the beer declined in popularity as new, lighter ales became available, although it has experienced a resurgence in recent years.

STOUT

Made famous by Dublin brewer Arthur Guinness in the late 18th century, dry stout is the best-known version of this beer, originally named stout (meaning strong) porter. Other variants include the stronger imperial stout, oatmeal stout and sweet 'milk' stouts, such as Mackeson.

BITTER

The classic British 'session' ale is clear amber-coloured and hoppy. It is naturally conditioned with a secondary fermentation in the cask. An ordinary bitter might be around 3.5% ABV, with best bitter weighing in at about 4%. Stronger bitters are also available.

MILD

This lightly hopped ale was a favourite with manual and agricultural workers owing to its relatively low alcohol content. This meant they could drink pints of it to refresh themselves without getting too drunk. It is harder to find these days, although some craft brewers have revived the style.

WHEAT BEERS

Wheat beers have a refreshing taste and may be spiced with flavours such as cloves, coriander, or dried orange peel. Traditional in both Belgium and Germany, in the late 20th century the style was dying out until brands like Hoegaarden discovered a younger audience and revived the market. The beers are often cloudy, hence the term *witbier*, weisse, or 'white' beer, but they can also be clear or even dark *dunkelweizen*.

FRUIT BEERS

Fruit has been added to beer for hundreds of years, producing interesting and refreshing drinks. Among the most well-known are Belgian lambic beers, which commonly use cherries and raspberries – or occasionally peaches or other fruit. In recent years, other brewers have taken to adding a fruity component to their beer, often as a fruit extract.

BARLEY WINE

Particularly strong beers were given the name barley wine, perhaps to align their quality and potency with wine. Strengths of between 8 and 12% ABV are common. Some beer writers see barley wines as a subset of old ales, or winter warmers, which are typically stronger than standard brews.

GOLDEN ALES

These beers offer the depth of flavour of an ale with the clarity and refreshment of a lager. They are fruity, fragrant and clean-tasting, but some – especially the Belgian-style blonde ales – can be deceptively strong.

IPA

By the 18th century, English maltsters were able to regulate kilning to produce lighter malt to create new, paler ales. India Pale Ale is a highly hopped, strong pale ale originally brewed to withstand export from England to India by ship. The term IPA became widely used by brewers mimicking the style, and it is now brewed around the world.

THE GLOBAL DRINK

Wherever you go in the world the locals have their own beers; finding out what they like to drink can be one of the joys of travelling. This book will help you.

Beer is the world's most widely consumed alcoholic drink. Wherever you go around the globe you will find people brewing, selling and, of course, drinking beer.

Frank Zappa said: 'You can't be a real country unless you have a beer and an airline. It helps if you have some kind of a football team, or some nuclear weapons, but at the very least you need a beer.'

Mr Zappa was – presumably – joking, but with the exception of a few countries in the Middle East, most countries do have a beer they call their own.

Why is beer so popular?

Every drinker can list their own answers to that question, but there are probably three main reasons:

Beer helps us to relax at the end of a hard day. It makes us feel good as we socialize with our friends.

It's refreshing and tastes good. Is there any better drink on a warm summer's day than an ice-cold pilsner? And who would not gladden at the prospect of drinking a comforting glass of stout in front of a pub fire on a winter's evening?

Finally, there is so much variety to choose from. 'I'll have a beer!' may be the common response to 'What are you drinking?' but which one to choose? Will it be a pale ale, porter, stout, fruit beer, cream ale, steam beer, best bitter, or barley wine? The choice is bewilderingly vast.

One of the great things about being a beer drinker is that there is always something

new to try. Wherever you go in the world, the question 'What's yours?' remains a delightful invitation to ponder what's on offer locally. This book is here to help you make that all-important decision.

It's refreshing and tastes good. Is there any better drink on a warm summer's day than an ice-cold pilsner?

With more than 400 of the world's best beers described inside, it will no doubt reacquaint you with a few old favourites as well as providing suggestions for some new beers to drink. The past few years have been incredibly exciting from a beer drinker's perspective. The rise of craft brewing has brought a new generation of inventive brewers to the fore who are combining the best of traditional know-how with innovative tastes and ingredients.

Even a small bar may now contain an array of beers from around the world, something that would not have been the case a few years ago. Beer drinkers' thirst for new experiences is driving the process.

This book will help you discover beers throughout the world. It takes a geographical approach, covering all the continents and the main beer-producing countries and looking at some of the most popular and distinctive beers available. For each beer it gives an overview of what to look out for and some tips on how best to enjoy it.

But that's not all. We'll also be looking at the history of beer and beer producers, the culture that surrounds beer in different countries, foods that go well with beer, and many fascinating beer facts to share with your friends the next time you're in a bar.

So pour yourself a glass, put your feet up and enjoy.

THE AMERICAS

Whether they are from the North or South of the continent, the European roots of America's culture show in the drinks they enjoy.

From Alaska in the North, through Canada and the rest of the US to Central and South America, beer reigns supreme. In a land so large and diverse, the range of beers is similarly broad, encompassing everything from pale ales and lagers to stouts and barley wine.

The United States is the second biggest producer of beer in the world, after China. It has more than 2,000 breweries, and beers such as Budweiser, Coors, Schlitz, Michelob and Miller are famous throughout the US and sell in huge quantities.

Today the US is experiencing a new American revolution in brewing with craft and microbreweries producing some of the most exciting and innovative beers around. Companies like Dogfish Head, Sierra Nevada, Samuel Adams and a host of others are now dropped into conversation when drinkers discuss American beer, and the tone of the conversation is usually laudatory.

The United States is the second biggest producer of beer in the world, after China.

Even before the craft brewing explosion, there were examples of US beers that stood out from the sea of weak lager. North

America's distinctive beer styles include Pennsylvania porter, American IPA, American amber ale, and steam beer.

Names like August Krug, founder of the Schlitz company, Eberhard Anheuser and Adolphus Busch of Anheuser-Busch, and Frederick Pabst of the Pabst Brewing Company demonstrate the importance of German know-how in American brewing. It is no surprise that when lager yeast arrived in the US in the mid-19th century brewers began to produce the pilsners and bocks of their homeland. American brewers often had to adapt their recipes to use the different types of barley and hops available to them. They also included corn and rice in the grain mix – and this resulted in the creation of American lager. This found a thriving market in such German strongholds as Ohio, Indiana, Illinois, Michigan, Missouri and Nebraska. More than five and a half million German immigrants arrived in the US between 1820 and 1910.

The German influence is also felt in Central and South America, where pale lager-style beers predominate. Breweries such as Bohemia in Brazil, Quilmes in Argentina and Modelo in Mexico were established by immigrants from Germany and Austria, and their brands still remain to this day.

Cool, refreshing, golden lagers are understandably popular in the hotter countries of South America, but they are not the whole story. Dark beers such as Brazil's Eisenbahn Dunkel and Peru's Cusqueña Malta demonstrate a taste for other styles. Meanwhile stout has always been popular in the Caribbean, where strong brews like Dragon Stout and Royal Extra Stout are a mainstay of the bar scene in Jamaica and Trinidad.

South America has not been immune to the growth in craft brewing. Inspired by the US, microbreweries, or *cervecerías*, are also opening up in most Central and South American nations. Antares in Argentina and DaDoBier in Brazil are just two of the names that have emerged, but there are many more.

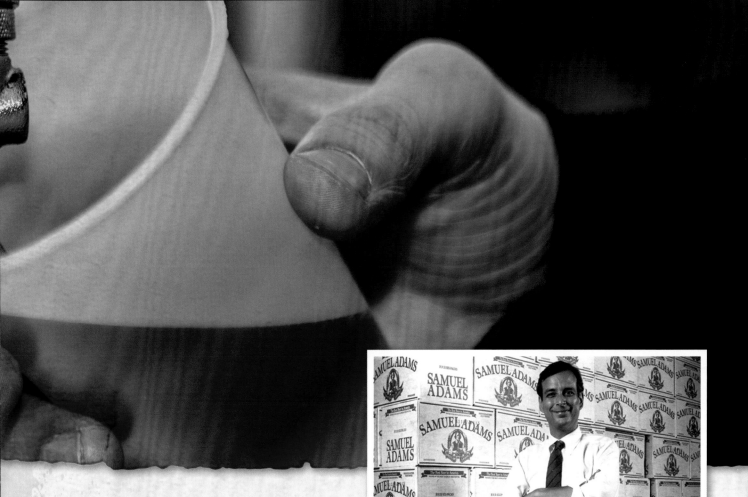

Inspired by the United States, microbreweries are opening up in most Central and South American nations.

To encourage this new breed of brewers, the first annual South Beer Cup was held in Buenos Aires, Argentina, in 2011. The competition aims to give those in South America the same sort of platform that their northern counterparts have enjoyed for some time. It provides a place to showcase what's new in South American brewing, share best practice and to allow some good-natured competition to emerge.

For the first competition, there were 280 beers entered in 20 categories, from 72 breweries, representing Argentina, Brazil, Chile and Uruguay. More than 40 medals were awarded.

The event continues to grow, as does the status of craft brewing, although it remains some way behind the US, which continues to

blaze a trail. Such is the vibrancy of the US scene that its brewers are now often cited as an influence on a new breed of European brewers, who are excited by the experimentalism and dynamism of the US.

Just as Britain took American blues and rock 'n' roll, and tweaked it to make it their own, so American brewers are doing something similar with beer.

And it is increasingly big business. Jim Koch (pictured), the creator of Samuel Adams, one of the original US craft beers, was recently listed in the Bloomberg Billionaires Index. In less than 30 years Sam Adams has grown from being a homebrew to become the largest US-owned brewery.

BEER: REBORN IN THE USA

Since the arrival of the first immigrants, beer has been a dynamic part of the American story. Virginia colonists were brewing ale from corn by 1587, before the first imports of beer arrived from England.

Fast forward to the mid-19th century and German lager started to take over from English-style ales and porters. However, as time went on, brewers such as Adolphus Busch noticed that Americans found all-malt beer too heavy. He set out to produce a lighter beer and experimented with corn and rice, eventually producing Budweiser. It is often assumed that using other ingredients was aimed at reducing costs. However, at the time Busch started using rice to produce his beer, it actually cost more.

As tastes have evolved, US drinkers now look for more character in their beer and new American brewers have started to produce beers that meet this demand. One of the best examples is American pale ale, a highly hopped derivative of India Pale Ale (IPA). American pale ale, using distinctive American hops, is now recognized as a style in its own right and is copied from Britain to Brazil.

Alaskan Amber

The Alaskan Brewing Company's flagship beer has been on every beer drinker's must-try list since it was voted Best Beer in the Nation in 1988. Alaskan Amber is based on a classic recipe for a beer the Alaskan gold miners used to drink around the turn of the 20th century. It's an Alt (old) style beer, a style that originated in Germany, using ale yeasts that ferment slowly and at colder temperatures than most ales.

Tasting notes: Heavy malt aroma, rich caramel taste with hints of soft peachy fruit. Try it with smoked salmon.
* ★ **Country:** USA ★ **Brewer:** Alaskan Brewing Co.
* ★ **Style:** Altbier ★ **Appearance:** Amber
* ★ **Alcohol:** 5.3% ★ **Serving temp:** 8–12°C

Anchor Old Foghorn Barley Wine

San Francisco's Anchor brewery was founded in the late 19th century and became famous for its California common beer or, as it is also known, steam beer. Old Foghorn is Anchor's take on classic British barley wine. Rich in sugars from two types of malt, the brewers balance out all that sweetness with bitterness and aroma from a mountain of Cascade hops – which lend their distinctive citrus aroma to many American beers.

Tasting notes: Strong caramel aroma and a long, dry, bitter finish. Try it with aged blue cheese or slow-cooked beef stew.
* ★ **Country:** USA ★ **Brewer:** Anchor Brewing Co.
* ★ **Style:** Barley wine ★ **Appearance:** Burnt copper
* ★ **Alcohol:** 8.8% ★ **Serving temp:** 8–13°C

🇺🇸 Anderson Valley Boont Amber Ale

The story of Anderson Valley brewery is a quintessentially American one. Starting in 1987 with a ten-barrel brewhouse beneath the bustling Buckhorn Saloon in Boonville, California, production quickly expanded and as of 2011 was 40,000 barrels per year. The Boont Amber Ale is typical of its style. A blend of malts that includes the darker crystal and the slightly paler two-row combine to give a brilliant copper appearance. Brewed with a blend of four hop varieties, the finished product is well balanced and subtly complex, with an easygoing, light bitter finish.

Tasting notes: Toffee, butterscotch and caramel flavours. One to drink alongside almost any meal.
★ **Country:** USA ★ **Brewer:** Anderson Valley Brewing Co.
★ **Style:** Amber ★ **Appearance:** Amber ale
★ **Alcohol:** 5.8% ★ **Serving temp:** 8–12°C

🇺🇸 Beer Valley Leafer Madness

Oregon's brewing scene is one of the most prolific in the world, with around 150 brewing companies. Such a hive of activity is bound to produce some outstanding beers and Leafer Madness by the Beer Valley Brewery is definitely one of them. A double or imperial pale ale – the generous quota of bittering hops help make this one of the few beers in the world that has 100 IBUs (International Bittering Units).

Tasting notes: Mouth-puckering bitterness, huge grapefruit citrus notes and probably best enjoyed without food.
★ **Country:** USA
★ **Brewer:** Beer Valley Brewing Co.
★ **Style:** Imperial IPA
★ **Appearance:** Hazy orange
★ **Alcohol:** 9% ★ **Serving temp:** 12–14°C

🇺🇸 Bell's Amber Ale

The kilning of malt is a very subtle part of the brewing process: just a few degrees' variation in temperature can produce very different flavours. Bell's Amber Ale, brewed in Michigan, is made with Munich malt – a rich variety that is most notably used in Oktoberfest beers in Germany. The higher kiln temperature imparts an intense, sweet flavour that is balanced out by floral and citrus hops to make a classic American amber ale.

Tasting notes: Intense, toasted flavours; great with a wide variety of food. Pure liquid bread.
★ **Country:** USA
★ **Brewer:** Bell's Brewery
★ **Style:** Amber ale
★ **Appearance:** Amber
★ **Alcohol:** 5.8%
★ **Serving temp:** 8–12°C

Big Sky Brewing Moose Drool Brown Ale

The ingredients used in this beer bring together the best from both sides of the Pond. It uses four types of malt and four hop varieties – including the famous Kent Goldings variety common in the UK's real ale scene. Moose Drool is easygoing and well balanced, and the lower alpha acids in the UK hops allow more sweetness to come through.

Tasting notes: Chocolate, light orange and caramel aromas with a nutty malt finish. Try with hearty foods like smoked sausage.
* **Country:** USA
* **Brewer:** Big Sky Brewing Co.
* **Style:** Brown ale
* **Appearance:** Deep brown
* **Alcohol:** 5.1%
* **Serving temp:** 10–12°C

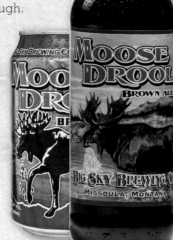

Brooklyn Lager

Since the late 1980s the Brooklyn Brewery has been at the forefront of the resurgence in American craft brewing. This Vienna-style lager was for a while the only craft lager in a marketplace dominated by big business. Production is now largely based at company headquarters in trendy Williamsburg. Brewing is overseen by Garrett Oliver – an aficionado of beer and food pairing – who has been Brooklyn's brewmaster since 1994. Brooklyn Lager is today an iconic product, a symbol of New York and a go-to beer for beer drinkers around the world.

Tasting notes: Firm, malty base provides a robust backdrop for floral, fragrant hops. Goes with anything you can find in your fridge.
* **Country:** USA * **Brewer:** Brooklyn Brewery
* **Style:** Vienna lager * **Appearance:** Dark amber
* **Alcohol:** 5.2% * **Serving temp:** 4–7°C

Budweiser

Known affectionately as Bud, Budweiser has claimed it is the 'King of Beers' since it became a world bestseller in the 1950s. This pale lager is brewed using up to 30% rice along with the barley malt to make it more cost-effective; this results in an incredibly 'lite' taste that needs to be drunk ice cold. Massive sales have helped Anheuser-Busch InBev become the world's largest brewing company, with more than 25% of market share worldwide.

Tasting notes: Very light aroma of grain and a carbonated texture in the mouth, with very little bitterness.
* **Country:** USA * **Brewer:** AB InBev
* **Style:** Pale lager * **Appearance:** Pale yellow
* **Alcohol:** 4.8% * **Serving temp:** 1–2°C

Coors Light

People in the late 1970s wanted a low-calorie beer to avoid the threat of beer belly. Coors Light was born during this time and by 1994 was one of a small number of pale lagers accounting for 35% of all beer sold in the USA. Brewed in Golden, Colorado, much is made of its use of Rocky Mountain water, where Adolph Coors founded his brewery in 1873. However, as with many North American mass-market beers, cheaper grains are used instead of some of the barley malt to keep costs low.

Tasting notes: Light corn sweetness and a thin texture that is best served ice cold.
* **Country:** USA * **Brewer:** Molson Coors
* **Style:** Pale lager * **Appearance:** Pale yellow
* **Alcohol:** 4.2% * **Serving temp:** 1–2°C

Dogfish Head
90 Minute Imperial IPA

One of the most important parts of any brewing process is the boil. This is the stage where hops are added for aroma, bitterness and preservation, and usually lasts one hour. Dogfish Head produces 60, 90 and 120 minute IPAs with varying levels of bitterness. The 90 minute version is a 9% ABV double IPA with extra malt to balance out the bitterness imparted by the extremely high level of hops.

Tasting notes: Sweet malt and pungent hops combine to create candied alcohol fruitcake-like flavours. Barbecue pulled pork would match well.
* **Country:** USA
* **Brewer:** Dogfish Head Brewery
* **Style:** Imperial IPA
* **Appearance:** Golden/orange
* **Alcohol:** 9%
* **Serving temp:** 8–12°C

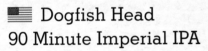

DID YOU KNOW?

President George Washington certainly appreciated beer – he had his own brewhouse in the grounds of his house at Mount Vernon, Virginia, and insisted that the soldiers in his Continental Army be permitted a quart of beer in their daily rations.

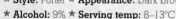 ## Duck-Rabbit
Baltic Porter

Beer specialists don't come with weirder names (or logos) than this! The Duck-Rabbit brewery in North Carolina brews specializes in dark beers, from amber ale to milk stout. There are no hoppy pale ales here. Duck-Rabbit's Porter and Baltic Porter are very much 21st-century American beers, only distantly related to the porters of 18th-century London.

Tasting notes: Earthy, nutty aromas with hints of spice and smoke. Medium bodied and easy to drink.
* **Country:** USA * **Brewer:** Duck-Rabbit Brewery
* **Style:** Porter * **Appearance:** Dark brown
* **Alcohol:** 9% * **Serving temp:** 8–13°C

El Toro Negro
Oatmeal Stout

Oats have a unique effect on beer. When added to the usual barley malts they give the beer a silky-smooth mouthfeel and viscous texture. When combined with darker, chocolatey malts, as in this Oatmeal Stout, the result is a fantastic chocolate milkshake effect with hints of vanilla and some coffee in the finish. A really comforting taste that's especially nice when winter starts to close in.

Tasting notes: Creamy chocolate, roasted coffee and light vanilla all blended in a sweet and subtle arrangement.
* **Country:** USA * **Brewer:** El Toro Brewing Co.
* **Style:** Stout * **Appearance:** Pitch black
* **Alcohol:** 5.5% * **Serving temp:** 10–14°C

THE WORLD BEER CUP

While the eyes of football-loving nations will be on the FIFA World Cup in Brazil in 2014, those of America's craft brewers will be fixed on Denver, Colorado, the location of the tenth World Beer Cup.

The competition was established in 1996 by the US Brewers Association, which promotes independent American brewers. The event is held every two years and claims to be the most prestigious beer competition in the world.

A total of 94 distinct styles are being judged in 2014, including such delights as pumpkin beer, chocolate beer, Belgian sour ale and American stout. Judges taste the beers blind and assess them according to how well they perform against the descriptions of each particular style.

Although the competition is open to brewers from around the globe, it is dominated by American entries. In 2012, 3,921 beers from 799 breweries in 54 countries were judged. US breweries swept up 208 awards, with Germany next in the pecking order with just 23. California and Colorado were the most productive states, with 524 and 274 entries respectively. California won 55 awards to Colorado's 27.

The competition also picks the best breweries. In 2012, Germany's Brauerei Michael Plank was named best small brewery, and Firestone Walker Brewing Company of Paso Robles, California, picked up the award for a medium-sized brewery. AB InBev was named best large brewing company.

Firestone Walker Double Barrel Ale

Using traditional methods of ageing dating back to the first IPAs made in Burton on Trent in the UK, Firestone Walker has based its flagship beer not on the modern, boldly hopped beers so popular in America, but on a style popular in Britain in the late 19th century. Rather than using stainless steel tanks, the beer is aged in oak barrels, which introduce slightly smokier, charred wood and vanilla flavours to produce a classic British-style pale ale.

Tasting notes: Toasted bread, caramel, wood and vanilla combine with a slight spice in the finish.
✶ **Country:** USA ✶ **Brewer:** Firestone Walker Brewing Co.
✶ **Style:** Premium pale ale ✶ **Appearance:** Dark amber
✶ **Alcohol:** 5% ✶ **Serving temp:** 8–12°C

DID YOU KNOW?

Pabst brewery produced the first six-pack of beer in the 1940s, after studies found that six cans were the ideal weight for the average housewife to carry home from the store.

Flying Dog Raging Bitch

Flying Dog is one of America's best-loved microbrewers. Adorned with the distinctive artwork of legendary British-born illustrator Ralph Steadman, its Raging Bitch Belgian IPA is perhaps not the ideal gift for your wife on Valentine's Day. It is, however, well worth a go on other occasions. The standout factor is the yeast – a Belgian strain known as Diablo that imparts a bubble gum and banana flavour combination often found in German wheat beers. Here it floats on a backdrop of hoppy American IPA to astounding effect, producing a unique beer.

Tasting notes: Banana, bubble gum and toffee. Like Banoffee pie in a bottle.
✶ **Country:** USA ✶ **Brewer:** Flying Dog Brew Co.
✶ **Style:** Belgian IPA ✶ **Appearance:** Dark amber
✶ **Alcohol:** 8.3% ✶ **Serving temp:** 8–12°C

Founders All Day IPA

Many American craft beers (especially IPAs) come with a high alcohol content that gets you drunk after one or two bottles. This beer is an exception, designed to have maximum flavour while keeping the ABV low enough to drink, well… all day! At only 4.7%, Founders has worked something of a miracle by creating a quaffable but delightful little flavour bomb that doesn't scare away the casual drinking crowd. A truly great beer.

Tasting notes: Lots of peach and grapefruit hop aromas in the nose and in the taste, well matched by sweet, doughy malts.
* **Country:** USA
* **Brewer:** Founders Brewing Co.
* **Style:** IPA
* **Appearance:** Golden yellow
* **Alcohol:** 4.7%
* **Serving temp:** 4–7°C

Goose Island IPA

It seems like the Goose Island brewery from Chicago has been delighting us with its IPA for ever. This was one of the first hoppy IPAs to become widely available. Goose Island is now owned by global brewing group AB InBev. Happily the recipe has not changed one bit since the buyout and hopefully it never will. A perfect balance of sweet, sour and bitter.

Tasting notes: Salted caramel popcorn, lovely floral hops with a hint of spice and a giant whiff of citrus in the nose.
* **Country:** USA
* **Brewer:** Goose Island Beer Co.
* **Style:** IPA
* **Appearance:** Hazy amber
* **Alcohol:** 5.9%
* **Serving temp:** 4–7°C

Grand Teton Bitch Creek ESB

In the Targhee National Forest in Idaho runs a restless vein of water popular with fishermen and kayakers for its beauty and character. This famous landmark gives its name to one of the most decorated beers in the USA. Grand Teton's Bitch Creek has won 12 gold medals at brewing awards throughout the country and is – so locals will tell you – as feisty and complex as its namesake. A rich American brown ale made with a blend of five malts for a very robust flavour and a satisfying baseline of rich caramels topped off with a spicy, pine resin hop finish.

Tasting notes: Caramel, nuts, orange and a slightly spicy finish. Try it with barbecued meats or aged Gouda cheese.
* **Country:** USA **Brewer:** Grand Teton Brewing
* **Style:** Brown ale **Appearance:** Brown
* **Alcohol:** 6.5% **Serving temp:** 10–12°C

Lagunitas IPA

Lagunitas IPA was first brewed in 1995 as a sessionable IPA that you could knock back for hours without wearying of being attacked by hops. More of a malt-forward, almost English-style IPA, Lagunitas proved so popular after its first batch that the brewery decided to make it an all-year-round brew, and now you can find it throughout America at the top of any craft beer list.

Tasting notes: Big toffee flavours, sweet, with a hoppy aroma that never overpowers you. Perfect with chargrilled meat.
* **Country:** USA
* **Brewer:** Lagunitas Brewing Co.
* **Style:** IPA
* **Appearance:** Amber
* **Alcohol:** 6.2%
* **Serving temp:** 4–7°C

Left Hand Brewing Milk Stout

Milk stouts are traditionally said to have certain health benefits. Sadly this isn't exactly true! They just include milk sugar (lactose) – a type of sugar that can't be fermented and therefore stays in the beer. Left Hand Brewing produces a fantastic version at its Colorado brewery. Like adding cream to your coffee, it might make you pile on a pound or two, but once you've tried it you won't go back to semi-skimmed milk any time soon.

Tasting notes: Sweet, creamy with big hints of chocolate and coffee. Like a boozy chocolate milkshake.
* **Country:** USA
* **Brewer:** Left Hand Brewing Co.
* **Style:** Milk stout
* **Appearance:** Black
* **Alcohol:** 6%
* **Serving temp:** 7–12°C

Magic Hat #9

Magic Hat's famous 'Not Quite Pale Ale' is almost impossible to describe, because there's never been anything quite like it. Put your scepticism aside until you try it though. The reason behind the #9 name is clouded in secrecy as part of the brewing sorcerers' image the Magic Hat brewery cultivates. It is a brewer with bags of personality and a wide range of impressive beers that always have that little special something.

Tasting notes: Perfume, light malt and a hint of citrus fruits in the nose are paired with sweet peach flavours on the tongue.
* **Country:** USA
* **Brewer:** Magic Hat Brewing Co.
* **Style:** Pale ale
* **Appearance:** Medium orange
* **Alcohol:** 5.1%
* **Serving temp:** 4–7°C

Maui CoCoNut PorTeR

Why the arbitrary capitalization in the name? Nobody knows. Apparently owner Garrett Marrero was 'just being weird one day'. Thankfully, the fairly weird idea of combining coconut and porter makes a whole lot of sense when tasted. Made with a blend of six different roasted malts, those classic American flavours of Cascade and Columbus hops and a whole heap of hand-toasted coconut, the weirdness becomes wonderful. The coconut flavour is never overpowering but remains subtly in the background, making this porter into something special. It is sold in Maui's kookily designed cans to keep it extra fresh.

Tasting notes: Dusty coconut and chocolate aroma, coffee and sweetness on the palate with more of that coconut subtly coming through at the end.
★ **Country:** USA ★ **Brewer:** Maui Brewing Co.
★ **Style:** Porter ★ **Appearance:** Black
★ **Alcohol:** 6% ★ **Serving temp:** 7–12°C

DID YOU KNOW?

President Jimmy Carter signed the bill to legalize homebrewing in 1978, but Americans have been brewing ever since English settlers reached the New World and they didn't stop – even during Prohibition!

Mendocino Black Hawk Stout

Technically this is an Irish-style dry stout, and the most important ingriedient is the dark roasted grain, which gives the matt black colour you'd expect in a pint of Guinness, the classic Irish dry stout. A fantastic example of traditional Irish-style beer from a modern American brewer.

Tasting notes: Dry roasted bitterness that balances the sweet dark malts. Great served with an Irish stew.
★ **Country:** USA
★ **Brewer:** Mendocino Brewing Co.
★ **Style:** Dry stout
★ **Appearance:** Black
★ **Alcohol:** 5.2%
★ **Serving temp:** 10–14°C

WHEN THE TAPS RAN DRY

The United States is the world's second greatest manufacturer of beer by volumes, but for a 13-year period in the early part of the 20th century, it was impossible to buy a beer legally in any of its states.

The US was not the only country to ban alcohol, but it was the largest and its version of Prohibition was one of the most far-reaching. Prior to the introduction of the 18th Amendment in January 1920, the US produced almost 60 million barrels of beer from more than 1,300 breweries.

While some brewers decided to sell up, others, such as Schlitz, Anheuser-Busch, Blatz and Pabst, switched production to malt beverages. This 'near beer' had a low alcoholic content of less than 0.5 per cent. Although it was not hugely popular, it kept brewing skills alive.

Another sideline was malt syrup. Advertised for use in baking, it was also a key ingredient for home brewers.

THE AMERICAN ISSUE
A Saloonless Nation and a Stainless Flag
WESTERVILLE, OHIO, JANUARY 25, 1919

Volume XXVI   Number 6

U.S. IS VOTED DRY
36th STATE RATIFIES DRY AMENDMENT JAN. 16

Nebraska Noses Out Missouri for Honor of Completing Job of Writing Dry Act Into the Constitution; Wyoming, Wisconsin and Minnesota Right on Their Heels

JANUARY 16, 1919, MOMENTOUS DAY IN WORLD'S HISTORY

The Volstead Act, which introduced Prohibition, contained allowances for the production of 'medicinal beer'. Companies that were granted a licence, like Anheuser-Busch, were in a better competitive position to sell this weak 3.2% ABV beer when Prohibition ended in December 1933.

Of course Prohibition failed, and led to a demand for illegal alcohol. Americans continued to drink illegally and while brewers suffered, bootleggers such as Al Capone made an estimated $1 billion tax free during the period.

Michelob Original Lager

First brewed in 1896 by the American godfather of brewing (for better or worse) Adolphus Busch, Michelob is pitched as a beer for the more discerning drinker. Named after a Czech brewer from Saaz (a region famous for its hops), Michelob is similar to many other pale lagers on the US market.

Tasting notes: Some light malt notes, hints of corn and light hints of earthy hop flavour.
* **Country:** USA
* **Brewer:** AB InBev
* **Style:** Pale lager
* **Appearance:** Clear yellow
* **Alcohol:** 5%
* **Serving temp:** 1–2°C

🇺🇸 Miller Lite

One of many beers from the US focusing on getting the calorie content down to avoid the dreaded beer belly, Miller Lite has only 96 calories per bottle. Originally called Gablinger's Diet Beer in 1967, this was the first beer of its kind in the US and quickly became market leader until Anheuser-Busch brought out Bud Light in the early 1980s – eventually usurping the majority share in the light beer market in 1994.

Tasting notes: Very light on the malt flavour and extremely easy to drink. Refreshing, crisp and good in hot weather.
* **Country:** USA
* **Brewer:** Miller Coors
* **Style:** Pale lager
* **Appearance:** Clear yellow
* **Alcohol:** 4.2% * **Serving temp:** 1–2°C

🇺🇸 Molson Coors Blue Moon

It would be wrong to talk about Blue Moon without mentioning the man who revived this style of beer in the 1960s. Pierre Celis put the Belgian village of Hoegaarden on the map when he began brewing Belgian *witbier* to an original recipe using wheat, orange and coriander. Blue Moon is a direct descendant, made with malted wheat and small quantities of oats for a smooth texture and mouthfeel.

Tasting notes: Zesty orange, mildly soapy with an almost celery-like finish. Classic with steamed mussels and fries.
* **Country:** USA
* **Brewer:** Molson Coors
* **Style:** Witbier * **Appearance:** Hazy yellow
* **Alcohol:** 5.4% * **Serving temp:** 4–7°C

🇺🇸 Odell Cutthroat Porter

High up in the Rocky Mountains there lives a freshwater fish named the Cutthroat trout. A favourite among anglers, it gives its name to Odell's London-inspired porter, brewed in Fort Collins, Colorado. A relatively easygoing beer for its style, a lightweight body belies its big flavour. This is one of Odell's regular beers and it has won various awards on both sides of the Atlantic.

Tasting notes: Slightly salty, savoury malt flavours work well with hints of coffee and chocolate.
* **Country:** USA * **Brewer:** Odell Brewing Co.
* **Style:** Porter * **Appearance:** Clear black
* **Alcohol:** 4.8% * **Serving temp:** 5–10°C

DID YOU KNOW?

In August 1997 a homebrewing club from Colorado scaled new heights in beer brewing when it brewed a batch of barley wine at 14,333ft on the summit of Mt Elbert (the highest peak in Colorado).

🇺🇸 Pabst Blue Ribbon

Pabst beer apparently won America's Best at the World's Columbian Exposition in Chicago in 1893. Since then, it has been known as Pabst Blue Ribbon, although the beer never actually won a blue ribbon. In fact, it's unclear whether it won any awards at all that year, with many official accounts claiming that only bronze medals were awarded. What is clear though is that this has established itself as one of America's go-to beers. Usually at the top of the list in any bar and attractively priced, PBR has had a surge in sales since it became popular among hipsters, artists and musicians.

Tasting notes: Plenty of toffee-like malt with a very mellow and refreshing aftertaste. To be drunk alongside live music!
* **Country:** USA
* **Brewer:** Pabst Brewing Co.
* **Style:** Pale lager
* **Appearance:** Pale yellow
* **Alcohol:** 5%
* **Serving temp:** 2–5°C

Pelican Imperial Pelican Ale

Adorned with a sketch of Phil the Pelican (the brewery mascot), Pelican's Imperial Pelican Ale is actually India Pale Ale, made with North America's trademark Cascade and Centennial hops for citrus aroma, and pale and caramel malts for malty sweetness. The Pelican's oceanfront pub and brewery in Pacific City, Oregon, is famous for fine cuisine from its executive chef, Ged Aydelott, and the fine beer of brewmaster Darron Welch. A must-visit attraction for any beer lover.

Tasting notes: Massive toffee and caramel in the nose coupled with fruity, citrus hops.
* **Country:** USA
* **Brewer:** Pelican Pub and Brewery
* **Style:** Imperial IPA
* **Appearance:** Light amber
* **Alcohol:** 8%
* **Serving temp:** 4–7°C

DID YOU KNOW?

John Harvard (1607–38), was born in Southwark, London. He emigrated to New England and when he died he left a large sum of money that helped found Harvard University. Harvard had its own brewhouse and five beer halls in 1674.

Rogue Dead Guy Ale

Brewers are often proud of their yeast and the brewers at Rogue are no exception. Its Pacman yeast is so named due to its extremely voracious nature – it eats a wide variety of sugars for a long time – making it perfect in the brewing of this German-style Helles (pale) lager. Using traditional Saaz and Perle hops from Europe together with four caramelized malts, Dead Guy Ale has all the bready character of a conventional Helles lager, but the brewers at Rogue have given it a slightly higher hop content for a fuller flavour.

Tasting notes: Grains, toasted bread and alcohol all contribute to the overall flavour of this beer, with a dry hoppy finish.
* **Country:** USA ✷ **Brewer:** Rogue Ales ✷ **Style:** Helles lager
* **Appearance:** Amber ✷ **Alcohol:** 6.6% ✷ **Serving temp:** 4–7°C

Sierra Nevada Pale Ale

Hugely popular in the United States, Sierra Nevada Pale Ale has also found favour with drinkers all over the world. This timeless interpretation of American pale ale has become something of a benchmark beer. As is common in many American pale ales, Sierra Nevada is dry-hopped with a generous helping of Cascade hops after the initial bittering hops have done their job, using the brewery's patented hop torpedo to impart all the fruity, citrus aromas of the plant without adding any further bitterness. The result is a nice balance of citrus fruits and bitter hops along with a helping of caramel flavours from the malts.

Tasting notes: Floral orange blossom on the nose, with a long, lingering bitter finish. Great with any spicy curry.
* **Country:** USA
* **Brewer:** Sierra Nevada Brewing Co.
* **Style:** Pale ale
* **Appearance:** Amber
* **Alcohol:** 5.6%
* **Serving temp:** 4–7°C

Ska Modus Hoperandi

There's nothing quite like a good beer-related pun. Ska Brewing's Modus Hoperandi is mainly found in cans – which some people might regard as inferior. In reality, though, cans keep a tighter seal so the beer stays fresher as well as cooling faster! Which is a good thing, as you'll want to drink this 6.8% American-style IPA as fresh and as cool as possible. One of the best American IPAs around.

Tasting notes: A pine-infused mix of grapefruit, citrus and sweet hearty malts. Perfect alongside a Thai curry. Even better with spicy kebabs.
* **Country:** USA
* **Brewer:** SKA Brewing
* **Style:** IPA
* **Appearance:** Deep orange
* **Alcohol:** 6.8%
* **Serving temp:** 4–7°C

🇺🇸 Samuel Adams Boston Lager

Samuel Adams Boston Lager is brewed from an old family recipe dating back to the 1870s. It was one of the leading lights in the American craft brewing revolution in the 1980s. Now a hugely recognizable brand that hasn't compromised on flavour and brewing know-how to cut costs, Sam Adams is an American institution and a six-pack would be a welcome sight in any beer-drinker's fridge. Best consumed while watching your favourite sports team.

Tasting notes: Toasty malt, toffee and caramel sweetness is balanced with refined hops.
★ **Country:** USA
★ **Brewer:** Samuel Adams Brewing
★ **Style:** Amber lager
★ **Appearance:** Amber
★ **Alcohol:** 4.9%
★ **Serving temp:** 4–7°C

SAMUEL ADAMS AND THE REBIRTH OF AMERICAN BREWING

It may seem strange for the biggest American-owned brewery in the US to be an inspiration to microbreweries, but Samuel Adams' backstory is the kind of tale that makes beer geeks want to quit their day jobs. So it's hardly surprising to learn that's exactly what founder Jim Koch did in 1984. A management consultant with a Harvard degree, he decided to pack it all in to brew beer using a family recipe.

At that time the American industry was dominated by mass-produced beers. Teaming up with a couple of Harvard buddies, Koch brewed his first batch of Samuel Adams Boston Lager in his kitchen and sold it bar to bar in Boston.

In its first year Boston Lager was voted 'Best Beer in America' and sales grew rapidly to the point where the company now produces more than two million barrels a year.

Samuel Adams has consistently produced a range of challenging and interesting beers, seeking to raise standards in American brewing.

Koch acts as a mentor to new brewers, providing advice and financial aid. His Longshot competition invites home brewers to have a beer brewed by Samuel Adams, and during the hops shortage of 2008, the brewery shared 20,000 pounds of hops with 108 craft brewers who risked going out of business.

WORKING UP A STEAM

California is associated with one of America's unique beer styles – steam beer. In fact, some people regard it as America's only native beer style.

When James Marshall found gold at Sutter's Mill, California, in 1848 it led to a rush of 300,000 gold seekers descending on the state by the following year. These '49ers' came in search of fortune; they also needed to be fed and watered.

Prospecting is thirsty work, so brewers also arrived in the Golden State on the lookout for a new market. At the time, lager was beginning to take over American brewing, so it is thought that some brewers arrived with lager yeast. However, at this point they encountered a problem.

Lager requires a period of fermenting at very low temperatures. In the hot Californian climate, this was not possible. There was no refrigeration and the nearest source of ice that could have been used to create a cooler fermenting environment was too far away to collect.

Brewers had to improvise, so they brewed with the lager yeast at ale temperatures, resulting in a hybrid beer style that combined elements of both lager and ale. Open fermenting tanks were used to cool the beer down. Because the fermenting tanks were sometimes on the roofs of buildings, the cooling beer would give off a steam in the mornings, which may be one source of the name 'steam beer'.

Another possibility is that it derives from a traditional German beer called Dampfbier, which literally means steam beer. Many American brewers were of German descent; they may have known that Dampfbier was also fermented at high temperatures and adapted the recipe.

After primary fermentation, the beer was transferred to kegs with live beer added, so that the beer continued to ferment. Before it could be poured the barrel had to be vented to remove excess carbonation. The resulting explosive release, not unlike a steam train's brakes, may be a further explanation for the name.

Like German steam beer, the American version was viewed as a rough-and-ready drink for working men; it was sometimes known as 'California common'.

Many different brewers produced the beer, which used local ingredients to keep costs down. It was generally an amber beer, often compared to Munich beer. Caramel malt, roast malt and caramelized sugar were used in combination to produce the distinctive colour.

Brewers had to improvise, so they brewed with the lager yeast at ale temperatures, resulting in a hybrid beer style that combined elements of both lager and ale.

As brewing technology improved, demand for this low-end drink subsided. Following Prohibition, one of the few brewers remaining was San Francisco's Anchor brewery, which had been established in 1896. However, after a period of decline, the business was about to fold in 1965. Alerted to the death throes of his favourite beer, Fritz Maytag (a Stanford graduate and heir to the washing machine business) bought a controlling share in the brewery and attempted to kickstart the business.

By altering the recipe of the beer and focusing on better quality control, Maytag helped revive Anchor. Bar owners had complained that the beer spoiled easily, so he developed a bottled version of Anchor Steam Beer, which was launched in 1971 to almost instant acclaim.

Throughout his ownership of the company Maytag deliberately kept its size relatively small to ensure that the beer quality remained great.

He can fairly be described as one of the godfathers of American craft brewing as he sought to help other microbreweries follow his example and develop products that were an alternative to mass-produced beer.

Because Anchor trademarked the term 'steam beer' in 1981, other brewers are not able to use it. They are stuck with the slightly more prosaic descriptor of 'California common beer'.

According to the Beer Judge Certification Program, a beer tasting examiner, the term California common beer is 'narrowly defined around the prototypical Anchor Steam example'. The style 'showcases the signature Northern Brewer hops (with woody, rustic or minty qualities) in moderate to high strength', and is fermented with a lager yeast that was selected to thrive at the cool end of normal ale fermentation temperatures. Traditionally it was fermented in open fermenters, a process that Anchor still uses.

Other brewers have sought to revive the style, which is no longer regarded as a cheap bottle of suds, but as a premium beer. Examples include Flying Dog Old Scratch Amber Lager and Linden Street Common Lager. The latter is brewed across the San Francisco Bay in Oakland and is described as a tribute to styles and brewing methods that originated in the Bay Area during the pre-Prohibition era.

Sly Fox 113

Based in Pennsylvania, Sly Fox is renowned for canning many of its products to keep them fresh as they are shipped around the world. It also serves beer on tap at its brewpub and eatery in Phoenixville. Its success has been swift – with production beginning in January 2012 it is a newcomer to the American craft-brewing scene. This is their year-round IPA. Made with hops grown in the Yakima Valley region of Washington state, the high alpha acid content guarantees big citrus, pine and bitterness.

Tasting notes: Powerful bitterness and lots of mixed fruity tones.
✶ **Country:** USA ✶ **Brewer:** Sly Fox Brewing Co. ✶ **Style:** IPA
✶ **Appearance:** Dark amber ✶ **Alcohol:** 7% ✶ **Serving temp:** 4–7°C

Stone Sublimely Self-Righteous Ale

Stone Brewing, based in Escondido, California, is rightly proud of its beers: one of its best-known brews is Arrogant Bastard Ale, an aggressively hoppy strong ale. The Sublimely Self-Righteous Ale is a black IPA that uses a dark chocolate malt usually associated with stouts and porters, with the mandatory mountain of hops added for tropical fruit aromas and a pine-like bitterness. A really good one to drink with sticky barbecue food, as any char on the meat works nicely with its flavour profile.

Tasting notes: Coffee, raisins and vibrant passionfruit aromas. Goes wonderfully well with barbecue and spicy jerk chicken.
✶ **Country:** USA
✶ **Brewer:** Stone Brewing Co.
✶ **Style:** Black IPA
✶ **Appearance:** Matt black
✶ **Alcohol:** 8.7%
✶ **Serving temp:** 7–10°C

The Bruery Mischief

American craft brewers are renowned for their habit of taking styles of beer from around the world and tinkering with them. The Bruery has taken a Belgian blonde strong ale and added extra fruity American hops during the boil stage of brewing, and also at the fermentation stage during the dry-hopping process. This adds another dimension to an already flavoursome and challenging style of beer. A delight at any dinner table – try it with crispy skinned duck or chicken.

Tasting notes: Dry and bubbling with big flavours of ripe peach and melon, sitting against a peppery backdrop.
✶ **Country:** USA
✶ **Brewer:** The Bruery
✶ **Style:** Belgian blonde ale
✶ **Appearance:** Golden
✶ **Alcohol:** 8.5%
✶ **Serving temp:** 4–8°C

Victory Golden Monkey

When they first met on the way to school in 1973, fifth-graders Bill Covaleski and Ron Barchet could scarcely imagine they'd end up starting one of America's best-loved breweries together. Their Golden Monkey is based on a classic Belgian abbey beer recipe but with that all-important American twist – extra hops. Spicy, bubbly and very refreshing – you'd never guess it was 9.5% ABV from its quaffable character.

Tasting notes: Ripened fruit, lots of bubblegum from the yeast and a full-bodied, bubbly character. Great with creamy cheese such as Brie.
* **Country:** USA
* **Brewer:** Victory Brewing Co.
* **Style:** Abbey tripel
* **Appearance:** Yellow-orange
* **Alcohol:** 9.5% * **Serving temp:** 4–7°C

Yards General Washington Tavern Porter

After homebrewing their way through their degrees, gaining experience at an English-style brewing company and spending every spare penny they had on beer, Tom Kehoe and Jon Bovit pooled their savings, maxed out their credit cards and in 1994 founded the Yards brewing company. This porter was created as part of their Ales of the Revolution series and is based on an original recipe from one of America's Founding Fathers, George Washington. A delicious lesson in American history.

Tasting notes: Buttery, chocolate, and with a slight hint of molasses. This would be great with slow-cooked brisket.
* **Country:** USA * **Brewer:** Yards Brewing Co.
* **Style:** Porter * **Appearance:** Clear brown
* **Alcohol:** 7% * **Serving temp:** 8–12°C

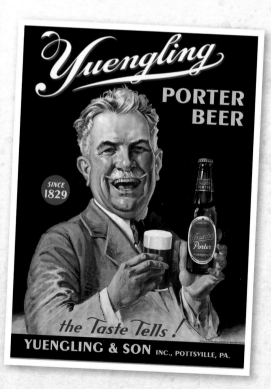

Yuengling Dark Brewed Porter

Originally called the Eagle Brewery when it was first established in 1829 in Pottsville, Pennsylvania, the Yuengling brewery is the oldest in the United States. After brewery fires, Prohibition and a whole host of hardships, the brewery surpassed two million barrels in 2009, making it not just the oldest, but also one of the most successful breweries in the US. This is its traditional, British-style porter and one of the flagship products.

Tasting notes: Notes of sweetened coffee, liquorice and a hint of chocolate.
* **Country:** USA * **Brewer:** D.G. Yuengling & Son
* **Style:** Porter * **Appearance:** Brown
* **Alcohol:** 5% * **Serving temp:** 8–13°C

🍁 Alexander Keith's India Pale Ale

Alexander Keith's IPA is unlike any other India Pale Ale. It's not particularly strong at only 5% ABV and has very low hop bitterness, so it doesn't resemble the modern American-style IPAs. It also lacks the fruitiness and full body associated with the traditional British style. But this IPA was around long before the current IPA revival. It has its own character and perhaps because of this has become Nova Scotia's most popular beer.

Tasting notes: Slight corn notes, very light hoppiness and a very smooth thin finish.
★ **Country:** Canada
★ **Brewer:** Oland Brewery
★ **Style:** IPA
★ **Appearance:** Golden
★ **Alcohol:** 5%
★ **Serving temp:** 8–12°C

🍁 Alley Kat Olde Deuteronomy

Alley Kat, founded in 1994, is one of the longest-running microbrewers in Canada, but is still a relatively new outfit. Founders Neil and Lavonne Herbst are brewing some of the most exciting beers in North America. Some are best drunk immediately to retain their fresh hop character, while others are best kept for lengthy periods in cool dark cellars so the malt flavours will develop. Olde Deuteronomy Barley Wine definitely falls into the latter category. Drink at around room temperature to feel its warming spiciness when the cold nights begin to draw in. A perfect beer to drink at Christmas.

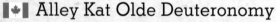

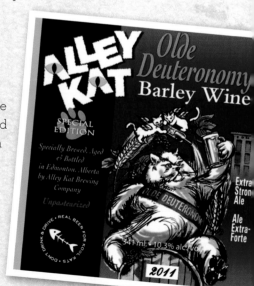

Tasting notes: Heavy on toffee, dark fruit, brown sugar and a heady dose of alcohol in the nose. Aged versions may take on woody notes.
★ **Country:** Canada ★ **Brewer:** Alley Kat Brewing Co.
★ **Style:** Barley wine ★ **Appearance:** Copper
★ **Alcohol:** 10.3% ★ **Serving temp:** 13–15°C

🍁 Amsterdam Boneshaker IPA

Some brewers aim for subtleties in their product that are only detectable to the seasoned beer lover. Amsterdam Brewery didn't care about subtleties when it made this continually hopped IPA. With an almost dangerous amount of Amarillo hops used, the question, 'How many hops can fit in one beer?' may never be 100 per cent settled but the Boneshaker IPA certainly comes close to providing the answer. Not for the faint of heart – hop lovers only.

Tasting notes: Pine-like resin aromas, forceful citrus fruits and a slight peppery spice from the hops.
* ★ **Country:** Canada ★ **Brewer:** Amsterdam Brewery ★ **Style:** IPA
* ★ **Appearance:** Hazy amber ★ **Alcohol:** 7.1% ★ **Serving temp:** 4–7°C

DID YOU KNOW?

Beer has a major role in the Canadian economy, with one in a hundred jobs being supported by beer sales.

🍁 Beau's Lug-Tread Lagered Ale

Named for the tyre treads of a small tractor that ploughs the fields of eastern Ontario, Lug-Tread Lagered Ale is somewhere between an ale and a lager. In Germany, the style is named Kölsch. The long maturation period at a cool temperature means the beer develops a crisp, dry character while retaining all the fruitiness you'd expect from a smooth golden ale. A good demonstration of how beer can truly be bread in liquid form.

Tasting notes: Soft, doughy aromas of proving bread and light toast with a subtle hint of peach-like fruit before the crisp, bitter finish.
* ★ **Country:** Canada ★ **Brewer:** Beau's All Natural Brewing Co.
* ★ **Style:** Kolsch ★ **Appearance:** Golden
* ★ **Alcohol:** 5.2% ★ **Serving temp:** 3–6°C

🇨🇦 Central City Red Racer IPA

Central City's Red Racer IPA is its flagship product and is served up by the bucketload at its chic little brewpub in Surrey, east of Vancouver, British Columbia. The brewery is named after a fictional city created by DC Comics as the home of its famous graphic novel character, The Flash.

Tasting notes: Floral, almost perfumed-like hops meld flowers and tropical fruit perfectly with a rich, biscuit toffee malt.
★ **Country:** Canada ★ **Brewer:** Central City Brewing Co.
★ **Style:** IPA ★ **Appearance:** Dark amber
★ **Alcohol:** 6.5% ★ **Serving temp:** 4–7°C

🇨🇦 Dieu du Ciel Péché Mortel

An incredibly rich and intense beer and not one for casual consumption. Péché Mortel is French for mortal sin – which is very appropriate in this instance. A hugely viscous and thick black body comes with the calorie count you'd expect from a 9.5% ABV Imperial stout. These flavoursome, warming strong stouts were originally brewed by English brewers for export to the Russian Tsar. Dieu du Ciel's version includes coffee in the brewing process. Be sure to drink this alongside a rich and dark chocolate dessert to get the intended sinful effect.

Tasting notes: Roasted coffee, sweet chocolate with hints of vanilla cream and spicy fruit. Great with vanilla ice cream on top for a beer float.
★ **Country:** Canada
★ **Brewer:** Dieu du Ciel
★ **Style:** Imperial stout ★ **Appearance:** Black
★ **Alcohol:** 9.5% ★ **Serving temp:** 8–13°C

🇨🇦 Driftwood Fat Tug IPA

The India pale ale style is one of the most popular in all of North America with very good reason. The Driftwood Fat Tug IPA is a typical example: it is intensely hopped to give vivid fruit flavours as well as a spicy bitterness at the end. Pairs superbly well with Mexican and other spicy fare.

Tasting notes: Grapefruit, melon and a healthy dose of spice sit atop a caramel malt base line.
★ **Country:** Canada ★ **Brewer:** Driftwood Brewing Co.
★ **Style:** IPA ★ **Appearance:** Dark amber
★ **Alcohol:** 7% ★ **Serving temp:** 4–7°C

DID YOU KNOW?

Beer is the most popular alcoholic beverage in Canada, accounting for around 8% of all household spending on food and drink. The biggest drinkers in Canada are those in Yukon territory, drinking 385 bottles per person per year!

🇨🇦 Flying Monkeys
Hoptical Illusion Almost Pale Ale

Not your standard-issue pale ale! So named because its aroma betrays a hoppy nature, with grapefruit and other citrus notes coming through strongly. However, it weighs in at only 32 IBUs. To put this in perspective, English-style pale ales usually start at around 25 IBUs while modern American-style pales are often 80+. All the aromatics with none of the mouth-puckering bitterness you'd expect, the name Hoptical Illusion is very appropriate.

Tasting notes: Grapefruit, orange peel and light caramel aromas with a light orange peel and sweet citrus flavour. Crisp, dry but short finish.
★ **Country:** Canada ★ **Brewer:** Flying Monkeys Craft Brewery ★ **Style:** Pale ale
★ **Appearance:** Orange amber ★ **Alcohol:** 5% ★ **Serving temp:** 4–7°C

🇨🇦 Granville Island Kitsilano Maple Cream Ale

Granville Island Brewing has been a mainstay in Canadian brewing since 1984, making it the oldest microbrewery in Canada and an inspirational success story. Its Maple Cream Ale isn't just a pretty name. It uses a hint of pure maple syrup in the brewing process in much the same way honey or sugar can be added during fermentation. The idea is to accentuate the naturally toffee-like flavours extracted from the caramel malt for an extra flavour dimension.

Tasting notes: Swirling caramel, sticky toffee and subtle hints of maple are balanced with the lightest of hop finishes.
★ **Country:** Canada ★ **Brewer:** Granville Island Brewing ★ **Style:** Amber
★ **Appearance:** Bronze ★ **Alcohol:** 5% ★ **Serving temp:** 4–7°C

🇨🇦 Great Lakes Crazy Canuck Pale Ale

When a beer is described as an American or West Coast-style pale ale, it tends to mean that its central attraction is the hops rather than the malt (as in an English or East Coast style). Crazy Canuck is Great Lakes' version of a West Coast pale ale, with a vivid hop personality and a relatively light malt content. Founded in 1987, the brewery is the oldest craft brewery in Toronto, with a large range of regular beers as well as a seasonal selection.

Tasting notes: Citrus, floral hops and a light maltiness in excellent balance. Great with a mild fish curry.
★ **Country:** Canada ★ **Brewer:** Great Lakes Brewery ★ **Style:** Pale ale
★ **Appearance:** Hazy amber ★ **Alcohol:** 5.2% ★ **Serving temp:** 4–7°C

🇨🇦 Labatt Blue

Without doubt the undisputed heavyweight brewer of Canada, Labatt Brewing Company sells more than any other in The Great White North – largely down to its flagship brand, Labatt Blue. Originally called Pilsener Lager when first introduced in 1951, the beer quickly gained the nickname 'Blue' from the colour of its label and the brewers' support of the Canadian Football League team, the Blue Bombers. Labatt Blue became Canada's bestselling beer by 1979. Although Budweiser now outsells it on home turf, this classic pale lager is still the most popular and bestselling Canadian beer in the world.

Tasting notes: Light malt and mild citrus aromas with the textbook crisp, clean pale lager taste. Serve it ice-cold with peanuts and your favourite sports team.
* ★ **Country:** Canada ★ **Brewer:** Labatt Brewing Company
* ★ **Style:** Pale lager ★ **Appearance:** Pale yellow
* ★ **Alcohol:** 5% ★ **Serving temp:** 1–2°C

DID YOU KNOW?

The oldest brewery in Canada is Molson's in Montreal, established in 1786 and strategically located to take advantage of the Scottish and English fur traders' preference for the ales and porters of their home countries.

🇨🇦 McAuslan St-Ambroise Oatmeal Stout

The McAuslan brewery began in early 1989 and quickly established itself as a big hitter in the microbrewing world with its St-Ambroise pale ale. Soon after, Peter McAuslan expanded his range to include this nigh-on perfect oatmeal stout. Adding a percentage of oats to the brew makes for a smooth body, while the dark roasted malts give hints of espresso coffee alongside a generous lug of chocolate and liquorice.

Tasting notes: The coffee and chocolate flavours are all at once bitter and sweet and are carried along by a smooth and sumptuous black body.
* ★ **Country:** Canada ★ **Brewer:** McAuslan Brewing
* ★ **Style:** Stout ★ **Appearance:** Black
* ★ **Alcohol:** 5% ★ **Serving temp:** 8–13°C

🇨🇦 Mill Street Tankhouse Ale

The Mill Street Brewery has been going strong since production started in 2002. Founders Steve Abrams, Jeff Cooper and Michael Diggan named it after the address 55 Mill Street in Toronto's historic distillery district. Its Tankhouse ale is made using a recipe for a hoppy, well-balanced modern American-style pale ale that the head brewer developed 20 years ago – it was such a favourite he saw no need to change it.

Tasting notes: Loaded with spicy hop aromas from the American Cascade variety used for both bitterness and finishing.
* ★ **Country:** Canada
* ★ **Brewer:** Mill Street Brewery
* ★ **Style:** Pale ale ★ **Appearance:** Copper red
* ★ **Alcohol:** 5.2% ★ **Serving temp:** 4–7°C

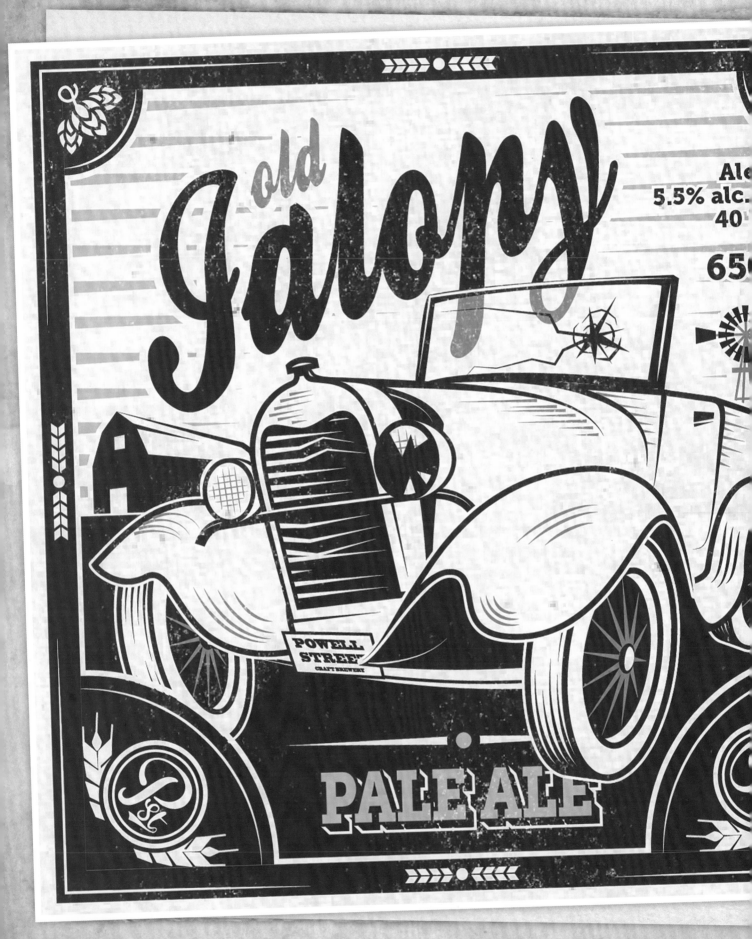

Molson Canadian Lager

The third bestselling pale lager in Canada, this is a beer with a string of awards to its name. As well as a gold medal in the North American Lager category at the Canadian Brewing Awards in 1989, 1990, 1991, 1997, 2001 and 2002, it also won Gold Medal Distinction from the Monde Selection – a sort of Michelin star guide for food and drink products. Not bad for a simple, clean, easy-drinking lager

Tasting notes: An easygoing blend of clean malts, a hint of lemon and a moreish sweetness that's hard to stop drinking.
- ★ **Country:** Canada
- ★ **Brewer:** Molson Coors
- ★ **Style:** Pale lager
- ★ **Appearance:** Pale yellow
- ★ **Alcohol:** 5%
- ★ **Serving temp:** 1–2°C

DID YOU KNOW?

To bolster national pride, Canadian beer company Molson placed beer fridges across Europe, containing a free supply of Canadian beer. The catch? – only Canadians can open the fridges by scanning their passports!

Powell Street Old Jalopy Pale Ale

The very definition of a microbrewer – technically a nano-brewery given its small production line – the husband-wife team of David Bowkett and Nicole Stefanopoulos began their Vancouver-based brewing adventure in 2012. A homage to the Burton on Trent beer styles, this beautifully made English-style pale ale is as balanced and refined as you'd hope for, with equal amounts of American hops and roasted caramel malts giving the perfect balance of bitter and sweet.

Tasting notes: Lots of sweet malts and zesty citrus in the aroma and much the same story in the taste. Excellent with a chargrilled steak.
- ★ **Country:** Canada ★ **Brewer:** Powell Street Craft Brewery
- ★ **Style:** Pale ale ★ **Appearance:** Orange
- ★ **Alcohol:** 5.5% ★ **Serving temp:** 4–7°C

🇨🇦 Propeller London Style Porter

Yet another tribute to the brewers of the British Isles, this traditional London porter is based on the drink the cabbies and porters of London used to drink after their late-night shifts. Propeller Brewery's version is just about perfect and extremely true to the original recipe of pale, roasted and chocolate malts levelled out with a sensible amount of hops from either side of the Atlantic. Much softer and easier to drink than you'd expect.

Tasting notes: Bitter chocolate, light toffee and liquorice notes in the aroma with a sweet, malty taste in the mouth. Great with roasted meats or blue cheese.
★ **Country:** Canada ★ **Brewer:** Propeller Brewery ★ **Style:** Porter
★ **Appearance:** Clear brown ★ **Alcohol:** 5% ★ **Serving temp:** 8–13°C

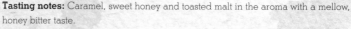

🇨🇦 Sleeman Honey Brown Lager

After a few years of running their own pub, John Sleeman and his English wife were visited by his Aunt Florian one fateful day. Clutching a bottle of his family's historic Sleeman beer, she proceeded to tell him about his heritage and on that day an empire was reborn. The Sleeman brewery reopened in 1988 and its Honey Brown Lager is brewed in the style of the cottage breweries of old, with a touch of natural honey being added toward the end.

Tasting notes: Caramel, sweet honey and toasted malt in the aroma with a mellow, honey bitter taste.
★ **Country:** Canada ★ **Brewer:** Sleeman Breweries. ★ **Style:** Amber lager
★ **Appearance:** Light amber ★ **Alcohol:** 5.2% ★ **Serving temp:** 4–7°C

DID YOU KNOW?

French herbalist Louis Hébert and his wife were Canada's first brewers – emigrating to Quebec in 1617, they were granted farmland to grow barley and wheat from which they brewed beer for themselves and their neighbours.

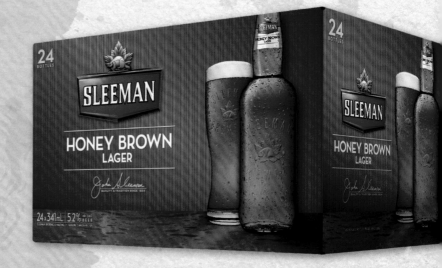

🍁 Unibroue La Fin du Monde

'La Fin du Monde' refers to the thoughts of the intrepid European pioneers who believed Canada was literally The End of the World. They brought with them a specific strain of yeast that had been used for centuries. La Fin du Monde first brewed in 1994, is Unibroue's recreation of one of those early beers and the first of its kind to be attempted in the Americas.

Tasting notes: Floral hops with aromas of honey, spice, coriander and a little orange peel coupled with a refreshing yeasty, dry finish.

★ **Country:** Canada ★ **Brewer:** Unibroue
★ **Style:** Abbey tripel ★ **Appearance:** Golden
★ **Alcohol:** 9% ★ **Serving temp:** 12–14°C

🍁 Wild Rose Cherry Porter

When you add whole cherries to the lusciously bitter and dark chocolate flavours and aromas of a classic London-style porter, then only good things can happen. Wild Rose's Cherry Porter does exactly that and is one of the best beers for a chilly winter evening. With a slightly smoky character as well as fruit, double cream and lashings of black cherry flavour, try pairing this award-winning beer with a big slice of Black Forest gateau.

Tasting notes: Rich chocolate, espresso coffee and a long-lasting impression of black cherry.

★ **Country:** Canada
★ **Brewer:** Wild Rose
★ **Style:** Cherry porter
★ **Appearance:** Dark burgundy
★ **Alcohol:** 6.6%
★ **Serving temp:** 12–14°C

THE CANADIAN ICE BEER WARS

The Canadian beer market is dominated by two brewers, Labatt and Molson, who together account for almost 80 per cent of sales. The companies have a history of going toe to toe in order to retain and increase their market share. Throughout the 1990s, brewers were experiencing declining sales and looked to new products and brands to awaken the interest of drinkers.

Labatt and Molson have tried light beer, dry beer, citrus beer and draught beer in bottles, to attract fickle drinkers. In the early nineties, they hit upon the idea of ice beer.

Ice beer was first developed by Labatt in 1993, based on German Eisbock beer. Using a low-temperature brewing process that caused unwanted proteins and tannins to precipitate more completely, it produced Labatt Ice. This was touted as a smooth-tasting brew with a high alcohol content of 5.6% ABV.

Molson quickly jumped on the bandwagon with Canadian Ice and Dry Ice, each at 5.7% ABV. Later that year Labatt upped the ante with Maximum Ice, an ice beer with 7.1% ABV.

Two months later, Molson launched its own high-alcohol beer, Molson XXX, with 7.3% alcohol. The high strength attracted heavy criticism, and ice beer fell out of fashion as quickly as it had appeared. However, you can still buy it.

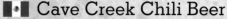 Baja Oatmeal Stout

Founded in 2007 by American-born brewing enthusiasts who fell in love with Mexico, the Baja Brewing Company is going from strength to strength, having found its feet in the brewing world. It now has three beach cantinas in the state of Baja California Sur and this oatmeal stout is served up in all of them, alongside some exciting Mexican food.

Tasting notes: Liquorice, tar and toffee in the aroma with ripe fruit, spice and banana on the palate.
★ **Country:** Mexico
★ **Brewer:** Baja Brewing Co.
★ **Style:** Stout ★ **Appearance:** Deep red
★ **Alcohol:** 7% ★ **Serving temp:** 10–13°C

Cave Creek Chili Beer

The fiery taste of chillies is ever-present in Central American food, so it's fitting that the Mexican beer world can provide us with the fabled chilli beer. Clearly not a beer for a spice hater, the flavour is completely dominated by chilli – making it a great beer to buy as a prank, or perhaps to order in a restaurant for the seasoned drinker who thinks he (or she) has seen it all.

Tasting notes: Chilli in the aroma. Chilli on the palate. Chilli. Pairs well with a… chilli.
★ **Country:** Mexico
★ **Brewer:** Cervecería Mexicana
★ **Style:** Chilli lager
★ **Appearance:** Golden orange
★ **Alcohol:** 4.7%
★ **Serving temp:** 1–2°C

MEXICAN BEER: WHY THE LIME?

Mexican beer brand Corona was launched in 1925 but became popular in the United States and Europe in the 1980s. The taste of this light lager was almost incidental to its stylish bottle topped with an obligatory slice of lime.

The clear glass bottles with directly printed labels made Corona stand out from dark glass bottles, encouraging drinkers to sup straight from the bottle.

But why is Corona served with a slice of lime?

One theory is that in a clear bottle the beer degrades more quickly, which can result in a stale smell. The lime helps to disguise this smell. Other theories are that the lime was

traditionally used to disinfect the top of the bottle, to keep flies away, or to remove rust left by metallic beer caps.

Mexicans rarely drink their beer with lime inserted in the bottle, although lime is an ingredient of a beer cocktail called a *michelada*. The lime could be simply a piece of clever marketing designed to bring attention to another beer in a crowded marketplace.

It has certainly worked for Corona, which is now the fourth biggest-selling beer in the world. Parent company Grupo Modelo sold a 50 per cent stake to global brewing company AB InBev for $20 billion in 2012.

Corona Extra

The number one bestselling beer in Mexico and increasingly popular worldwide, Corona is easily recognizable in bars all over the world thanks to the lime wedge that plugs the top of the bottle once opened. Some say this used to be a smart way of keeping flies out of your beer in hot weather – not to mention adding a citrus taste of lime to the beer. Nowadays (and in most cooler climes) this lime wedge is largely not needed but is a popular gimmick nonetheless.

Tasting notes: Very light and refreshing with small hints of citrus and light hay-like grains. A twist of lime is optional.
- ★ **Country:** Mexico
- ★ **Brewer:** Grupo Modelo
- ★ **Style:** Pale lager
- ★ **Appearance:** Yellow
- ★ **Alcohol:** 4.6%
- ★ **Serving temp:** 1–2°C

Dos Equis XX Lager Especial

Originally brewed by the German-born Mexican brewer Wilhelm Hasse in 1897, this brand was so named with Roman numerals to commemorate the turn of the 20th century. Just in case you didn't work it out, 'Dos Equis' also literally translates as 'two X's' in Spanish. The brand was first exported to the USA in 1973.

Tasting notes: Pale malt, sweet bread and toasted cereal. A slightly dry finish that doesn't last long.
- ★ **Country:** Mexico
- ★ **Brewer:** FEMSA
- ★ **Style:** Pale lager
- ★ **Appearance:** Yellow
- ★ **Alcohol:** 4.45% ★ **Serving temp:** 3–5°C

Minerva Imperial Tequila Ale

There are many oak-aged beers around the world but not many are aged in old tequila casks.

The Minerva Imperial Tequila Ale is a unique taste experience you're unlikely to find anywhere else. Hints of oak and vanilla are just about matched blow for blow with a rounded tequila finish. One of the most memorable beers you'll ever try.

Tasting notes: Oak, vanilla and hints of caramel and fresh tobacco and water chestnuts. Tequila-like finish.
- ★ **Country:** Mexico
- ★ **Brewer:** Cervecería Minerva
- ★ **Style:** Imperial tequila ale
- ★ **Appearance:** Hazy amber
- ★ **Alcohol:** 7% ★ **Serving temp:** 4–7°C

🇲🇽 Modelo Especial

Following their mission statement to create a 'model' beer, the brewers of Modelo started with this pilsner-like pale lager in 1925. At the turn of the new millennium, Modelo had become the third most-imported beer to the USA after Corona and Heineken. Its flavour is classic German-style pilsner. Dry in the finish with light and bready notes and a low hop character.

Tasting notes: Very light and refreshing with a slight sourness and a tart lemon edge to the finish.
★ **Country:** Mexico ★ **Brewer:** Grupo Modelo ★ **Style:** Pale lager
★ **Appearance:** Golden ★ **Alcohol:** 4.4% ★ **Serving temp:** 3–5°C

🇲🇽 Red Pig Mexican Ale

Brewed in Tecate, Mexico, this is amber ale with a twist. With its deep, amber-red colour and malty sweetness, on first sip you'd think the Red Pig Mexican Ale is a standard amber ale. It's not until the finish that the pleasantly smoky presence comes in to give you a surprising taste of Mexico.

Tasting notes: Smoky peat, roasted corn, grains and light yeast flavours. Lovely with a spicy taco.
★ **Country:** Mexico ★ **Brewer:** Cervecería Mexicana ★ **Style:** Amber ale
★ **Appearance:** Clear amber ★ **Alcohol:** 5.4% ★ **Serving temp:** 3–5°C

 Bohemia Weiss

A beer inspired by the 'Old World' brewers of Europe. Harking back to the German *Hefeweizen* (yeast wheat) style, Bohemia Weiss uses a combination of malted wheat and hops with the strain of yeast so famous for making German wheat beers. The result is a brilliantly refreshing balance of banana, cloves and spice.

Tasting notes: A super bubbly and refreshing beer that goes well with spicy dim sum.
* **Country:** Brazil
* **Brewer:** AB InBev
* **Style:** Hefeweizen
* **Appearance:** Hazy yellow
* **Alcohol:** 5.6%
* **Serving temp:** 3–5°C

DaDo Bier Original

Few breweries outside Germany profess to follow the *Reinheitsgebot* – an ancient German purity law that restricts the ingredients allowed in brewing beer to barley, hops, water and yeast. The brewers at DaDo Bier – set up in 1995 – follow this law to the letter and in the process created their flagship beer. This easygoing pilsner is a homage to the lagers of Germany.

Tasting notes: Grassy hops that don't overwhelm, light toasted grain notes and creamy-white bubbly head.
* **Country:** Brazil
* **Brewer:** DaDo Bier
* **Style:** Pilsner
* **Appearance:** Bright yellow
* **Alcohol:** 4.5% ★ **Serving temp:** 3–5°C

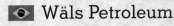 Wäls Petroleum

Don't be put off by the name. Not a budget brand of fuel for your car but a Russian-style imperial stout with some serious clout. So named because of its thick, almost gloopy texture and velvety smoothness. This is achieved by adding extra cacao and roasted Belgian malts. Very much a sipping beer at 12% ABV.

Tasting notes: Long smooth toffee flavour, caramel and chocolate. Perfect with a chocolate dessert.
* **Country:** Brazil ★ **Brewer:** Cervejaria Wäls ★ **Style:** Imperial stout
* **Appearance:** Hazy brown ★ **Alcohol:** 12% ★ **Serving temp:** 10–14°C

🇦🇷 Antares Imperial Stout

The Antares brewery is named after the brightest star in the constellation Scorpio, which was traditionally used as a point of reference for sailors to find their way home – or, rather more fantastically, to find their destiny. A little weaker than many Russian imperial-style stouts, at 8.5% ABV, it still packs a fruity and slightly boozy punch.

Tasting notes: Rum-soaked raisins with hints of blackened toast and smoky campfire aromas.
★ **Country:** Argentina ★ **Brewer:** Antares ★ **Style:** Imperial stout
★ **Appearance:** Dark brown ★ **Alcohol:** 8.5% ★ **Serving temp:** 10–14°C

🇦🇷 Otro Mundo Strong Red Ale

The best brewers often have humble beginnings. Founded in 2004, the Otro Mundo Brewing Company is an Argentinian gem that began operations in a dilapidated former brewery in the small town of San Carlos in Santa Fe. This red ale gets its amber colour and caramel notes from its blend of malts, fermented with an ale yeast for a full, fruity flavour.

Tasting notes: Sweet, yeasty toffee notes with a caramel sweet finish.
★ **Country:** Argentina ★ **Brewer:** Otro Mundo Brewery Co.
★ **Style:** Strong amber ale ★ **Appearance:** Light amber
★ **Alcohol:** 7.5% ★ **Serving temp:** 8–10°C

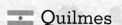

🇦🇷 Quilmes

Often known as Quilmes Cristal, this is without doubt the most famous Argentinian beer, with a massive 75 per cent of the market share in the country, as well as strong international sales. The colours of its label match those of the Argentinian flag and it comes from a brewery that was founded in 1888 by a German immigrant.

Tasting notes: Malted grain, toasted grains and a sweet caramel aroma. Pairs well with spicy barbecued meat.
★ **Country:** Argentina
★ **Brewer:** Cervecería y Maltería Quilmes
★ **Style:** Pale lager
★ **Appearance:** Yellow
★ **Alcohol:** 4.9%
★ **Serving temp:** 2–5°C

▌▌ Cusqueña

First brewed in 1888, this pale lager has a particularly interesting bottle design. The design embossed in the glass is based on the Twelve Angle Stone in the Hatun Rumiyoc Street in Cusco – a city in south-eastern Peru. This stone is a famous example of ancient Inca architecture and reflects how proud Peruvians are of their Inca roots. Without doubt the most famous beer in the country, the water used is sourced in the Peruvian Andes from a spring 18,000ft (5,486m) above sea level.

Tasting notes: Light corn flavours, malted grain and other cereals. Very refreshing.
★ **Country:** Peru
★ **Brewer:** Cervecería del sur del Peru
★ **Style:** Pale lager ★ **Appearance:** Yellow
★ **Alcohol:** 4.9% ★ **Serving temp:** 2–5°C

DID YOU KNOW?

Excavations in a pre-Inca brewery in Peru show that hundreds of gallons of beer were brewed every week by elite women from the noble class, using corn and Peruvian pepper-tree berries.

▌▌ Cusqueña Malta

The same trademark bottle as regular Cusqueña is filled with an altogether different beer. Made with Saaz hops – a variety found most often in the Bohemian pilsners of the Czech Republic – this black beer also uses four types of dark malt to achieve its distinctive dark colour, burnt caramel flavours and long, dry, hoppy finish.

Tasting notes: This rich dark lager needs to be paired with smoky barbecued meat or spicy seafood to bring out its best.
★ **Country:** Peru
★ **Brewer:** Cervecería del sur del Peru
★ **Style:** Black beer
★ **Appearance:** Black
★ **Alcohol:** 5.6%
★ **Serving temp:** 4–7°C

▌▌ Pilsen Polar

Don't be misled by the polar bear on the label. There's nothing icy about this *Schwarzbier* (black beer), which is brewed in the capital city of Peru, Lima. With pronounced flavours coming from the roasted malts, it has a warming character that makes it perfect for a Peruvian sunset.

Tasting notes: Chargrilled pork chops, steaks and smoky barbecue sauces go nicely with this beer.
★ **Country:** Peru
★ **Brewer:** Backus y Johnston
★ **Style:** Black beer
★ **Appearance:** Black
★ **Alcohol:** 5.5%
★ **Serving temp:** 4–7°C

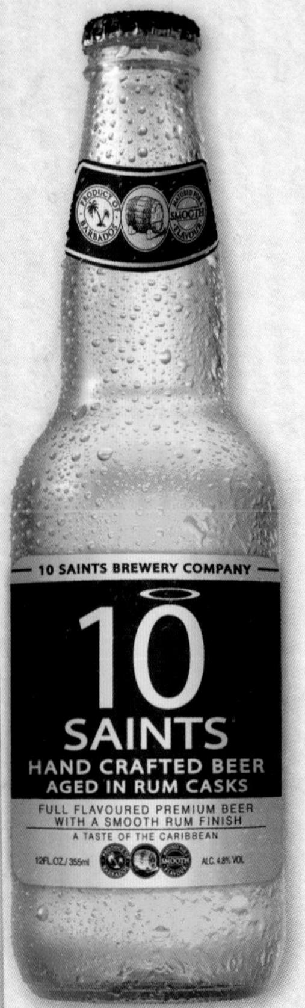

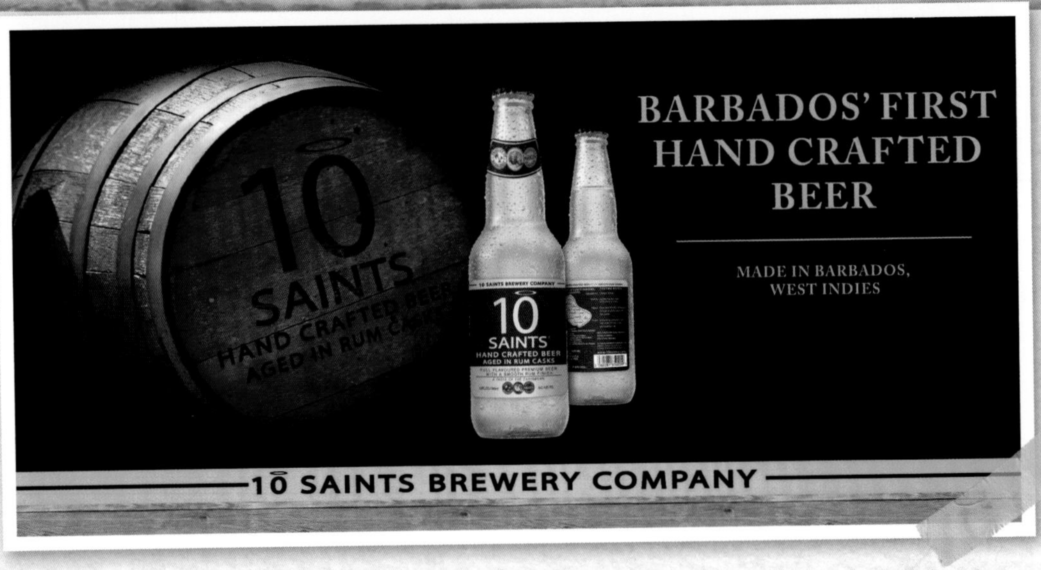

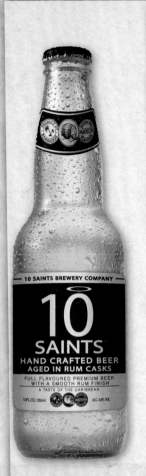

10 Saints

This classy-looking beer is a lager with a difference. Many darker, stronger beers get the barrel-aged treatment, but there aren't many barrel-aged beers accessible to people who don't want to drink high-alcohol brews. 10 Saints lager fills this gap. Aged in Mount Gay Special Reserve rum casks for 90 days, it comes in at an easy-drinking 4.8% ABV.

Tasting notes: Sweet vanilla, light spice and hints of rum overlay the clean flavours of pale lager.
★ **Country:** Barbados ★ **Brewer:** 10 Saints Brewery Co. ★ **Style:** Premium lager
★ **Appearance:** Gold ★ **Alcohol:** 4.8% ★ **Serving temp:** 2–5°C

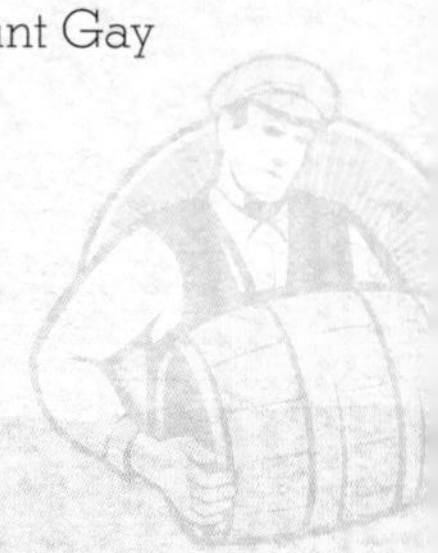

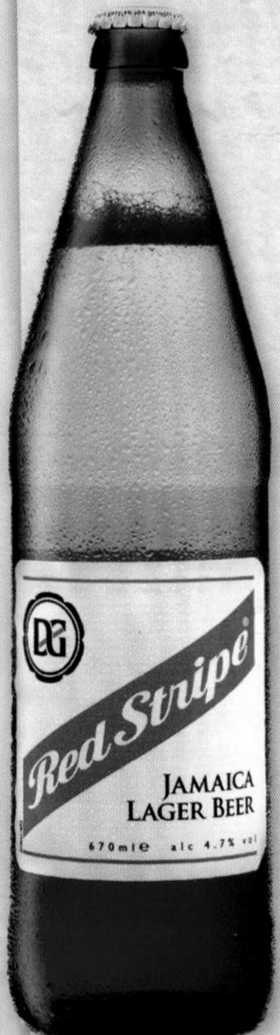

Red Stripe

One of the most famous exports of the Caribbean, Red Stripe made its name in the reggae dance halls of the 1990s and has kept on going. First brewed in 1938, its invasion of the USA and Europe was on the back of success stories like Budweiser, Heineken and other pale lagers. Accessible, easy to drink and a true taste of Jamaica.

Tasting notes: Light notes of brown bread and corn with a very light hop finish.
★ **Country:** Jamaica
★ **Brewer:** Desnoes & Geddes
★ **Style:** Pale lager
★ **Appearance:** Light gold
★ **Alcohol:** 4.7%
★ **Serving temp:** 1–2°C

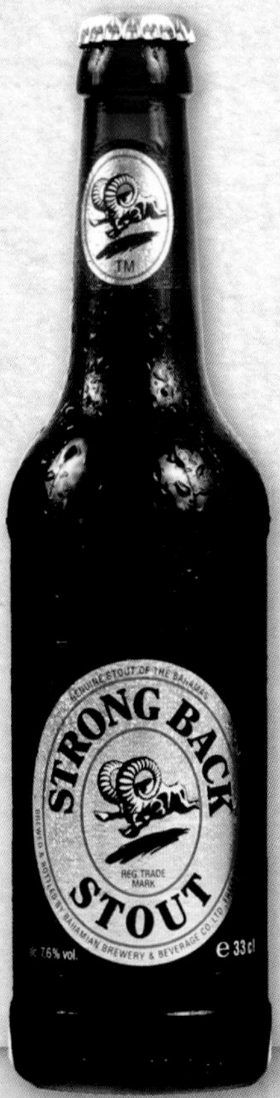

Bahamian Strong Back Stout

'Drink Strong Back every day 'cause it keeps the heart attacks away,' was the exclamation of one happy Bahamian shipyard worker. While that might not be strictly true, Strong Back is an export strength stout designed to appeal to men and women – despite the ultra-macho charging ram on the label. Brewed on the island of Grand Bahama.

Tasting notes: Aromas of raisins, caramel and cocoa with hints of chocolate and spice on the palate.
★ **Country:** Bahamas
★ **Brewer:** Bahamian Brewery & Beverage Co.
★ **Style:** Export stout
★ **Appearance:** Dark brown
★ **Alcohol:** 7.6%
★ **Serving temp:** 8–13°C

Cristal

The taste of an ice-cold lager is particularly welcome in countries where the climate is hot. Cristal lager has become the most popular beer in all of Cuba. Crisp and clean on the palate, the goal is refreshment rather than overwhelmingly big flavour. Great to have alongside spicy barbecued food to dowse any chilli afterburn.

Tasting notes: Very light flavour profile of crisp malt, lightly bitter hops and a thin texture.
★ **Country:** Cuba
★ **Brewer:** Cervecería Bucanero
★ **Style:** Pale lager
★ **Appearance:** Pale gold
★ **Alcohol:** 4.9% ★ **Serving temp:** 1–2°C

Carib Lager

If you're going to drink a lager on the isles of Trinidad and Tobago then it's safe to assume you'll be drinking Carib Lager. First brewed in 1950, it's been a mainstay of island life for decades and is the Carib brewery's flagship product. Pale and refreshing with the easygoing taste you'd expect from a tropical island beer.

Tasting notes: Slightly malty flavours with a soft carbonation and a thin texture. Very lightly bitter.
★ **Country:** Trinidad and Tobago
★ **Brewer:** Carib Brewery
★ **Style:** Pale lager
★ **Appearance:** Pale yellow
★ **Alcohol:** 5.2%
★ **Serving temp:** 1–2°C

Ironshore Bock

One of the official beers of the Cayman Islands' famous Caybrew Cardboard Boat Race, this German-style bock (a strong lager) uses American-grown Cascade hops alongside Munich malts to create an amber lager with a powerful, sweetish flavour. This malty lager pairs well with any spicy food and nutty cheddar as well as a good traditional German bratwurst and sauerkraut.

Tasting notes: Light toffee, caramel and molasses.
★ **Country:** Cayman Islands
★ **Brewer:** The Cayman Islands Brewery
★ **Style:** Dunkler bock
★ **Appearance:** Dark amber
★ **Alcohol:** 7%
★ **Serving temp:** 4–7°C

Bière Lorraine

Also known as Lorraine Blonde, this beer takes its name from the region of Lorraine in north-eastern France, a region famous for its beer and where the creator of this beer learned his craft in the early 20th century. The island of Martinique may be thousands of miles from its parent country – but a little piece of French brewing culture is alive and well in Bière Lorraine.

Tasting notes: Sweet malts with notes of sweetcorn and grassy hops.
★ **Country:** Martinique ★ **Brewer:** Brasserie Lorraine
★ **Style:** Pale lager ★ **Appearance:** Medium yellow
★ **Alcohol:** 5% ★ **Serving temp:** 1–2°C

EUROPE

Europe is the home of most beer styles enjoyed in the world today, from refreshing pale lagers to warming strong ales.

In terms of the importance of brewing culture, the diversity of beers available, and the influence of its brewing traditions on the rest of the world, Europe remains the most important brewing region.

Europeans certainly love beer: Europe accounts for 15 of the top 20 beer-consuming countries by capita in the world, including the first four places. The Czech Republic tops the league table with an average of 132 litres of beer drunk per person every year.

Culturally, beer is an essential part of European society. It is consumed in a wide range of settings, as an accompaniment to food, to help relax and socialize, while watching sport

Scottish and Irish brewers have beers that reflect their own brewing traditions, such as heather ales and stouts.

or other events, and as a way of celebrating. Although consumption has been falling in recent years, the continent still produces 25 per cent of all the beer in the world – 427 billion litres a year.

Quantity isn't everything, however, and Europe can rightly claim to have a greater range of beer styles than anywhere else in

the world. It is home to some of the biggest beer brands in the world, such as Heineken, Guinness and Kronenbourg, but also to beers so local that they don't travel much beyond the shadow of the brewery.

For the beer tourist, a road trip through Europe is strewn with possibility.

England is the home of real ale – beer that is conditioned in the cask or bottle. It is a style that remains central to UK pub culture: most bars will have at least one, and usually several ales on offer. Despite reaching

a nadir in the 1970s when keg bitter and lager threatened to wipe it out, real ale is now in rude health. Brewers such as Adnams, Fuller's, Greene King and Timothy Taylor continue to create typically British-style beers.

Scottish and Irish brewers have beers that reflect their own brewing traditions, such as heather ales and stouts. Scotland has also emerged as the unlikely home of the brewers of the world's strongest beer. Craft brewer BrewDog set a record with its End of History beer, which had a strength of 55%

ABV. However, this was superseded by a 67.5% brew called Snake Venom, from the nearby Brewmeister brewery.

Across the English Channel in Belgium, a long history of brewing has produced distinctively different results. From Trappist and abbey beers to strong ales and lambic beers fermented with wild yeast, Belgium has a huge number of beer styles. Belgians have resisted the seemingly invincible onward march of pilsner lager, even though Stella Artois, its best-

known beer, is just that. Alongside the ubiquitous lager, Belgium has maintained its rich brewing tradition.

The heat of Spain makes beer one of the most popular drinks and the country is in the top 10 beer producers in the world.

Germany is sometimes thought of as the home of lager, and the image of foaming steins of golden beer is iconic. While that is what is served at the world's largest beer festival, Oktoberfest in Munich, German beer offers much more. Wheat beers are a speciality and are available in dark and light varieties. Other local brews include Cologne's Kölsch, the Altbiers of the Rhine, and regional specialities like Gose, which is centred on Leipzig.

Even traditional wine-drinking nations in Europe are waking up to beer. The heat of Spain makes beer one of the most popular drinks and

the country is in the top 10 beer producers in the world. Italy has a growing reputation as a destination for beer-themed tourism as a new generation of microbreweries has sprung up in the past 20 years. While large brewers like Peroni and Moretti cater for the mass market, Italy's craft brewers are creating beers to be savoured and which can be paired particularly well with food.

These are just a few of the beers on offer. There is a new beer to be discovered around every corner in Europe and something for every taste.

EUROPEAN BEER FACTS

* Europe has more than 5,000 years of brewing tradition

* There are more than 4,000 breweries in Europe

* There are an estimated 40,000 beer brands in the EU

* There are around 100 different beer styles

* The brewing industry employs more than two million people in the EU

* Europe's brewers generate €106 billion in sales or 0.42% of EU GDP

* Beer generates more than €50 billion in tax each year

* 50% of the world's hops are grown in Europe

* 20% of Europe's barley is used for beer

* Beer is brewed in all 28 EU member states

(Source: European Parliament Beer Club)

✚ Adnams Broadside

A heartwarming example of Great British brewing. Adnams brewery in Southwold, Suffolk, was founded in 1872 and it really knows its craft. Broadside is a multi-award-winning English strong ale rich in fruity, Christmas cake-like aromas and sweetness from the pale ale malts and First Gold hops. A fantastically authentic taste of the British Isles.

Tasting notes: Booze-soaked fruitcake and a healthy dose of floral hops to balance it out.

* ✱ **Country:** England
* ✱ **Brewer:** Adnams
* ✱ **Style:** Strong bitter
* ✱ **Appearance:** Dark ruby
* ✱ **Alcohol:** 6.3%
* ✱ **Serving temp:** 8–12°C

✚ Beavertown Smog Rocket

Started by the son of Led Zeppelin frontman Robert Plant and a foodie friend from his American adventures, Beavertown Brewery (named after the De Beauvoir area of Hackney) is fast becoming renowned not just for its excellent brewing creations – like this flavoursome and smooth smoked porter – but also for the creative food pairings served up in its American bar and grillhouse, Duke's Brew and Que in Hackney, London.

Tasting notes: Smoky, campfire-like aromas together with hints of coffee and a light body that's perfect served cellar-cool or slightly warmer.

* ✱ **Country:** England
* ✱ **Brewer:** Beavertown Brewery
* ✱ **Style:** Smoked porter
* ✱ **Appearance:** Dark brown
* ✱ **Alcohol:** 5.4%
* ✱ **Serving temp:** 4–12°C

✚ Courage Best

The flagship beer of a former brewing powerhouse and now owned by UK brewing group Wells and Young's, Courage Best is a simple 3.8% ABV English-style bitter. It really doesn't come more traditionally British than this. Despite a sharp decline in sales as more modern-style beers begin to gain popularity, Courage Best is still among the top ten bestselling beers in England.

Tasting notes: Light notes of hay, toast and caramel in the nose with a smooth and sweet finish.

* ✱ **Country:** England
* ✱ **Brewer:** Wells and Young's
* ✱ **Style:** Bitter
* ✱ **Appearance:** Amber
* ✱ **Alcohol:** 3.8%
* ✱ **Serving temp:** 8–13°C

✚ Dark Star Revelation

Regarded by many in the business as one of the best brewers in the world, Dark Star's Rob Jones named his first brew for Dark Star brewery (then called Skinners) after a Grateful Dead song. The name stuck and became the name of the brewery soon after. Revelation is an American-style pale ale made with four North American hop varieties for that instantly recognizable fresh citrus aroma.

Tasting notes: A cheesecake biscuit-like base is followed by a wave of citrus fruits, pine and butterscotch.

* ✱ **Country:** England
* ✱ **Brewer:** Dark Star Brewing
* ✱ **Style:** American pale ale
* ✱ **Appearance:** Deep amber
* ✱ **Alcohol:** 5.7%
* ✱ **Serving temp:** 6–10°C

🏴󠁧󠁢󠁥󠁮󠁧󠁿 Fuller's London Pride

A beer that's synonymous with the city in which it is brewed, and highly regarded by its devotees. Fuller's London Pride is one of the most popular real ales in Britain and has won a multitude of awards from beer enthusiasts and CAMRA (Campaign for Real Ale) since it was first brewed in the 1950s.

Tasting notes: Spices, nuts and tea-like aromas from the dark malts, together with woody hops and peach.
✳ **Country:** England ✳ **Brewer:** Fuller's ✳ **Style:** Premium bitter
✳ **Appearance:** Golden ✳ **Alcohol:** 4.7% ✳ **Serving temp:** 8–12°C

🏴󠁧󠁢󠁥󠁮󠁧󠁿 Greene King Abbot Ale

Brewed atop the ruins of an ancient monastery, Greene King's Abbot Ale is a tribute to the brewing heritage of the Great Abbey in Bury St Edmunds. The *cerevisiarii* or ale brewers would brew on behalf of the Abbot of the monastery; they drew water from the same chalk wells still used today by the brewers at Greene King. They use only English ingredients, including the famous hop varieties Fuggles, Goldings and Challenger for an authentically English taste.

Tasting notes: Hints of elderflower and dark berries are subtly woven into a brown sugar-rich malt background.
✳ **Country:** England
✳ **Brewer:** Greene King
✳ **Style:** Premium bitter
✳ **Appearance:** Amber
✳ **Alcohol:** 5%
✳ **Serving temp:** 8–12°C

DID YOU KNOW?

Before the invention of thermometers brewers used their thumbs to estimate the right temperature at which to add yeast to their mix, thus giving rise to the phrase 'the rule of thumb'.

✚ Greene King Old Speckled Hen

The name of this beloved English premium bitter is nothing to do with the egg-laying farmyard fowl. It was first brewed in 1979 to mark the 50th anniversary of the MG car factory in Abingdon and the name came from a paint-speckled car used as a runaround by the factory workers – which they affectionately named the Ol' Speckl'd 'Un.

Tasting notes: Sweet light caramel aromas with a little orchard fruitiness and a softly bitter finish.
* ✱ **Country:** England
* ✱ **Brewer:** Greene King
* ✱ **Style:** Bitter
* ✱ **Appearance:** Light brown
* ✱ **Alcohol:** 5.2%
* ✱ **Serving temp:** 7–12°C

✚ Ilkley Mary Jane IPA

'Tastes like happiness' is the byline for this transatlantic IPA from Ilkley in Yorkshire. Using their blonde ale Mary Jane as a base and traditional English hops for bittering, Mary Jane IPA includes floral and fragrant American hops from the Yakima Valley to give it a distinctly modern aroma and pleasantly sharp bitterness.

Tasting notes: Hints of orange blossom and pine resin together with elderflower and honey-enriched malt.
* ✱ **Country:** England
* ✱ **Brewer:** Ilkley Brewery
* ✱ **Style:** IPA
* ✱ **Appearance:** Hazy gold
* ✱ **Alcohol:** 6%
* ✱ **Serving temp:** 4–7°C

✚ Magic Rock Cannonball

Magic Rock is a Yorkshire-based microbrewery set up in 2010 by two brothers with a love for beer, together with brewmaster Stuart Ross. Cannonball is one of Magic Rock's more restrained IPAs at 7.4% ABV. The Double IPA Human Cannonball weighs in at 9.2% while their 2013 Triple IPA Un-Human Cannonball is a massive 11%. This is a brewery that does everything but the ordinary.

Tasting notes: Tropical flavours of passionfruit and more resinous pine-like qualities balancing beautifully with a sweet malty backbone.
* ✱ **Country:** England
* ✱ **Brewer:** Magic Rock Brewing
* ✱ **Style:** IPA
* ✱ **Appearance:** Hazy amber
* ✱ **Alcohol:** 7.4% ✱ **Serving temp:** 4–7°C

DID YOU KNOW?

The London Beer Flood occurred in October 1814, when a vat containing more than 135,000 imperial gallons of beer ruptured. The resulting tidal wave demolished houses and killed nine people, one from alcohol poisoning.

✚ Marble Dobber

The bestselling beer in the Marble brewery's range is Dobber – a 5.9% ABV IPA flavoured with hops native to New Zealand for an exotic taste that Mancunians and the rest of the UK are lapping up. This Manchester-based brewery also runs three brewpubs in the city – The Beerhouse, 57 Thomas Street and the Marble Arch. The latter was the inspiration for starting a brewery in the first place, in order to save a beloved local venue from extinction – though they nearly turned it into a karaoke bar instead.

Tasting notes: Ripe tropical fruits and buttery toffee caramel balanced with a dry, hoppy, bitter finish.
* **Country:** England * **Brewer:** Marble * **Style:** IPA
* **Appearance:** Hazy orange * **Alcohol:** 5.9% * **Serving temp:** 4–7°C

THE PUB LEAGUE

For as long as drinking establishments have existed, their patrons have been keen to mix drinking with play. Consequently, Britain has a rich and varied history of pub games.

Traditional games such as cards, darts, skittles and dominoes remain popular and are played in a multitude of different ways, with rules varying from region to region or even from pub to pub.

Many 'British' pub games actually arrived from overseas. Draughts came with the Romans; dominoes were originally from China, via Italy, and billiards was probably conceived in France.

As well as entertaining drinkers, games are a great way for landlords to keep customers in the pub spending money.

Not surprisingly, this has not gone down well with the authorities over the years. Both Henry VII and Cromwell passed laws banning games.

However, drinkers continued to develop their own pastimes, including the weird and wacky – such as dwyle flunking, gnurdling, bumble puppy and wellie wanging. Some games have died out due to lack of space or changing modern tastes. Pipe smoking contests are rare these days, although some indoor shooting leagues continue.

The introduction of satellite TV sport in pubs may have focused the competitive spirit onto a screen rather than a cribbage board, but the desire to team beer with light-hearted competition remains.

🏴 Marston's Pedigree

Pedigree is the flagship brand of a brewing powerhouse, with sales hitting a peak of nearly 150,000 hectolitres in 2010. The traditional aromas from English hop varieties are teamed with Marston's yeast and fermented in a unique 19th-century system of huge oak barrels, called the Burton Union system.

Tasting notes: Caramel malts and hedgerow-like grassy hops with a smooth texture and easygoing finish.
* ✹ **Country:** England
* ✹ **Brewer:** Marston's
* ✹ **Style:** Bitter
* ✹ **Appearance:** Amber
* ✹ **Alcohol:** 4.5%
* ✹ **Serving temp:** 8–13°C

🏴 Meantime Yakima Red

Based on the cusp of the Greenwich Meridian, the Meantime brewery has gone from being a small-batch microbrewer to the definitive modern English brewery. This hoppy red ale gets its colour from a combination of German and English malts and is balanced with five of the fruitiest hops the Yakima Valley region of the USA can offer.

Tasting notes: Well-roasted malts and a plethora of hoppy fruit flavours make this a great match for crispy roast pork belly.
* ✹ **Country:** England
* ✹ **Brewer:** Meantime Brewing Co.
* ✹ **Style:** Amber ale
* ✹ **Appearance:** Dark amber
* ✹ **Alcohol:** 4.3% ✹ **Serving temp:** 4–7°C

🏴 O'Hanlon's Thomas Hardy's Ale

Here we have a beer that demands a measure of patience to enjoy it at its best. When just brewed, Thomas Hardy's Ale has a sharp and boozy edge that will soften and develop if you let it rest in the cellar for at least a decade. If you can wait that long, you'll be rewarded with an incredibly complex and full-bodied flavour.

Tasting notes: Notes of brandy and sherry with lots of earthy fruit and caramel. Drink with strong blue cheese.
* ✹ **Country:** England
* ✹ **Brewer:** O'Hanlon's
* ✹ **Style:** Barley wine
* ✹ **Appearance:** Mahogany red
* ✹ **Alcohol:** 11.7%
* ✹ **Serving temp:** 10–14°C

CRAFT BEER: ATLANTIC CROSSING

Britain has a great tradition of brewing that stretches back hundreds of years. In recent decades this has been reinvigorated by an upsurge in interest from a new group of brewers. Step forward the craft brewer.

It is hard to pin down the definition of craft brewing and craft beer. For some people, it relates to the size of a brewery, with craft equalling small and passionate teams producing low amounts of high-quality beer using the very best ingredients. Others see independence from large-scale brewing companies as one of the main criteria. Or maybe it relates to the type of beer that is being produced, typically taking existing styles and adding a dash of experimentalism.

In reality, craft beer is probably a mix of all of these things, and some more besides. The roots of the movement can be traced to the United States, where in the 1970s and 80s pioneering brewers started to produce beers that provided drinkers with an alternative to the high-volume American lagers that dominated the marketplace.

Key names include Fritz Maytag, saviour of the Anchor Brewing Company, Jack McAuliffe, who started the first American microbrewery, the New Albion, Jim Koch, creator of Samuel Adams, and Ken Grossman, who founded the Sierra Nevada Brewing Company. They helped establish the framework for a new industry in the US, leading to an explosion of microbreweries and brewpubs. Where they led, breweries like Dogfish Head, Stone Brewing, New Belgium Brewing, Rogue Ales and many others have followed.

Although Europe has a more varied beer tradition, and one to which US craft brewers have looked for inspiration, European brewers have not been immune to the charms of the US. Indeed, America's craft-beer movement has now become a model for a new generation of brewers.

They helped establish the framework for a new industry in the US, leading to an explosion of microbreweries and brewpubs.

Craft beer geeks in the US have become experts at experimenting with somewhat side-lined beer types, such as fruit beers, barley wine and imperial stouts, producing imaginative results. Unusual recipes, seasonal specials, and highly hopped versions of old favourites such as pale ale are all hallmarks of the craft-beer scene. UK brewers such as Dark Star, Meantime, Marble and BrewDog have paid homage to this approach.

The craft sector has also been a marketing success story. Although beer-obsessed cognoscenti will claim 'it's all about the beer', it's hard to deny that part of craft beer's allure is its cool, even sexy, status. It is brewed by

young, hip guys for a well-heeled group of customers who see themselves as connoisseurs of beer rather than simply consumers.

Branding of beers by companies such as Thornbridge, St Peter's and the Camden Town Brewery is modern and intriguing. In the same way that New World wines made those of traditional winemakers seem dull, the iconography of craft beers often makes them stand out in a crowded market.

Craft beer has also embraced kegs, which is another point of difference with real ale loyalists, who insist on cask conditioning as a badge of authenticity. Craft brewers have been more ready to use kegs to keep their beer fresh, as well as bottles and even cans.

A further reason that small-scale brewing has taken off in the UK is that the sliding scale of duty has made it more economically viable for producers with lower volumes to start up.

Whatever the reasons, craft beer is in the ascendancy. Established brewers such as Fuller's and Adnams have already collaborated with exponents of craft beer, both from the UK and the US. Other brewers, such as Ringwood, have rebranded to emphasize that they too are brewing 'craft' beer.

Only the future will tell if the title of 'craft beer' still holds meaning, or whether the sector simply becomes part of a wider and more varied beer market.

UK CRAFT BREWERS TO LOOK OUT FOR:

BrewDog
Based in – Aberdeenshire
Try – Punk IPA, Dogma Scotch ale

Thornbridge
Based in – Derbyshire
Try – Jaipur IPA, Kill Your Darlings

Marble
Based in – Manchester
Try – Manchester Bitter, Ginger 6

Meantime
Based in – Greenwich, London
Try – London Lager, Chocolate Porter

Dark Star
Based in – West Sussex
Try – American Pale Ale, Dark Star Original

Bristol Beer Factory
Based in – Bristol
Try – Milk Stout, Seven

Wild Beer Company
Based in – Somerset
Try – Madness IPA, Fresh

Camden Town Brewery
Based in – Camden, London
Try – Camden Hells lager, Camden Pale Ale

Williams Brothers
Based in – Alloa, Scotland
Try – Fraoch Heather Ale, Williams 80 Shillings

St Peter's Brewery
Based in – Suffolk
Try – Golden Ale, Cream Stout

⊞ Oakham JHB

Named after the diminutive court jester Jeffrey Hudson, Oakham JHB is an award-winning bitter that was crowned Supreme Champion Beer of Britain 2001. This is traditional bitter with a modern twist. More hop-led than traditional-style bitters; it has a familiar buttery and biscuity-sweet malt base to give it real mass appeal.

Tasting notes: Pithy, citrus-infused hops at the forefront in both aroma and taste, with toasted malt afterthought.
✱ **Country:** England ✱ **Brewer:** Oakham Ales
✱ **Style:** Golden ale ✱ **Appearance:** Pale yellow
✱ **Alcohol:** 4.2% ✱ **Serving temp:** 6–10°C

⊞ Redemption Trinity

It's often a good measure of how skilled a brewer is when you see how much flavour can be packed into a low ABV beer. If Trinity is anything to go by, then Andy Moffat, head brewer at Redemption brewery, is nothing short of a genius. At only 3% ABV, Trinity is a beer that you'll be able to (and want to) drink all evening.

Tasting notes: Doughy white bread and crackers with a citrus hit of Seville orange and lime zest.
✱ **Country:** England
✱ **Brewer:** Redemption Brewing Co.
✱ **Style:** Golden ale
✱ **Appearance:** Medium orange
✱ **Alcohol:** 3%
✱ **Serving temp:** 8–13°C

⊞ Samuel Smith's Oatmeal Stout

The Samuel Smith brewery based in the small brewing town of Tadcaster in Yorkshire has always done things the old-fashioned way. This includes delivering beer to local venues by horse and cart, serving their product 'straight from the wood' where possible and using traditional Yorkshire slate square vessels to ferment their varied range of beers – including this silky oatmeal stout.

Tasting notes: Smooth, milky chocolate and roasted almonds are carried off with a thick and viscous texture in the mouth.
✱ **Country:** England
✱ **Brewer:** Samuel Smith Old Brewery
✱ **Style:** Oatmeal stout
✱ **Appearance:** Deep brown
✱ **Alcohol:** 5%
✱ **Serving temp:** 8–13°C

✚ Sambrook's Wandle

Great breweries (and some bad ones) are often started with the founder quitting a boring City job for a radical career change. That's what happened to Duncan Sambrook when he began the Sambrook's brewery in 2010. His light and extremely quaffable session bitter, Wandle, is named after the river that runs through south-west London and into the Thames. Indeed, all the Sambrook's beers are named for local landmarks.

Tasting notes: Easygoing peach-like hop flavours with a light vanilla hint from the pale English malt. Great with fish and chips.
* ✱ **Country:** England ✱ **Brewer:** Sambrook's Brewery ✱ **Style:** Bitter
* ✱ **Appearance:** Orange ✱ **Alcohol:** 3.8% ✱ **Serving temp:** 8–13°C

✚ Sharp's Doom Bar

Doom Bar is Sharp's biggest-selling beer, accounting for nearly 90 per cent of all its sales. Named after a dangerous sandbank in North Cornwall that is notorious for getting sailors into tricky situations, Doom Bar is rather controversially sold in a clear bottle that offers very little protection from harmful UV rays in sunlight, but which shows off the beer's distinctive amber colour.

Tasting notes: Roasted caramel and honey with hints of orange blossom. A good match for roast chicken.
* ✱ **Country:** England ✱ **Brewer:** Sharp's Brewery ✱ **Style:** Bitter
* ✱ **Appearance:** Amber ✱ **Alcohol:** 4.3% ✱ **Serving temp:** 8–13°C

✚ St Austell Korev

Proper lager should be stored for anything from one to five months in order for the lager yeast to do its job properly. Korev is a very well-made version from the St Austell brewery in Cornwall. Made with 100 per cent locally grown barley and stored or 'lagered' at low temperatures for a lengthy maturation, Korev is easily distinguishable from most of the lagers you find in the average British pub. Full of fresh white bread aromas and a wonderfully crisp, bitter finish, it can pair nicely with a wide selection of dishes, from charcuterie to sushi.

Tasting notes: Doughy white bread, creamy marshmallow and a little lemony citrus fruit. Pure, clean and uncomplicated.
* ✱ **Country:** England ✱ **Brewer:** St Austell Brewery ✱ **Style:** Lager
* ✱ **Appearance:** Orange ✱ **Alcohol:** 4.8% ✱ **Serving temp:** 4–6°C

⊞ The Kernel Table Beer

Table beer was once a prominent style in Belgium and other parts of Europe. Table beer has a low alcoholic strength (traditionally only 1–2% ABV) and is served up in large quantities at the dinner table. The Kernel's version is a little stronger – typically 2.7% – and uses plenty of American hops for a fresh aroma and bitter finish. Widely regarded as one of the best brewers in the British Isles for its artisanal and passionate approach to craft brewing.

Tasting notes: Considerable passionfruit aromas together with mandarins and peach, rounded off with a short sharp bitter finish.
* ✶ **Country:** England ✶ **Brewer:** The Kernel Brewery
* ✶ **Style:** Table beer ✶ **Appearance:** Hazy gold
* ✶ **Alcohol:** 2.7-3% ✶ **Serving temp:** 4–7°C

⊞ Theakston Old Peculier

Old Peculier owes its origin to the strong, dark stock beers that were brewed around 200 years ago in the cool winter months. These stock beers were kept to provide a base for the beers brewed in the summer months to give them stability in the warmer temperatures. It is still brewed using traditional methods in the Masham brewery in North Yorkshire, in an area known as Paradise Fields.

Tasting notes: Sweet bread pudding with rich fruit overtones of cherry and figs. Perfect paired with a dark stew.
* ✶ **Country:** England
* ✶ **Brewer:** T. & R. Theakston
* ✶ **Style:** Old ale
* ✶ **Appearance:** Deep ruby
* ✶ **Alcohol:** 5.6%
* ✶ **Serving temp:** 7–12°C

⊞ Thornbridge Jaipur

One of the most highly regarded brewers in the UK, Thornbridge was one of the first to take the exciting modern and hoppy beers of the USA and refine them with English sensibilities. The original brewery opened in the grounds of Thornbridge Hall, Derbyshire, in 2005; it has now been joined by a new, state-of-the-art brewery.

Tasting notes: Grapefruit and elderflower with a balance of white bread and honey. Perfect with a spicy Indian curry.
* ✶ **Country:** England
* ✶ **Brewer:** Thornbridge Brewery
* ✶ **Style:** IPA
* ✶ **Appearance:** Pale gold
* ✶ **Alcohol:** 5.9%
* ✶ **Serving temp:** 4–7°C

✚ Timothy Taylor's Landlord

Four times Champion Beer of Britain at the Great British Beer Festival, Timothy Taylor's Landlord is also well known as being the preferred tipple of pop star Madonna. Initially created in the 1950s for the mining communities of West Yorkshire in order to compete with a local rival brew, Landlord won the miners over and is still going strong.

Tasting notes: Toasted white bread and cereals together with botanic floral hops. Try it with pork sausages and mashed potato.

* **Country:** England
* **Brewer:** Timothy Taylor
* **Style:** Pale ale
* **Appearance:** Golden orange
* **Alcohol:** 4.3%
* **Serving temp:** 4–7°C

HOME BREWS

Once upon a time, the majority of beer would have been served where it was brewed, often in the alewife's house.

Over the years, as brewing became more professional and commercial, the distance between the brewery and the place where the beer was drunk has increased. By the 1970s in Britain there were only a handful of pubs left that brewed their own beer. The oldest is thought to be the Blue Anchor in Cornwall, which has been brewing since 1400.

However, in recent years there has been a switch back to a more localized approach. Access to small-scale brewing equipment, a sliding scale of duty for smaller producers and the desire of enthusiasts to produce their own beer has led to a reversal of history. In brewing, bigger is not necessarily better, and both brewers and drinkers are now beginning to appreciate this.

Brewpubs have now sprung up throughout the UK, and the number is increasing every week. They range from hip city pubs such as Manchester's Marble Arch and London's Camden Town Brewery, to country boozers like Hampshire's The Flowerpots or Kent's The Swan on the Green.

Ironically, one of the biggest recent influences on British brewpub growth has been the envious glances across the Atlantic at the US scene, where brewpubs have been producing their versions of classic British styles for the past 20 years.

🏴󠁧󠁢󠁥󠁮󠁧󠁿 Windsor & Eton Knight of the Garter

Launched to mark the annual 'Ceremony of the Garter' at the royal residence of Windsor Castle in Berkshire. Awarded by the monarch, the Order of the Garter has only 24 members and is the most prestigious level of the honours system in England. Thankfully the beer is good enough to live up to its noble title.

Tasting notes: Lightly hoppy with a bready sweetness, making it perfect with roast chicken.
* ✷ **Country:** England
* ✷ **Brewer:** Windsor & Eton
* ✷ **Style:** Golden ale
* ✷ **Appearance:** Golden
* ✷ **Alcohol:** 3.8%
* ✷ **Serving temp:** 7–10°C

🏴󠁧󠁢󠁥󠁮󠁧󠁿 Worthington's White Shield

The only pale ale still being made from the golden age of brewing in the 19th century, William Worthington's White Shield was first brewed to export to India and had to be highly hopped in order to survive the long journey. As a result, this traditional pale ale ages rather well in bottle.

Tasting notes: Earthy hops and bitterness with a toffee, honeyed white bread from the malt.
* ✷ **Country:** England
* ✷ **Brewer:** Coors UK
* ✷ **Style:** IPA
* ✷ **Appearance:** Golden
* ✷ **Alcohol:** 5.6%
* ✷ **Serving temp:** 8–13°C

DID YOU KNOW?

Porter and stout were originally a murky brown colour, until the drum roaster was invented in 1817 by Daniel Wheeler. The black patent malt he created changed the colour and flavour of porter for ever.

🏴󠁧󠁢󠁥󠁮󠁧󠁿 Wychwood Hobgoblin

Known for its fantastical artwork of witchcraft, wood nymphs and wily goblins, Wychwood Brewery has been a success story since its inception in 1983. Brewed near Wychwood Forest in Oxfordshire, its flagship brand Hobgoblin is a dark ruby-red ale with as much character and sense of mischief as the crafty character that adorns the label. A dark ale that's loaded with complex flavour.

Tasting notes: Toffee pudding with hints of sharp lemon and bitter chocolate with a light tobacco aftertaste.
* ✷ **Country:** England
* ✷ **Brewer:** Wychwood Brewery
* ✷ **Style:** Ruby ale
* ✷ **Appearance:** Ruby red
* ✷ **Alcohol:** 5.2%
* ✷ **Serving temp:** 8–12°C

⚔ Arran Blonde

On one of Scotland's many small but beautiful islands there is a brewer that positions itself at the centre of the local community. Arran Blonde is drunk at Highland games, in small folk clubs and along the many hiking trails of Arran. Thankfully, the island doesn't keep all the supply of this wonderful golden ale to itself.

Tasting notes: Brown bread with notes of honey, peppery bitterness and a herbal grassy hop finish.
* ✱ **Country:** Scotland
* ✱ **Brewer:** Isle of Arran Brewery
* ✱ **Style:** Golden ale
* ✱ **Appearance:** Golden
* ✱ **Alcohol:** 5%
* ✱ **Serving temp:** 4–7°C

⚔ Belhaven Best

John Johnstone started Belhaven in 1719 and this traditionally run brewery remained in his family until its sale to Greene King in 2005. Belhaven Best may have changed over the years but it's still rated as one of the best bitters in Scotland. With its easygoing, bready flavours, it is one for any occasion.

Tasting notes: Crackerbreads, toasted grains with a hint of cooked vegetable.
✱ **Country:** Scotland ✱ **Brewer:** Belhaven ✱ **Style:** Bitter
✱ **Appearance:** Amber ✱ **Alcohol:** 3.5% ✱ **Serving temp:** 7–12°C

SCOTLAND'S SHILLING SYSTEM

The country may have gone decimal in 1971, but in Scotland beer is still sometimes referred to by the old money term of shillings.

The shilling system dates from the mid-19th century, when the taxes on malt and sugar in the United Kingdom were replaced by Beer Duty. The shilling names referred to the price of a hogshead (about 50 imperial gallons) of the ale.

Brewers produced a number of beers of differing styles and alcohol content. 40/- ale was a very light beer often supplied to farmhands. The 50/- and 60/- beers were also reasonably light. 70/-, 80/- and 90/- were progressively stronger beers, known as 'heavy' and 'export'. The strongest Scotch ales, known as 'wee heavy', could be up to 160/- with an alcohol content of 9–10% ABV.

The shilling system continued to be used to indicate the beers' quality and was legally recognized in 1914. The system gradually declined in use after World War II. The terms 'Light', 'Heavy' and 'Export' came to denote beer types and strengths.

Scottish brewers resurrected the terms when cask ale experienced a resurgence in the 1970s. Today they can be seen in such beers as Belhaven 80/-, Caledonian 80/- as well as in North American Scotch ale-style beers.

The system was unique to Scotland and as such provides one of the purely Scottish contributions to the overall history of brewing.

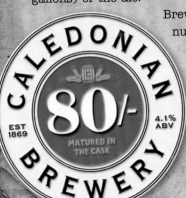

✠ BrewDog Punk IPA

Known for their brash marketing strategy, Scotland's 'punk' brewers BrewDog really caused a stir when they emerged, wild and restless, into the UK brewing scene in the early 2000s. Thankfully they weren't all mouth and no trousers. Punk IPA is still regarded as one of the best of the new wave of IPAs the UK has produced. All the exciting grapefruit and tropical flavour you'd expect from an American-style IPA, with a dry, mouth-puckering bitter finish to boot. Mohawk and nose rings not required to enjoy this one.

Tasting notes: Tropical fruit flavours from the blend of American and southern hemisphere hops.
✼ **Country:** Scotland ✼ **Brewer:** BrewDog ✼ **Style:** IPA
✼ **Appearance:** Light golden ✼ **Alcohol:** 5.6% ✼ **Serving temp:** 4–8°C

✠ Fyne Ales Jarl

One of the first beers in the UK to demonstrate the potential of the vibrant Citra hop, Jarl is a very drinkable session beer. The Nordic name refers to the Norwegian Earls (Jarls) who, in the 12th century, claimed much of the land that now surrounds the Fyne Ales brewery in Argyll.

Tasting notes: Citrus and grassy hop flavours are at the forefront, with a light and quickly diminishing finish.
✼ **Country:** Scotland ✼ **Brewer:** Fyne Ales
✼ **Style:** Blonde ale ✼ **Appearance:** Golden
✼ **Alcohol:** 3.8% ✼ **Serving temp:** 4–7°C

✠ Harviestoun Schiehallion

It's often hard to get excited about drinking a lager, but when it is as well made as Harviestoun's Schiehallion it becomes a little easier. First brewed in 1994, nobody envisioned the wild success of this Scottish favourite – now available all over the world – especially considering the tricky-to-pronounce name (pronounced 'She-hali-on'), which takes its name from a local mountain.

Tasting notes: Aromas of grass and caramelized apples with smaller hints of mango. A very crisp and fresh finish.
✼ **Country:** Scotland ✼ **Brewer:** Harviestoun Brewery ✼ **Style:** Lager
✼ **Appearance:** Yellow ✼ **Alcohol:** 4.8% ✼ **Serving temp:** 4–7°C

🏴󠁧󠁢󠁳󠁣󠁴󠁿 Orkney Dark Island Reserve

Ageing its award-winning Dark Island ale for three months at low temperatures in old Orkney whisky casks, the Orkney Brewery works some serious magic into this highly decorated beer. It is made in limited quantities and will age very nicely at home, so be in no great rush to drink it.

Tasting notes: Soft, peaty notes with a touch of oak and plenty of bitter chocolate and coffee.
* **Country:** Scotland * **Brewer:** The Orkney Brewery
* **Style:** Barley wine * **Appearance:** Deep brown
* **Alcohol:** 10% * **Serving temp:** 8–15°C

🏴󠁧󠁢󠁳󠁣󠁴󠁿 Orkney Raven Ale

Based in a former schoolhouse, the Orkney Brewery was founded in 1988 by Roger White and still brews at the same site. This is its classic bitter, which is laced with intense grainy aromas – a result of the high-quality pale ale malt used in the brewing process. A very refreshing and easy drink.

Tasting notes: Sweet biscuit and light pine hoppiness in the aroma followed by more of the same on the palate.
* **Country:** Scotland
* **Brewer:** The Orkney Brewery
* **Style:** Blonde ale
* **Appearance:** Golden
* **Alcohol:** 3.8%
* **Serving temp:** 4–7°C

🏴󠁧󠁢󠁳󠁣󠁴󠁿 West St Mungo Lager

Owned by German-born Petra Wetzel, the West brewery is located in the heart of Glasgow, and specializes in lagers and wheat beers. St Mungo Lager, the flagship brand of the company, follows the principles of the German purity law or *Reinheitsgebot*: only barley, hops and yeast are used for an authentic German-inspired flavour and character. A real taste of Bavaria via Scotland!

Tasting notes: Crisp and clean with a toffee note and equal parts of sweet fruits, toasted grain and nuttiness.
* **Country:** Scotland * **Brewer:** West * **Style:** Lager
* **Appearance:** Clear orange * **Alcohol:** 4.9% * **Serving temp:** 4–7°C

🏴 Traquair House Ale

Traquair House Ale is brewed with patience and care: the beer is fermented in oak vessels, some of which are 200 years old. Currently brewing only around 600 barrels per year, Traquair is the very definition of small-scale brewing and its House Ale is definitely a rarity to be savoured.

Tasting notes: Lots of roasted malts, liquorice and caramel, with a smooth spicy finish.
* ✫ **Country:** Scotland ✫ **Brewer:** Traquair
* ✫ **Style:** Scotch ale ✫ **Appearance:** Dark red
* ✫ **Alcohol:** 7.2% ✫ **Serving temp:** 8–13°C

🏴 Williams Brothers Fraoch Heather Ale

Described by the brewers Williams Brothers as the 'Original Craft Beer', Fraoch is based on an ancient Gaelic recipe for heather ale – a recipe that dates back over 4,000 years. Williams Brothers is the only brewery that produces this rarity and distributes it worldwide. The brewery is noted for many other interesting styles, including a Scots pine ale, a tayberry beer and a chocolate seaweed ale. Froach is perhaps the most popular, thanks to its delicate but pronounced honey-like flavours. A proper taste of the Highlands.

Tasting notes: Herbal, honey flavours combine with bready malts and a slight spicy ginger finish.
* ✫ **Country:** Scotland ✫ **Brewer:** Williams Brothers ✫ **Style:** Heather ale
* ✫ **Appearance:** Golden ✫ **Alcohol:** 5% ✫ **Serving temp:** 8–13°C

DID YOU KNOW?

The world's strongest beer comes from Scotland – Brewmeister's Snake Venom has a whopping 67.5% ABV, achieved by the use of smoked peat malt, beer yeast and champagne yeast. It's expensive too, at £50 per bottle.

Beamish Stout

The flagship beer of Cork-based brewery Beamish and Crawford, Beamish Stout is a traditional Irish stout. In a similar vein to Ireland's most famous and bestselling dry stout, Guinness, Beamish has a drier flavour and is noted for its large creamy head that laces the glass to the last drop. Great with a hearty Irish stew.

Tasting notes: Slightly smoky in the nose with notes of burnt coffee, Beamish has an oily texture and a quick, dry finish.
* **Country:** Ireland
* **Brewer:** Heineken Ireland
* **Style:** Dry stout
* **Appearance:** Dark brown
* **Alcohol:** 4.1% ✶ **Serving temp:** 6–10°C

Elbow Lane Angel Stout

A relative newcomer to the world of microbrewing, Elbow Lane produced its first beer, Angel Stout, in 2012, soon followed by Elbow Lager and Wisdom Ale. In the wonderful Angel Stout, brewed with dark burnt malts and the strong Herkules hop variety, Elbow Lane has created a truly authentic taste of Irish dry stout.

Tasting notes: Thick bitter chocolate, coffee and a firm, spicy hop profile.
* **Country:** Ireland
* **Brewer:** Elbow Lane ✶ **Style:** Dry stout
* **Appearance:** Deep brown
* **Alcohol:** 5% ✶ **Serving temp:** 8–13°C

Harp Lager

Marketed with the Brian Boru harp as its logo, a bottle of Harp could, at a glance, be confused with Guinness. Unlike Guinness though, this is a pale lager and not nearly as widely available as the famous Irish stout. Known for being the default lager option in many Irish pubs, its taste will be familiar to any Irish lager lover. Crisp, clean with a dry finish.

Tasting notes: Easy to drink with light malts, fresh fruity citrus hints on the nose and a very smooth aftertaste.
* **Country:** Ireland
* **Brewer:** Dundalk Brewery
* **Style:** Pale lager
* **Appearance:** Yellow
* **Alcohol:** 4.3% ✶ **Serving temp:** 2–5°C

Galway Bay Buried at Sea

Buried at Sea from Galway Bay Brewery is a sweet milk stout made with added lactose (milk sugar). Since lactose can't be consumed by yeast during fermentation, it remains in the beer and gives a sweetish taste. The sweetness works brilliantly with the chocolatey flavours of a stout. A real after-dinner treat for grown-ups.

Tasting notes: Surprisingly light with hints of hazelnut, dark chocolate and milk. Prime candidate for a scoop of vanilla ice cream.
* **Country:** Ireland * **Brewer:** Galway Bay Brewery
* **Style:** Milk stout * **Appearance:** Deep brown
* **Alcohol:** 4.5% * **Serving temp:** 7–12°C

Guinness

Guinness is as famous around the world as it is in its native Ireland. With its distinctive thick tan head and matt black body, it has a reputation for being a meal in a glass – yet surprisingly it is lighter in calories than most lagers. Guinness is known for its exceptionally creamy taste. The archetypal Irish stout.

Tasting notes: Creamy beige head with aromas of coffee, dark chocolate and sugar. Uncomplicated bliss.
* **Country:** Ireland
* **Brewer:** Guinness Brewery
* **Style:** Dry stout
* **Appearance:** Matt black
* **Alcohol:** 4.1%
* **Serving temp:** 7–12°C

Metalman Pale Ale

Like many microbreweries, Metalman was set up when its founders became disillusioned with lack of choice, lack of flavour and seeing the same old beers over and over again. This American-style pale ale is its only permanent beer, but it releases seasonal beers every few weeks to keep its range as interesting as possible. The pale ale manages to keep a fairly low alcohol content, while still offering a large array of citrus fruit and tropical hops with a deliciously bitter aftertaste. Perfect with a curry of any kind.

Tasting notes: Grapefruit and tinned mandarins from the hops, with a spicy bitter finish.
* **Country:** Ireland * **Brewer:** Metalman Brewing Co. * **Style:** American pale ale
* **Appearance:** Dark gold * **Alcohol:** 4.3% * **Serving temp:** 4–7°C

Murphy's Irish Stout

Known simply as Murphy's to drinkers around Ireland, Murphy's Irish Stout was intended to be lighter and less bitter than its famous compatriot Guinness. However, Murphy's has a textbook dry stout finish. The lively rivalry between the two is famous in recent Irish folk history.

Tasting notes: Strong hints of chocolate and coffee suggest a milky cappuccino flavour.
* ✱ **Country:** Ireland
* ✱ **Brewer:** Heineken Ireland
* ✱ **Style:** Dry stout ✱ **Appearance:** Black
* ✱ **Alcohol:** 4% ✱ **Serving temp:** 4–7°C

Porterhouse Oyster Stout

Traditionally, oysters were not seen as the luxurious aphrodisiac they are perceived as today. On the contrary, they were so cheap and plentiful they'd be added to pies and stews to bulk them out. Oysters and stout are a great pairing. Here, oysters are added to the conditioning tank for a subtle savoury touch.

Tasting notes: Roasted malt aroma with a smooth, salty and bread-like flavour. Unsuitable for vegetarians!
* ✱ **Country:** Ireland ✱ **Brewer:** Porterhouse Brewing Co.
* ✱ **Style:** Oyster stout ✱ **Appearance:** Black
* ✱ **Alcohol:** 5.2% ✱ **Serving temp:** 8–13°C

Trouble Brewing Dark Arts Porter

Trouble Brewing, based in Co. Kildare, brewed its first beers in 2010. Using an open-source computerized system to control its brewing mechanism, it is able to be precise about every detail of the brewing process. This easy-drinking porter is made with a low and sessionable alcohol content, while keeping the flavour intense and in balance. Dark Arts Porter is one of the regular beers, joined by seasonal specials at different times of the year. The first brewery in Ireland to accept payment in Bitcoins.

Tasting notes: Long-lasting fresh coffee and bitter chocolate without being heavy. Easy-drinking porter.
* ✱ **Country:** Ireland ✱ **Brewer:** Trouble Brewing ✱ **Style:** Porter
* ✱ **Appearance:** Deep brown ✱ **Alcohol:** 4.4% ✱ **Serving temp:** 8–13°C

 Brains Bitter

Usually requested by drinkers with the sentence 'A pint of Brains, please!' this long-standing flagship brew sells at a rate of 12 pints per minute. Not surprisingly it's the Brains brewery's – and indeed Wales's – biggest selling cask beer. It's made with a smart mix of those classic British hops, Goldings and Fuggles – though they are harvested not in Kent, but in the heartlands of Wales.

Tasting notes: Soft peach and apple orchard fruits combined with pale, bready malt.
* ★ **Country:** Wales ★ **Brewer:** Brains
* ★ **Style:** Bitter ★ **Appearance:** Light brown
* ★ **Alcohol:** 3.7% ★ **Serving temp:** 8–13°C

Celt Experience Dark-Age

Formerly one of Wales's most popular styles of beer, the decline of mild beers coincided with that of the coal mining industry, as these usually low-alcohol beers were the preferred beer of coal miners. Thankfully the resurgence in craft brewing has seen milds return with a bang. This one is light in body, sweet, bitter and warming. Perfect after a day of hard work.

Tasting notes: Mild chocolate and sweetness with a very easy finish. Nice with chocolate desserts.
* ★ **Country:** Wales
* ★ **Brewer:** Celt Experience
* ★ **Style:** Mild
* ★ **Appearance:** Dark brown
* ★ **Alcohol:** 4%
* ★ **Serving temp:** 8–13°C

Celt Experience Ogham Willow Magestic IPA

As more and more IPAs began to be brewed in the American style, increasing amounts of hops were added, which often made the beers incredibly bitter. To counteract all that bitterness, brewers began using more malt for sweetness, which increased the alcohol content, and the imperial or double IPA was born. Celt's Magestic IPA is a definitive example.

Tasting notes: Lots of New World hoppy bitterness counteracted with brown sugar.
* ★ **Country:** Wales
* ★ **Brewer:** Celt Experience
* ★ **Style:** Imperial IPA
* ★ **Appearance:** Amber
* ★ **Alcohol:** 8.8%
* ★ **Serving temp:** 8–13°C

DID YOU KNOW?

The patron saint of Ireland, St Patrick, evangelized pagan Ireland in the 5th century. Having a brewmaster in his missionary team may have helped as he wooed the tribal chieftains with his tasty beer.

Evan Evans CWRW

The Buckley family began brewing beer in 1767 and the Evan Evans brewery in Llandeilo is run by Simon and James Buckley, the seventh and eighth generations of the family – still flying the flag for traditional Welsh beer. Cwrw, the Welsh word for beer, has won a string of awards in the Best Bitter category.

Tasting notes: Malty backbone is complemented by gentle but very definite earthy hop flavours.
* ✹ **Country:** Wales ✹ **Brewer:** Evan Evans
* ✹ **Style:** Bitter ✹ **Appearance:** Amber
* ✹ **Alcohol:** 4.2% ✹ **Serving temp:** 8–13°C

Felinfoel Double Dragon

In the 1830s, David John bought a pub in the village of Felinfoel. He brewed his own beer, as did most pubs of the time. The difference? His was just that much better. Soon he was selling his beer to all the pubs in the region and was able to build an imposing brewhouse on the river Lliedi. Double Dragon is still brewed there today.

Tasting notes: Lots of toffee and malty notes in the flavour with a slightly floral hop note and a thin body.
* ✹ **Country:** Wales ✹ **Brewer:** Felinfoel Brewery Co. ✹ **Style:** Bitter
* ✹ **Appearance:** Amber ✹ **Alcohol:** 4.2% ✹ **Serving temp:** 8–13°C

DID YOU KNOW?

Felinfoel Brewery was the first outside the USA to commercially can beer, in 1931. During World War II it was a major supplier to the armed forces as cans saved space and weight.

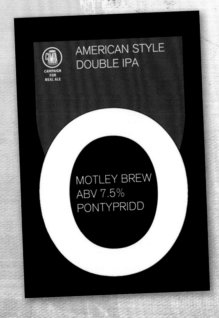

Otley Motley Brew

The Otley brewery believes strongly in bottle-conditioned beers and this double IPA is no exception. When the beer is bottled, all the yeast is left in so the beer continues to ferment and mature in the bottle. As it ferments, carbon dioxide is produced, which gives the beers their carbonation. It's this 100 per cent natural quality that makes good ale, 'real ale'.

Tasting notes: Fruit salad sweets, orange, grapefruit and hints of pine.
* ✹ **Country:** Wales ✹ **Brewer:** Otley
* ✹ **Style:** Imperial IPA
* ✹ **Appearance:** Cloudy amber
* ✹ **Alcohol:** 7.5% ✹ **Serving temp:** 4–7°C

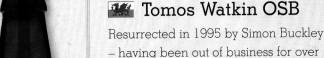 Tiny Rebel Hadouken

Tiny Rebel is a very modern and accomplished brewery that is causing quite a stir in its native Wales and beyond. Hadouken was brewed in collaboration with a famous craft beer bar in London and is named for the finishing move of a 1990s' arcade game. A true American-style, hoppy IPA and one of Tiny Rebel's most famous creations.

Tasting notes: Big caramel and biscuit malt flavour with a pine resin, oily hop counterbalance.
* **Country:** Wales
* **Brewer:** Tiny Rebel Brewing Co.
* **Style:** IPA
* **Appearance:** Hazy amber
* **Alcohol:** 7.4%
* **Serving temp:** 4–7°C

 Tomos Watkin OSB

Resurrected in 1995 by Simon Buckley – having been out of business for over a century – Tomos Watkin quickly became one of the fastest-growing brands in Wales. Buckley left the company in 2002 and went on to open Evan Evans, while Tomos Watkin has gone from strength to strength and now brews a wide range of beers, including OSB, Old Style Bitter

Tasting notes: Light orange and grassy hop aromas quickly give way to butterscotch and caramel, with an oily texture.
* **Country:** Wales
* **Brewer:** Tomos Watkin
* **Style:** Bitter
* **Appearance:** Clear amber
* **Alcohol:** 4.5%
* **Serving temp:** 8–13°C

 Waen Blackberry Stout

The crown jewel in a spectacular range of beers from this tiny young microbrewery based in Llanidloes, Wales, Waen's Blackberry Stout is a multi-award winner. You wouldn't expect mind-blowing flavour from a beer with such a low alcohol content. Nevertheless, every last drop of flavour is squeezed out of dark roasted malts and plump and juicy blackberries to produce a rich coffee-chocolate taste with a subtle hint of dark berries. And the best thing is you could drink this one all evening without worrying about the hangover.

Tasting notes: Coffee, chocolate with a nice amount of dark blackberry fruit and an easy-drinking texture.
* **Country:** Wales
* **Brewer:** Waen Brewery
* **Style:** Stout
* **Appearance:** Purple black
* **Alcohol:** 3.8%
* **Serving temp:** 8–13°C

Altenburger Schwarze

The Altenburger brewery has been in operation since 1871 at its present location in the Kauerndorf district of Altenburg. Altenburger Schwarze is a black beer, a style of lager that is always deep brown to black in colour, with low sweetness and bitterness and very little fruitiness. The flavours are fairly subdued, making it an easy drink that is consumed in large quantities at mealtimes in the beer halls of Germany. Drink with dark and sticky pretzels and sauerkraut to get the full effect.

Tasting notes: Bready flavours, with notes of chocolate and a nutty aroma. A smooth and subtle caramel finish.
* **Country:** Germany
* **Brewer:** Altenburger
* **Style:** Schwarzbier
* **Appearance:** Dark brown
* **Alcohol:** 4.9%
* **Serving temp:** 8–13°C

Astra Urtyp

A favourite in the docklands of Hamburg, Astra Urtyp is one of the first drinks that sailors and tourists might enjoy when they get off the ferry from the North Sea. A classic pilsner-style lager, its trademark is its excellent, creamy head, which will last all the way to the bottom of the glass. A very crisp, refreshing beer to start an evening with.

Tasting notes: Malted grains, light hay aromas and baked white bread. Easy to pair with almost anything at dinner.
* **Country:** Germany
* **Brewer:** Carlsberg
* **Style:** Pilsner
* **Appearance:** Medium orange
* **Alcohol:** 4.9%
* **Serving temp:** 2–3°C

DID YOU KNOW?

The Roman historian Tacitus wrote about the early Germanic tribes' addiction to beer and suggested they might more easily be conquered by giving them as much to drink as they wanted rather than using weapons!

GERMAN BEER PURITY

'*Gebraut nach dem deutschen Reinheitsgebot*'
Translation – 'Brewed according to the German Purity Law'

These words on German beer labels carry a promise of purity that dates back to 1516 and represent the world's oldest piece of food legislation still in use.

Known as the *Reinheitsgebot*, the law was introduced in Bavaria to set standards for the sale and composition of beer. At the time, quality was variable and brewers used whatever was to hand to make beer, including such questionable additives as henbane, fly agaric mushrooms, nettles and even soot.

Under the new law the only ingredients that could be used in the production of beer were water, barley and hops. Brewers who transgressed would have their beer confiscated.

When Germany unified in 1871, Bavaria insisted that the *Reinheitsgebot* be applied throughout the country as a precondition to its entry. The rules were also adopted by the former German colony of Namibia and by Greece, whose King Otto was Bavarian.

Critics of the *Reinheitsgebot* claim its restrictions killed off other German brews such as spiced beer and cherry beer, and led to the domination of lager. It has never applied to wheat beer.

In recent years the restrictions have been lifted somewhat, primarily to allow foreign beers to enter the German market. However, German brewers still make much play of their adherence to the *Reinheitsgebot* as the ultimate guarantee of quality.

▬ Augustiner Helles

The Augustiner brewery is certainly one of the most distinguished in Germany. When people speak of Augustiner, they generally refer to this extremely popular Helles (pale) lager. This drink is given a secondary fermentation over a long period to allow its superb liquid bread character to develop fully. A perfect example of how bready and wholesome the Helles style can be.

Tasting notes: Pure liquid bread! Aromas of proving dough dominate the nose, with a smooth, light bitter aftertaste.
* ✱ **Country:** Germany
* ✱ **Brewer:** Augustiner-Bräu München
* ✱ **Style:** Helles ✱ **Appearance:** Golden
* ✱ **Alcohol:** 5.2% ✱ **Serving temp:** 4–6°C

▬ Ayinger Jahrhundert

The Ayinger brewery prides itself on its absolute mastery of the brewing process. Aware that the smallest change in temperature can affect the extraction of sugar from the malt, they use the most up-to-date equipment and techniques to produce this superb Dortmund-style Helles. First brewed in 1978 to celebrate the 100th anniversary of the Ayinger brewery.

Tasting notes: Bready malts, sweet brown bread and hints of honey and grains.
* ✱ **Country:** Germany
* ✱ **Brewer:** Ayinger
* ✱ **Style:** Dortmund Helles
* ✱ **Appearance:** Straw
* ✱ **Alcohol:** 5.2%
* ✱ **Serving temp:** 4–6°C

Beck's

The world's bestselling German beer, Beck's is instantly recognizable: it was the first beer in Germany to use a green glass bottle. A brewing powerhouse, Beck's is sold in around 90 countries as well as its native Germany; the largest markets are the UK and the USA. The 'key' logo is derived from the Bremen city coat of arms.

Tasting notes: Light malt with a very subtle hop aroma. Very easy to drink with a relaxed flavour profile.
* **Country:** Germany
* **Brewer:** Beck's
* **Style:** Pale lager
* **Appearance:** Golden
* **Alcohol:** 4.8%
* **Serving temp:** 1–2°C

Berliner Pilsner

Here we have a good example of a traditional German pilsner. The differences between Czech and German-style pilsners are subtle but important. While Czech pilsners use Saaz hops to impart an earthy, herbal aroma that needs balancing with more malt, German styles are lighter in hops and use harder water, which results in a much longer-lasting bitter finish.

Tasting notes: Crisp, refreshing with a long bitter finish. Very light, with high carbonation.
* **Country:** Germany
* **Brewer:** Berliner Kindl Schultheiss
* **Style:** Pilsner
* **Appearance:** Golden
* **Alcohol:** 5%
* **Serving temp:** 3–5°C

Bitburger Premium Beer

'Bit in the evening, fit in the morning' is a slogan of the Bitburger brewery in the Rhineland – implying rather dubiously that enjoying Bitburger will not give you a hangover. What it will give you is a light, grassy hops aroma, smooth, toasted malts and a long, dry, bitter finish. In other words, Bitburger is a classic German-style pilsner. But at 4.8% ABV, drinking a few of them will definitely give you a hangover – regardless of the brewery slogan.

Tasting notes: Light malt, light hops and light taste. Serve very cold and drink before dinner.
* **Country:** Germany
* **Brewer:** Bitburger Braugruppe
* **Style:** Pilsner
* **Appearance:** Pale gold
* **Alcohol:** 4.8%
* **Serving temp:** 3–5°C

Diebels Pils

Despite brewing over one million hectolitres of beer in 2005, the Diebels brewery had been in sharp decline since 2001 – largely due to the decreased demand for its former flagship product, the copper-coloured Diebels Altbier. A pilsner-style lager was introduced in 2005 and is now its main product, much to the annoyance of beer enthusiasts in the lower Rhineland.

Tasting notes: Toasted malt, hay notes and a light hoppy citrus aroma, all in a very good balance.
- ✻ **Country:** Germany ✻ **Brewer:** Brauerei Diebels
- ✻ **Style:** Pilsner ✻ **Appearance:** Clear yellow
- ✻ **Alcohol:** 4.9% ✻ **Serving temp:** 3–5°C

Erdinger Dunkel

Erdinger Dunkel is a great example of a dark wheat beer. *Dunkelweizen* (dark wheat) uses dark malted wheat as well as malted barley. The *Reinheitsgebot* of 1516 decreed that barley was the only grain brewers could use – but wheat beer, made in royal breweries, was exempt. Royal control was loosened in the 1870s, and brewers such as Erdinger began to make wheat beers.

Tasting notes: Very light hints of malted wheat make it through rich and sweet banana flavours.
- ✻ **Country:** Germany
- ✻ **Brewer:** Erdinger Weissbräu
- ✻ **Style:** Dunkelweizen
- ✻ **Appearance:** Dark brown
- ✻ **Alcohol:** 5.3%
- ✻ **Serving temp:** 8–10°C

Flensburger Pilsener

Today the Flensburger brewery is still owned by the two families who founded it in 1888, the Petersens and the Dethleffsens. Back then, the brewers needed to take huge blocks of ice from frozen lakes in the winter to keep underground storage facilities cool in summer. Today's Flensburger Pilsener is fermented at cool temperatures using modern refrigeration methods.

Tasting notes: A very traditional German pilsner with low malt and hop profiles and a long crisp finish.
- ✻ **Country:** Germany ✻ **Brewer:** Flensburger Brauerei ✻ **Style:** Pilsner
- ✻ **Appearance:** Light yellow ✻ **Alcohol:** 4.8% ✻ **Serving temp:** 3–5°C

BEER STEINS

Pictures of Germans drinking beer will almost inevitably feature a large, foam-topped stein.

The drinking vessels have long been a feature of the country's drinking culture, dating from the 14th century when bubonic plague raced through Europe. In an attempt to prevent disease-carrying flies from infecting food and drinks, some German regions passed laws requiring that foodstuffs be covered. This led to the introduction of the pewter-lidded tankard, which allowed the drinker to open and close it.

Steins are made from a variety of materials, including pottery, glass, pewter, wood, and even silver. However the classic stein is made of stoneware, which accounts for the name – *Stein* means stone in German. Starting out as relatively plain drinking tankards, steins became more and more elaborately decorated, often featuring historical and allegorical scenes. Glass has been the main material for steins since the 19th century. Stoneware and ceramic steins are still manufactured in huge numbers, but mainly as souvenirs and collectables.

The largest stein in the world is a 1.2-metre tall, 32-litre capacity monster produced by Zöller & Born, which features the words, 'He who can empty this stein is truly a man.'

Although the stein remains quintessentially German, the world record for stein-carrying was set in Australia in 2008 by German-born Reinhard Wurtz, who carried 20 one-litre steins of beer for 40 metres.

Franziskaner Hefe-Weissbier

This is a great example of the light German wheat beer style called *Hefeweizen*. Made with pale malted wheat and malted barley, the yeast flavour breaks through, revealing spiced notes of clove and soft fruits – most notably banana. The Franziskaner is loaded with both spice and fruit and is certainly one of the best *Hefeweizens* on the market.

Tasting notes: Banana, cloves and very light malty wheat. Little hints of citrus in the aroma.
★ **Country:** Germany
★ **Brewer:** Spaten-Bräu Franziskaner
★ **Style:** Hefeweizen
★ **Appearance:** Hazy yellow
★ **Alcohol:** 5% ★ **Serving temp:** 3–5℃

Freiburger Pils

Freiburger Pils gets its name from the city of Freiburg where the Ganter brewery is based. During the world wars in the 20th century, the Ganter brewery was largely destroyed in bombing raids. A reconstruction was undertaken in 1979 and today the brewery is as strong as ever. Its pilsner is classically light in the German tradition.

Tasting notes: Crackerbread, hints of honey and a light toasted bread aroma with low hop bitterness.
★ **Country:** Germany
★ **Brewer:** Ganter Brauerei
★ **Style:** Pilsner
★ **Appearance:** Yellow
★ **Alcohol:** 4.9%
★ **Serving temp:** 3–5℃

Früh Kölsch

Kölsch is one of the more interesting beers to come out of Germany – specifically Cologne. It is first fermented like an ale at a warm 13–21°C, and then cold-matured or lagered. The result is the best of both the lager and the ale styles. Früh Kölsch has a very light golden colour with aromas of grassy hops and a slightly sour hint. A medium-bodied beer, much like bready ale, with the long bitter finish you'd expect from a good lager. Delicious with cold meat.

Tasting notes: Mild malt, faint grassy hops and a sweet bready corn flavour. Long bitter finish.
* ★ **Country:** Germany ★ **Brewer:** Cölner Hofbräu
* ★ **Style:** Kölsch ★ **Appearance:** Clean gold
* ★ **Alcohol:** 4.8% ★ **Serving temp:** 3–5°C

GERMAN BAR SNACKS

Beer may be known as 'liquid bread' but that doesn't mean that drinkers don't also need a little extra sustenance. That's particularly true in Germany, where beer and food seem to go hand in hand.

The classic German snack to go along with an ice-cold pilsner or a *Weissbier* is a pretzel, ideally served up with mustard sauce. German pretzels are a soft and delicious bread, and a substantial snack in their own right.

Although a staple of Germany, and Bavaria in particular, it is thought that pretzels were first baked by Italian monks in the 7th century to use up leftover scraps of bread dough. The twisted knot shape is said to represent arms crossed in prayer.

Visitors to Munich's Oktoberfest will see *Brotfrauen*, or bread ladies, moving from table to table selling baskets of the extra-large pretzels, which are ideal fare for soaking up the litres of beer consumed.

Another perfect complement to a German beer night is some form of *Wurst*, or sausage. Germany is rightfully proud of its sausages and many are ideal for snacking with beer. None more so than bockwurst which, as the name suggests is traditionally eaten with strong, malty bock beer.

Other sausages commonly consumed with beer include currywurst, bratwurst and frankfurter. Served up with potato salad and sauerkraut, they go great with beer.

Hacker-Pschorr Weisse

Hacker-Pschorr uses 60% malted wheat and 40% malted barley in the mash. After the grains have released their sugars, hops are added and the beer is fermented. It undergoes a secondary fermentation in the bottle, resulting in a yeasty sediment, so pour it carefully or you'll get a mouthful of yeast.

Tasting notes: Mild yeast, banana and a hint of citrus and spice. Great to pair with Chinese food like shrimp chow mein.
* ✲ **Country:** Germany
* ✲ **Brewer:** Hacker-Pschorr
* ✲ **Style:** Hefeweizen
* ✲ **Appearance:** Cloudy yellow
* ✲ **Alcohol:** 5.5%
* ✲ **Serving temp:** 3–5°C

Hasseröder Premium Pils

The sixth-bestselling brewery in Germany, Hasseröder is a well-known brand. This is its flagship product. A premium German-style pilsner described by the brewery as 'beer for men, honest and strong'. In reality of course, it is simply a lager beer and one to serve as an aperitif for refreshment rather than to pair with any food.

Tasting notes: Light baked crackerbreads, hints of honey and a pithy, dry hop aroma.
* ✲ **Country:** Germany
* ✲ **Brewer:** Hasseröder Brauerei
* ✲ **Style:** Pilsner
* ✲ **Appearance:** Pale yellow
* ✲ **Alcohol:** 4.8%
* ✲ **Serving temp:** 3–5°C

Hofbräu Münchner Weisse

For many years, the Purity Law forbade brewing wheat beer in order for the government to control grain supplies. However, certain noble families were allowed to break the rules! The Hofbräuhaus (Royal Court Brewery) relished this freedom, holding a monopoly on wheat beer in Bavaria for 200 years. The sheer quality of this beer speaks of its history.

Tasting notes: Bananas, cloves, citrus and malted wheat in perfect balance.
* ✲ **Country:** Germany
* ✲ **Brewer:** Hofbräu München
* ✲ **Style:** Hefeweizen
* ✲ **Appearance:** Hazy yellow
* ✲ **Alcohol:** 5.1%
* ✲ **Serving temp:** 4–7°C

DID YOU KNOW?

Germany's Veltins-Arena stadium has a beer pipeline that connects the many bars and supplies thirsty soccer fans with roughly 52,000 litres of beer on match days.

OKTOBERFEST:
THE FESTIVAL OF BEER FESTIVALS

There are many beer festivals around the world, but perhaps the most famous is Munich's Oktoberfest.

Every year, more than six million people attend the event, which is held in Munich's vast Theresienwiese parkland. It is spread over 16–18 days, depending on which day German Unification Day falls, and actually begins in late September.

To understand Oktoberfest you need to know a little history.

Oktoberfest commemorates the celebrations that were held in October 1810 for the marriage of Bavaria's Prince Ludwig and Princess Therese of Saxe-Hildburghausen. In honour of the union, a huge party was held for the Munich citizens, featuring a parade, horse racing and beer drinking.

The time of year also coincided with the recommencement of brewing following the summer lay-off. Before refrigeration, summer was not a good time to brew German beers, which require cold fermentation. Instead, producers brewed a surplus of beer in spring, known as Märzen (March beers), to last until fresh brews were made in the cooler autumn.

The teaming of a royal wedding and the new season ale was such a winning combination that

the good burghers of Munich decided to make it an annual event. It has been that way ever since, with a few missed years due to war and cholera outbreaks. The 2013 Oktoberfest was the 180th to be held.

In honour of the marriage of Prince Ludwig a huge party was held for the Munich citizens, featuring a parade, horse racing and beer.

Over the years the date slipped to a September start to take advantage of the last of the summer weather. The event gradually evolved to include a carnival and a parade as well as horse racing, although horse races were dropped in 1960.

OKTOBERFEST IN NUMBERS

6.4 million visitors

€400 million spent

7.4 million litres of beer drunk

1,000 tons of garbage

1,800 toilets

2,500 items of lost property

93 lost children

2,031 police interventions

7,551 helped by the Red Cross

638 cases of alcohol poisoning

508,958 chickens eaten, as well as…

115,015 pairs of pork sausages

116 roasted oxen

85 roasted calves

Oktoberfest kicks off at noon on the first Saturday, with the Lord Mayor of Munich opening the first barrel of beer and making the traditional Bavarian announcement 'O'zapft is' meaning 'It has been tapped'.

The following day, a parade marks the ceremonial opening, with a procession of the

Oktoberfest staff and breweries. The parade, which started in 1887, is led by the Münchner Kindl, or Munich Child, who features on the city's emblem holding a mug of beer and a radish. Following are horse-drawn coaches and drays adorned with flowers, the bands of the festival tents, waitresses on decorated carriages and up to 9,000 people in folk costume.

Inside the festival visitors drink officially designated Oktoberfest Beer. This must conform to the *Reinheitsgebot* purity laws and is quite strong, at about 6% alcohol by volume. The beer must also be brewed within the city limits by six breweries: Spaten, Löwenbräu, Augustiner-Bräu, Hofbräu-München, Paulaner and Hacker-Pschorr.

Oktoberfest kicks off at noon on the first Saturday, with the Lord Mayor of Munich opening the first barrel of beer.

Drinkers consume it in huge steins by the litre or 'Maß', although a smaller half litre, or 'Halbe' is on offer. Originally a dark Märzen lager, Oktoberfest beer has become progressively lighter and is now golden in colour.

Each of the breweries has its own tent and in total there are 14 large tents, which can seat up to 6,000 drinkers, as well as a number of smaller

IF YOU CAN'T MAKE OKTOBERFEST — OTHER BEER FESTIVALS

The Great British Beer Festival, London
CAMRA's showcase event for real ale

The Great American Beer Festival, Denver, Colorado
America's biggest festival of craft beer

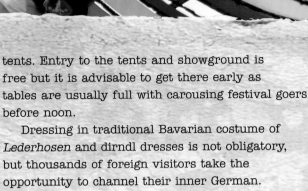

tents. Entry to the tents and showground is free but it is advisable to get there early as tables are usually full with carousing festival goers before noon.

Dressing in traditional Bavarian costume of *Lederhosen* and dirndl dresses is not obligatory, but thousands of foreign visitors take the opportunity to channel their inner German.

As well as becoming an item on many people's bucket lists, Oktoberfest has also spawned celebrations around the world, with around 2,000 spin-offs globally. However, there is only one original.

The Belgian Beer Weekend, Brussels
A celebration of Belgian beer

Pilsner Fest
The home of lager, Pilsen has held an annual festival for 200 years

Qingdao International Beer Festival
China's home of Tsingtao beer holds a beachside celebration during the last two weeks of August

Holsten Pilsener

First brewed in accordance with the Beer Purity Law, Holsten Pilsener was created in 1953 and became a big success in Germany. Since then, the Holsten business has expanded steadily – it now owns seven breweries in Germany. The name Holsten derives from an old Germanic tribe who lived in the north of Germany in a region now called Holstein.

Tasting notes: Lightly baked crackerbreads, cereal and hints of earthy, peppery hops.
* **Country:** Germany
* **Brewer:** Holsten Brauerei
* **Style:** Pilsner
* **Appearance:** Clear yellow
* **Alcohol:** 4.8%
* **Serving temp:** 3–5°C

Jever Pilsener

The word *Lager* is German for storeroom, and derives from the long period of maturation, or storage, that lagers traditionally underwent. In the case of Jever Pilsener, this maturation period is a massive 90 days. The word '*Herb*' on the label does not mean it contains herbs: *herb* is the German word for dry or bitter, and this is a particularly hoppy pilsner.

Tasting notes: Herby hop aromas with light biscuit-like malt flavours. Great with a salad or sushi.
* **Country:** Germany
* **Brewer:** Jever   * **Style:** Pilsner
* **Appearance:** Clear yellow
* **Alcohol:** 4.8%
* **Serving temp:** 3–5°C

DID YOU KNOW?

In the drinking game *Stiefeltrinken* sips of beer are taken in turns from a glass boot; as the level drops you must avoid splashes by twisting the boot, or the next round's on you!

König Pilsener

Known affectionately as 'KöPi' by the Duisberg locals, König Pilsener has been a mainstay in Germany since 1911. The pilsner style of golden lager – created in Plzen in Bohemia in 1842 – was initially slow to catch on in Germany, but once it did there was no stopping it and it is now the most widely drunk type of beer in all of Germany.

Tasting notes: Fresh fruity aromas with hints of toast, flowers and grain. The taste is buttery, light and softly carbonated.
* **Country:** Germany
* **Brewer:** König Brauerei
* **Style:** Pilsner
* **Appearance:** Medium yellow
* **Alcohol:** 4.9%
* **Serving temp:** 3–5°C

Kostritzer Schwarzbier

The Köstritzer Schwarzbierbrauerei has always been famed for its black beer – with the first recorded example being brewed in 1543. The style almost died out, but when the Bitburger brewery bought Köstritzer in 1991, this beer was re-introduced to great critical acclaim. Drink with blackened pork loin or washed-rind cheeses.

Tasting notes: Lots of roasted malt aroma, berries and light smoke. All this is evident in the taste too with a peppery background.

* **Country:** Germany
* **Brewer:** Köstritzer Schwarzbierbrauerei
* **Style:** Schwarzbier
* **Appearance:** Black
* **Alcohol:** 4.8%
* **Serving temp:** 4–7°C

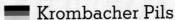

Krombacher Pils

The Krombacher brewery has brewed this pilsner in exactly the same way since the beginning of the 20th century. The brewery was sold to Otto Eberhardt in 1898, and Krombacher Pils was single-handedly responsible for building the company's fortunes. Since 1922 the brewery has been running as a family business after Bernhard Schadeberg assumed the management of the company.

Tasting notes: Fresh notes of citrus, lemony bubbles and a healthy dose of sweet grains and cereal.

* **Country:** Germany
* **Brewer:** Krombacher Brauerei
* **Style:** Pilsner
* **Appearance:** Golden
* **Alcohol:** 4.8% * **Serving temp:** 3–5°C

Löwenbräu Original

Löwenbräu beers have been served at every single Oktoberfest in Munich since 1810. Along with five other breweries that operate in Munich, the brewery produces a special Oktoberfestbier to go alongside its regular range. The most recognizable beer from Löwenbräu though is its Original Helles lager – brewed in accordance with the famous Purity Law of 1516. The brewery traces its history back to 1524, so you're drinking a small part of German brewing history when you open a Löwenbräu Original.

Tasting notes: Dry hops, a lightly malty background and a fine white head. One of the more classic Helles in Germany.

* **Country:** Germany * **Brewer:** Löwenbräu Munich
* **Style:** Helles * **Appearance:** Light yellow
* **Alcohol:** 5.2% * **Serving temp:** 3–5°C

BACK TO THE GARDEN

Drinking a beer out of doors is a pleasure to us all, especially in the summer when the sun is shining.

In Germany, drinkers can take to their nearest shady *Biergarten* – beer garden – to enjoy a glass or two. These outdoor seated areas are found next to many restaurants and beer halls.

Today they provide a pleasant location to relax and enjoy a beer and food, but beer gardens originally served another very practical purpose. Bavarian brewers planted broad-leaved chestnut or linden trees on their land to keep their beer cellars cool during the hot summer months. German beers traditionally require a lengthy period of 'lagering' when the beer matures at a low temperature, and in the days before refrigeration this was an ingenious way to keep the ground cool.

Brewers started to sell their beer directly to the public, so chairs and tables were placed in the gardens. Brewers were prohibited from selling food, so customers brought their own, a practice that continues today.

Many beer gardens are up to 200 years old and Munich alone is home to 180 beer gardens of various sizes, including the largest in the world. Königlicher Hirschgarten is an old hunting lodge which now seats 8,000 people. Drinkers can also try Viktualienmarkt at the city market, or enjoy the Airbräu Biergarten at Munich airport.

Lübzer Pils

All pilsners are bottom-fermented. This means the yeast used in the brew sinks to the bottom of the fermentation tank and has minimal contact with the air outside. The long fermentation time produces more carbon dioxide and gives the beer a beautiful foamy head that will last all the way down. Enjoy with light food such as steamed clams or chicken.

Tasting notes: Sweet, mellow grain flavours, herbal hoppy notes and a long-lasting bitterness in the finish.
* ★ **Country:** Germany
* ★ **Brewer:** Mecklenburgische Brauerei Lübz
* ★ **Style:** Pilsner
* ★ **Appearance:** Clear gold
* ★ **Alcohol:** 4.9%
* ★ **Serving temp:** 3–5°C

Maisel's Weisse Original

One of the proudest family brewers in all of Germany. Founded in 1887 by two brothers, the brewery remains in the family to this day largely due to the success of this fantastic *Hefeweizen*, Maisel's Weisse Original. The beer is one of the archetypal examples of the style, which literally translates as 'yeast wheat' – the two main flavour components of the beer.

Tasting notes: Bananas, bubble gum, vanilla and cloves. A very refreshing drink in hot weather.
* ★ **Country:** Germany
* ★ **Brewer:** Brauerei Gebruder Maisel
* ★ **Style:** Hefeweizen
* ★ **Appearance:** Hazy gold
* ★ **Alcohol:** 5.4%
* ★ **Serving temp:** 3–5°C

DID YOU KNOW?

A heat-damaged but still-sealed bottle of Löwenbräu, taken from the wreckage of the German airship *Hindenburg* in 1937, reached over $16,000 at auction in 2009, setting a record for the most expensive bottle of beer.

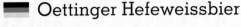 Oettinger Hefeweissbier

Many beer purists would say that unless the yeast strain *Torulaspora delbrueckii* is used, then the beer shouldn't be called a *Hefeweizen*. It's this specific strain of yeast that imparts the banana, bubble gum and clove flavours that are evident in this example from Oettinger. A good one to drink with Chinese dim sum.

Tasting notes: Lightly spiced banana with hints of bubble gum, clove and a bubbly malted wheat finish.
* **Country:** Germany
* **Brewer:** Oettinger Brauerei
* **Style:** Hefeweizen
* **Appearance:** Hazy gold
* **Alcohol:** 4.9%
* **Serving temp:** 3–5°C

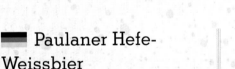 Paulaner Hefe-Weissbier

The extremely pale wheat used in the mash alongside the barley in a *Hefeweizen* allows the yeast flavour to come through more strongly than in other styles of beer. The light citrus flavours of Paulaner Hefe-Weissbier also provide a great contrast for meaty dishes like Wiener schnitzel, veal sausage and spicy tacos.

Tasting notes: Light creamy vanilla toffee with banana flavours and hints of spice.
* **Country:** Germany
* **Brewer:** Paulaner Brauerei
* **Style:** Hefeweizen
* **Appearance:** Cloudy orange
* **Alcohol:** 5.5%
* **Serving temp:** 3–5°C

Paulaner Salvator

One of the older beers to come out of the Paulaner brewery, the name Salvator means 'saviour' in Latin. The name may suggest that the Paulaner monks who established the brewery would drink this strong beer instead of food in times of fasting. The recipe is little changed since Brother Barnabus, the most famous Paulaner monk, first brewed this beer in the 18th century.

Tasting notes: Strong malty flavours, with traces of honey, caramel and bread dough.
* **Country:** Germany
* **Brewer:** Paulaner Brauerei
* **Style:** Doppelbock
* **Appearance:** Cloudy brown
* **Alcohol:** 7.9%
* **Serving temp:** 8–10°C

▬ Plank Dunkler Weizenbock

Strong, dark and made with high proportions of malted wheat, this Weizenbock's malt flavours take centre stage. Though the *Weizenbock* (wheat bock) style is often noted for high levels of esters, which provide fruity flavours, Michael Plank's wholesome version is all about the malted grains in a very smooth, silky beer, which aims to warm your heart rather than refresh.

Tasting notes: Bread, pepper with light hints of raisin and toasted pecans. Pair with apple strudel for a pleasant combination.
* **Country:** Germany
* **Brewer:** Brauerei Plank-Laaber
* **Style:** Weizenbock * **Appearance:** Dark red
* **Alcohol:** 7.5% * **Serving temp:** 8–10°C

▬ Radeberger Pilsner

This classic pilsner has something of a distinguished history. Elevated to 'Kanzier-Brau' (Chancellor-brew) in 1887 by the first German Chancellor, Otto Von Bismarck, the beer also became the favourite drink of King Frederick Augustus III of Saxony in 1905. In the early 21st century, however, the beer had a rather less noble following – being the beer of choice for Charlie Sheen's character in the TV series *Two and a Half Men* doesn't have quite the same ring to it! A fantastic example of a good pilsner nonetheless.

Tasting notes: Easygoing malty flavour, toasted sweet grains with a slightly buttery finish.
* **Country:** Germany * **Brewer:** Radeberger Exportbierbrauerei
* **Style:** Pilsner * **Appearance:** Medium yellow
* **Alcohol:** 4.8% * **Serving temp:** 3–5°C

▬ Schlenkerla Rauchbier Märzen

Famous among German beer enthusiasts, Schlenkerla Märzen is known for its pungent aroma, achieved by smoking the barley malt before adding it to the mash tun. Distinctive, almost meaty, flavours emerge as a result and it's not something many enjoy on first taste. In Bamberg they say that before you decide whether you like or dislike the flavour of the Rauchbier, you must first drink your own bodyweight in it – though presumably not all in one sitting.

Tasting notes: Bacon, smoke and sweet malt. Try boiling some bratwurst in this beer for 10 minutes before grilling them.
- ✳ **Country:** Germany ✳ **Brewer:** Brauerei Heller
- ✳ **Style:** Smoked beer ✳ **Appearance:** Dark brown
- ✳ **Alcohol:** 5.1% ✳ **Serving temp:** 8–10°C

▬ Schneider Aventinus

The archetypal *Weizenbock*, Schneider has been brewing this strong, dark, wheat beer since 1907. The beer takes its name from the 16th-century historian Johannes Aventinus. Schneider was sold the right to brew wheat beers in 1872. Before that, only the royal family and those with special permission were allowed to use wheat – an ingredient prohibited in beer by the *Reinheitsgebot*. Schneider is largely credited with saving wheat beer from extinction in the face of competition from golden lager.

Tasting notes: Sweet plums, ripe soft banana with hints of spice and raisins.
- ✳ **Country:** Germany
- ✳ **Brewer:** G. Schneider & Sohn
- ✳ **Style:** Weizenbock
- ✳ **Appearance:** Dark brown
- ✳ **Alcohol:** 8.2% ✳ **Serving temp:** 8–10°C

GOSE: THE BEER THAT CAME BACK FROM THE BRINK

While Germany is famous for its lagers and wheat beers, one regional speciality remains little appreciated.

Gose is a sour wheat beer brewed since the 16th century in Goslar in Lower Saxony, from where its name derives. Because the beer was brewed using saline water from the local aquifers, it has a salty taste. It is traditionally flavoured with coriander, while the lactic acid bacteria used in fermentation produce a distinctively tart, lemony flavour.

The drink became a favourite of Leipzig drinkers and by 1900 there were 80 Gose taverns in the city. With the arrival of Pilsner lager, Gose, always an acquired taste, began to lose favour. Soon after World War II, commercial production all but died out in Leipzig, which was now behind the Iron Curtain in East Germany.

However, in 1980 a local bar owner decided to revive the style, and the beer has gradually

returned from the brink of extinction. Now several German brewers produce it, including Gasthaus & Gosebrauerei Bayerischer Bahnhof in Leipzig. For drinkers who find the drink too sour, Gose can be served with syrups such as cherry or raspberry.

Gose has also appeared on the American craft beer scene. Its complexity and quirkiness are a challenge for new brewers, and variations have been produced by Upright Brewing, Portsmouth Brewery and Cascade Brewing.

Spaten Oktoberfest

One of the six breweries that provide beer for the Munich Oktoberfest, the Spaten-Franziskaner brewery brews this Märzen (March) beer in the spring to allow it to mature in time for autumn. 'Spaten' literally translates as spade in German – a tool all brewers are familiar with after shifting tons of malt around all day. Its Oktoberfest beer is a great example of the style.

Tasting notes: Flavoursome lager. Sweet bready malts give way to a crisp, clean aftertaste with a touch of spice.
* **Country:** Germany
* **Brewer:** Spaten-Franziskaner Bräu
* **Style:** Märzen
* **Appearance:** Medium yellow
* **Alcohol:** 5.9%
* **Serving temp:** 4–5°C

Spezial Rauchbier Märzen

Bamberg is famous for its smoky beers. In fact, it's said that even if you try to make a plain pilsner in Bamberg, the residual smoke in the area will make it taste of smoke anyway. The Brauerei Spezial purposely treats its malt to a good lick of smoke before piling it into the mash. The result is this peppery beer with rich leathery hints.

Tasting notes: Smoked leather, pepper and caramel with lighter hints of orange and walnut.
* **Country:** Germany
* **Brewer:** Brauerei Spezial
* **Style:** Smoked
* **Appearance:** Dark copper
* **Alcohol:** 5.3%
* **Serving temp:** 8–10°C

Veltins Pilsener

This German brewery has been going strong since it first opened its doors as a guesthouse in 1824 under the name Franz Kramer. The Veltins family bought the brewery in 1852 and today is directed by Susanne Veltins. Their flagship product is this classic German-style pilsner, one of the country's top ten best-selling beers.

Tasting notes: Sweet malts, toasted grain and a buttery aroma. Long, bitter aftertaste.
* **Country:** Germany
* **Brewer:** Brauerei C. & A. Veltins
* **Style:** Pilsner
* **Appearance:** Medium yellow
* **Alcohol:** 4.8%
* **Serving temp:** 3–5°C

GOOD SINCE 1040

Beer has been around for thousands of years, but the title of the oldest brewery in the world is more recent, relatively speaking.

Given its beer heritage, it is perhaps no surprise that Germany – specifically Bavaria, one of the oldest states in Europe – claims to be home of the world's oldest continuously operating brewery. The Weihenstephan Brewery was originally a monastery brewery for Benedictine monks and was licensed by the City of Freising in 1040. However, documentation dating from 768 refers to a hop garden in the area paying a tithe to the monastery, indicating an even earlier brewing history.

When the monastery and brewery were secularized in 1803 ownership passed to the State of Bavaria. Since 1923, the Bavarian State Brewery Weihenstephan has cooperated with Munich University to both produce and study beer. It brews wheat beer, pilsners and bock, and in 2010 teamed with Samuel Adams of Boston, Massachusetts to produce Infinium, a 10.5% ABV champagne-style beer.

Warsteiner
Premium Verum

Tasting notes: Very light flavour with a profile of corn, malt and grassy hops. A great beer to have cold as an aperitif.
★ **Country:** Germany ★ **Brewer:** Warsteiner Brauerei
★ **Style:** Pilsner ★ **Appearance:** Clear yellow
★ **Alcohol:** 4.8% ★ **Serving temp:** 3–5°C

The largest privately owned brewery in Germany, Warsteiner has been in the Cramer family since the 1750s and is still going strong, with Catharina Cramer at the helm. Its most popular product is this fresh-tasting premium pilsner made with 100% naturally sourced spring water and the best quality two-row summer barley malt.

DID YOU KNOW?

In medieval Bavaria official beer bouts could be ordered by the *Burgermeister* (mayor) to settle disputes; the contesting parties drank for three hours without standing up, and the steadiest at the end was the winner.

Weihenstephaner Hefeweissbier

Ancient documents from the year 768 refer to a hop garden in the Freising district of Bavaria. Many take this as proof of the claim that Weihenstephan, the location of the Weihenstephan monastery is the world's oldest operational brewery. What is certain is the quality of Weihenstephan Hefeweissbier – a perfect example of cloudy German wheat beer at its best.

Tasting notes: Banana, cloves, pepper and hints of orange. A great match for Weisswurst sausage.
✱ **Country:** Germany ✱ **Brewer:** Bayerische Staatsbrauerei Weihenstephan
✱ **Style:** Hefeweizen ✱ **Appearance:** Cloudy yellow ✱ **Alcohol:** 5.4% ✱ **Serving temp:** 3–5°C

Weihenstephaner Pilsner

Even the world's oldest brewery has to follow trends to some extent. But as long as it takes the same care and attention to brew the ubiquitous pilsner that it does with the rest of its historic beers, it still retains every inch of the integrity it has become famous for. A perfectly rounded and traditionally-made pilsner.

Tasting notes: Brewer's mash, light caramel and hints of honey and lemon.
✱ **Country:** Germany
✱ **Brewer:** Bayerische Staatsbrauerei Weihenstephan
✱ **Style:** Pilsner
✱ **Appearance:** Light yellow
✱ **Alcohol:** 5.1%
✱ **Serving temp:** 3–5°C

Wernesgrüner

The Wernesgrüner brewery was founded in 1436 by the Schorer family; it began life as a tavern serving only one beer. It changed hands many times over the centuries and was an early adopter of the pilsner style, which brought the company huge success. The beer would later become Wernesgrüner Pils. A light, tangy and refreshing pilsner, it is sold in Germany as Wernesgrüner Pils Legende.

Tasting notes: Light honey malt, corn and subtle hops blend together in perfect balance.
✱ **Country:** Germany ✱ **Brewer:** Wernesgrüner Brauerei ✱ **Style:** Pilsner
✱ **Appearance:** Light yellow ✱ **Alcohol:** 4.9% ✱ **Serving temp:** 3–5°C

◼◼ Abbaye Des Rocs Brune

Steak-lovers everywhere rejoice! There is a beer to rival red wine when it comes to matching your favourite dinner and it comes in the form of this Abbaye Des Rocs beer. This fruity, woody and hugely flavoursome beer has all the body and rich dark colour you need with a robust meaty dish. The brewmasters created such a complex taste by using seven types of malt and three different hop varieties. One of the most underrated beers in Belgium.

Tasting notes: Some dark fruits, oaky wood and caramel flavours. Savour with dark, bloody meat.
* ★ **Country:** Belgium
* ★ **Brewer:** Abbaye Des Rocs
* ★ **Style:** Belgian strong ale
* ★ **Appearance:** Deep ruby
* ★ **Alcohol** 9%
* ★ **Serving temp:** 8–13°C

◼◼ Affligem Tripel

The tiny Flemish village of Opwijk is the home of this luxurious Abbey-style tripel. Affligem Tripel gets a second fermentation in the bottle so it carries on maturing after it's bottled. This makes it a prime candidate for storage to allow its flavours to develop further. High alcohol content but somehow still fantastically refreshing.

Tasting notes: Candy floss, banana and cane sugar. Serve with a plate of ham and Brie.
★ **Country:** Belgium ★ **Brewer:** Brouwerij Affligem ★ **Style:** Tripel
★ **Appearance:** Light amber ★ **Alcohol** 9.5% ★ **Serving temp:** 8–10°C

■■ Belle-Vue Kriek

Even for the most ardent beer haters, Kriek, or cherry lambic, styles are extremely drinkable. With their inviting, deep fruity colours and sweet/sour balance, you could be forgiven for thinking you'd opened a particularly tangy fruit juice rather than a beer. Belle-Vue Kriek is a great example of the style. Made with whole cherries, this is a beer that anyone can enjoy.

Tasting notes: Sour cherries, lemon and a tangy mouth-puckering finish. Try with a piece of dark chocolate.
★ **Country:** Belgium
★ **Brewer:** Belle-Vue ★ **Style:** Kriek
★ **Appearance:** Deep ruby ★ **Alcohol** 5.2% ★ **Serving temp:** 4–7°C

■■ Blanche de Bruxelles

Blanche de Bruxelles is a Belgian-style wheat beer, also known as a *witbier*, or white beer. These differ from the more restrained German wheat beers because brewers in Belgium can use other ingredients besides just malt, hops, water and yeast. Blanche de Bruxelles is made with a combination of malted wheat and barley with coriander and orange peel thrown in for good measure.

Tasting notes: Light, bubbly and very refreshing with notes of lemon and very light spice. Perfect with mussels and fries.
★ **Country:** Belgium
★ **Brewer:** Brasserie Lefebvre
★ **Style:** Witbier
★ **Appearance:** Hazy yellow
★ **Alcohol** 4.5% ★ **Serving temp:** 4–7°C

DID YOU KNOW?

The Museum of Belgian Beers in Lustin, south of Namur, displays more than 20,000 bottles and 18,000 glasses of Belgian beer as well as beermats, ashtrays, posters and advertisements for Belgian beers.

■■ Boon Kriek

While some sour cherry lambics include a measure of sweetness to make them more approachable, Book Kriek is a more 'serious' brew. With a much more subtle and complex flavour, Boon Kriek retains all the sourness with slightly less sugar. Still very drinkable – especially alongside a piece of dark chocolate or vanilla ice cream – but definitely one for the more experienced lambic lover.

Tasting notes: Sour barnyard-type aromas with sweet black cherries and acidic lemon juice.
★ **Country:** Belgium ★ **Brewer:** Brouwerij Boon
★ **Style:** Kriek ★ **Appearance:** Deep red
★ **Alcohol** 4% ★ **Serving temp:** 4–7°C

■■ Brugse Zot

For many, Brugse Zot is the archetypal Belgian blonde beer. The only beer to be both brewed and matured in the centre of Bruges, this crisp, refreshing, pale blonde ale is labelled with its affectionate tribute to the people of Bruges – a city once dubbed 'one big fools' house' by the Emperor of Austria. This explains the literal translation: the Bruges Fool.

Tasting notes: Light lemon, with subtle spices and orange and a long and defined malty sweetness.
* ★ **Country:** Belgium
* ★ **Brewer:** Huisbrouwerij De Halve Maan
* ★ **Style:** Belgian blonde
* ★ **Appearance:** Golden
* ★ **Alcohol** 6%
* ★ **Serving temp:** 4–7°C

■■ Cantillon Kriek

Making Kriek is a great way of using up all the cherries that grow in Belgium. Take an 18-month-old lambic beer, add a vast quantity of cherries, and their natural sugars and yeast kick-start fermentation as well as imparting flavour. Cantillon Kriek is made in the old-fashioned way with oak barrels and decades of know-how.

Tasting notes: Acidic, lemon juice, sour cherry and subtle barnyard-like aromas. Drink with brown bread and white cheese.
* ★ **Country:** Belgium
* ★ **Brewer:** Cantillon
* ★ **Style:** Kriek
* ★ **Appearance:** Cherry red
* ★ **Alcohol** 5%
* ★ **Serving temp:** 4–7°C

■■ Celis White

Pierre Celis, a milkman from the village of Hoegaarden, revived the Belgian wheat beer or *witbier* (white beer) style in the 1960s using a recipe that included coriander and orange peel. When a fire forced him to sell off his brewery to AB InBev (owners of today's Hoegaarden), he moved to Austin, Texas, to brew Celis White. He granted this brewery the right to make it in Belgium.

Tasting notes: Fresh grassy wheat with notes of orange peel and coriander. A great match for any seafood.
* ★ **Country:** Belgium
* ★ **Brewer:** Brouwerij Van Steenberge
* ★ **Style:** Witbier
* ★ **Appearance:** Hazy gold
* ★ **Alcohol** 5%
* ★ **Serving temp:** 4–7°C

DID YOU KNOW?

Belgium has six of the eight Trappist breweries in Europe: Chimay, Orval, Rochefort, Westmalle, Westvleteren and Achel. They are strong and famous for ales produced using centuries-old methods.

■■ Chimay Blue

To be deemed a Trappist ale, the beer must be made within the walls of the monastery by a member of the monastic community. In addition, the proceeds from any sales must go towards providing for the community or other local charitable projects. Monks at Notre-Dame de Scourmont Abbey, near the town of Chimay, began brewing in 1862. The range includes Chimay Red (7% ABV), best enjoyed within a year, and Chimay Blue, their most famous and highly-rated beer, which can mature for several years.

Tasting notes: Malty caramels, boozy raisins and toffee apple with just a hint of bitterness. Matures with age.
★ **Country:** Belgium ★ **Brewer:** Chimay
★ **Style:** Belgian strong ale
★ **Appearance:** Muddy brown
★ **Alcohol** 9% ★ **Serving temp:** 8–10°C

■■ Corsendonk Pater

The name refers to the Priory of Corsendonk, which was in operation from 1398 to 1784 and was rebuilt as a hotel complex in the 1960s. The 'Dubbel' abbey beer style usually means a strong, rich brown ale. This example is extremely complex owing to its blend of multiple hops and malts; the less pronounced yeast flavours allow the malts to take centre stage.

Tasting notes: Light spice and caramel malts with a solid fruity flavour. A great beer for roasted game dishes like venison.
★ **Country:** Belgium
★ **Brewer:** Brasserie Du Bocq
★ **Style:** Abbey dubbel
★ **Appearance:** Rusty brown
★ **Alcohol** 7.5%
★ **Serving temp:** 8–10°C

■■ De Dolle Stille Nacht

Called a Christmas beer by many, De Dolle Stille Nacht is a fabulous beer in its own right without any seasonal gimmicks needed to make it stand out. It has an unusually high density of texture owing to its long boil time (five hours) and added candy sugar. There is also an interesting sourness that develops as the beer matures. Keep this one in the cellar for a year or two.

Tasting notes: Sweet candyfloss, sour yeast and a hop balance for bitterness. A perfect flavour triangle.
★ **Country:** Belgium
★ **Brewer:** De Dolle Brouwers
★ **Style:** Belgian strong ale
★ **Appearance:** Dirty brown
★ **Alcohol** 12%
★ **Serving temp:** 8–10°C

De Koninck

Not all Belgian beers are going to blow your head off with a high ABV and sickly richness. De Koninck keeps things pretty restrained, the flagship beer of its range. Brewed with barley malt, water, yeast and hops, this is a 100% natural product with a smart hoppy finish from the Czech-sourced Saaz hops. A good beer to start the evening.

Tasting notes: Easygoing with notes of sweet malts, a little sourness and a subtle bitter finish from the hops.

★ **Country:** Belgium
★ **Brewer:** De Koninck
★ **Style:** Belgian ale
★ **Appearance:** Dark copper
★ **Alcohol** 5.2% ★ **Serving temp:** 4–5°C

A GLASS OF ITS OWN

For some drinkers it's all about the beer and it doesn't matter how it is served up. Not so with Belgian beers, where each drink has its own bespoke glass and bars are expected to use them.

The chalice or goblet is often used to serve Trappist beers such as Chimay. It has a thick wall and scored bottom to promote development of the head.

Tulip glasses and brandy-style glasses are also popular for Belgian beers, encouraging the drinker to linger over the beer's aroma. Wheat beers such as Hoegaarden are served in more robust tumblers.

Probably the most famous Belgian beer glass is the Pauwel Kwak glass, which to British eyes resembles a miniature yard of ale in a wooden stand. Some bars require drinkers to leave a shoe behind the bar to ensure that they return the handsome glass. Apparently the glass was designed to be hung from the side of coaches in the 18th century as coachmen were not allowed to leave their station at a stop.

The tradition of strange glassware continues with Mea Culpa, a Belgian pale ale that is designed to be served in an elegant chalice that is supported by a swan's neck stem attached to the side of the glass.

It might all seem like a marketing gimmick, but proponents of proper glasses maintain that the beer tastes better if served in the right glass.

■■ De Ryck Arend Tripel

A mother and daughter team is one you find all too rarely in the world of brewing. The De Ryck brewery has been family-run for several generations and is now in the hands of An De Ryck, with a fantastic range of beers. This Abbey tripel is very well balanced with a gorgeous sweet but sour flavour.

Tasting notes: Alcohol and orchard fruit in the aroma are rounded off with a sweet, sour and spicy taste.
★ **Country:** Belgium
★ **Brewer:** Brouwerij De Ryck
★ **Style:** Abbey tripel
★ **Appearance:** Hazy gold
★ **Alcohol** 8%
★ **Serving temp:** 4–7°C

■■ Delirium Tremens

With its trademark white speckled bottle, you might be forgiven for mistaking Delirium Tremens for a funky bottle of salad dressing. Thankfully, a masterfully smart but very potent blend of spice, boozy apples and three tangy types of yeast await you when you pop the lid. Given the 1998 World Beer Championship gold medal, it has a reputation fully deserved.

Tasting notes: Apples, orange and grape in the nose with a sharp citrus tang in the taste. Great with spicy seafood dishes.
★ **Country:** Belgium ★ **Brewer:** Brouwerij Huyghe
★ **Style:** Belgian strong ale ★ **Appearance:** Hazy yellow
★ **Alcohol** 8.5% ★ **Serving temp:** 4–7°C

DID YOU KNOW?

Belgian brewery Brasserie Ellezelloise produces a world-classic Russian stout named after the famous Belgian detective Hercule Poirot – however, Poirot himself never drank beer, preferring herbal tisanes and blackcurrant cassis.

■■ Duvel

This strong golden pale ale is exported to more than 40 countries around the world. The name comes from the Flemish word 'duivel' which translates as devil. There's certainly a devilish aspect to Duvel as despite its 8.5% ABV, it's extremely easy to drink – making it a dangerous beer indeed. Handle with care.

Tasting notes: Smooth, crisp and refreshing with a dry finish. Great with soft creamy cheeses.
★ **Country:** Belgium ★ **Brewer:** Duvel Moortgat ★ **Style:** Belgian strong ale
★ **Appearance:** Clear yellow ★ **Alcohol** 8.5% ★ **Serving temp:** 4–5°C

▌▌ Fantôme

The Fantôme brewery produces several variations of the *saison* style. Originally created for farm workers to drink in the summer months, *saisons* were traditionally very refreshing, with complex earthy and herbal notes developing from their yeasts. Fantôme's flagship product is a tribute to this style but a little stronger – not just in its alcohol content but also in its very intense flavours and pronounced sourness. Not for the faint of heart.

Tasting notes: Strong peach, strawberry and bitter orange flavours with a pronounced sourness.
★ **Country:** Belgium
★ **Brewer:** Brasserie Fantôme
★ **Style:** Saison
★ **Appearance:** Hazy yellow
★ **Alcohol** 8%
★ **Serving temp:** 4–7°C

▌▌ Grimbergen Blonde

Grimbergen Abbey, north of Brussels, was founded in 1128. Over the centuries it was destroyed by fire and rebuilt several times, hence the phoenix emblem. Only the finest Gatinais barley is used for the mash as the hop profile is so light. A lovely yeast flavour rounds this beer off nicely.

Tasting notes: Light citrus fruits, hints of spice from the yeast and a creamy and fast-collapsing head.
★ **Country:** Belgium
★ **Brewer:** Alken-Maes
★ **Style:** Belgian blonde
★ **Appearance:** Clear gold
★ **Alcohol** 6.7%
★ **Serving temp:** 3–5°C

▌▌ Gulden Draak

Belgian brewers are noted for their willingness to experiment and innovate. Gulden Draak (golden dragon) uses a wine yeast in its secondary fermentation – giving it a unique flavour and also making it very versatile in cooking. Try using a bottle in a bordelaise sauce or a rich stew and you'll be astounded. Pure indulgence as an aperitif or with dessert.

Tasting notes: Very sweet with notes of berries, yeast and alcohol. A dry hoppy ending.
★ **Country:** Belgium
★ **Brewer:** Brouwerij Van Steenberge
★ **Style:** Belgian barley wine
★ **Appearance:** Deep brown
★ **Alcohol** 10.5%
★ **Serving temp:** 8–10°C

HOLY ORDERS

Monasteries have been involved in brewing since the Middle Ages, when they began to recognize it as a useful method of raising money and also serving their local communities.

This process continues today in the Trappist breweries of Belgium, the Netherlands and Austria. The monks at the eight authentic Trappist breweries produce some of the most exquisite beers available.

The Trappists are a branch of the Cistercians who broke away from the main order in the 17th century to pursue a more devout version of the faith. Their name comes from the abbey of La Grande Trappe in Normandy, France, which began to institute reforms in 1664.

Beer was an important part of monastic life for several reasons. In medieval times, water quality was not always good, so beer was a better bet as a daily drink. Monasteries were places where travellers could find shelter, food and drink, so beer was a saleable product. Trappist monks were among the most active brewers, with many monasteries producing their own beer.

Over the years, the monks built up an impressive knowledge of beer-making, especially the ability to brew stronger beers. There was no way of measuring the alcoholic strength of beer, but monks realized that by doubling or tripling the ingredients, they could make stronger beer. This led to the *enkel*, *dubbel* and *tripel* (single, double and triple) naming system, which indicates progressively stronger brews.

Trappist beers became increasingly popular in Belgium, where most of the brewing monasteries are located, especially when spirits were banned in bars in 1919. Drinkers in search of a stronger drink turned to the high-alcohol Trappist beers, and production increased to keep pace with demand.

However, the popularity of Trappist beer led to other brewers launching their own 'Trappist' beers. These were not brewed according to Trappist principles, and in 1962 a Ghent brewer was sued for passing off his beer as Trappist.

In 1997, the Trappist abbeys of Belgium (Orval, Chimay, Westvleteren, Rochefort, Westmalle and Achel), Koningshoeven in the Netherlands and Mariawald in Germany formed the International Trappist Association (ITA) to safeguard the Trappist name. Trappist abbeys can use a logo on bottles of beer and other products such as cheese and wine to show their authenticity. Trappist beer must be brewed within the walls of the abbey, either by the monks or under their control. The economic purpose of the brewery must be directed toward charity and not toward financial profit.

The monks built up an impressive knowledge of beer-making, especially the ability to brew stronger beers.

This guidance relates to how the beer is produced, but the type of beer is not described. Consequently there are a number of different beer styles under the Trappist umbrella. Most are top-fermented and bottle-conditioned, but the beers range from blonde through amber to very dark ales. Alcohol content is similarly varied, although most Trappist beers are much stronger than normal 'session' beers. Rochefort's 10 beer has 11.3% ABV.

The monasteries also sometimes brew a lower-strength beer for consumption by the monks. Known as *patersbier*, this is usually only available at the abbey.

Since the introduction of the ITA designation, non-Trappist beers are sometimes called abbey beers. They can be similar in style to monastic beers, but are produced by a non-Trappist monastery or by a commercial brewery under an arrangement with an existing monastery. Some have no connection to existing religious orders.

The newest Trappist brewery only received its ITA affiliation in 2012. Stift Engelszell in Austria was founded in the 13th century but the monastery was dissolved by the emperor in the 18th century. Re-founded in the 20th century, it has recently started brewing after the monastery teamed up with a local, family-run brewer, Brauerei Hofstetten. It produces two beers, both using the abbey's own honey.

Stift Engelszell may not be the last of the Trappist breweries as other monasteries are in the process of adding brewing capacity. Abdij Maria Toevlucht in the Netherlands will produce a copper blonde beer, while St Joseph's Abbey in Massachusetts hopes to have the first American Trappist beer.

It seems the Trappist tradition is set to continue.

■■ Jupiler

Generally speaking, the people of Belgium have escaped the dominance of pale lager in the latter part of the 20th century. Traditional methods and beers prevailed. Jupiler is something of an exception to the rule and has become the biggest-selling beer in Belgium, according to the brand owners AB InBev. Sometimes, a simple crisp lager is all you need.

Tasting notes: Refreshing, carbonated and crisp pale malts give way to a dry but only lightly bitter finish.
★ **Country:** Belgium ★ **Brewer:** Brasserie Piedboeuf ★ **Style:** Pale lager
★ **Appearance:** Golden ★ **Alcohol** 5.2% ★ **Serving temp:** 3–5°C

■■ Pauwel Kwak

This fruity Belgian ale comes with its own masterful glass and stand – a commodity that many people took to stealing after a night on the Kwak. To combat the problem, some pub landlords asked drinkers to part with their shoes before using the glass and stand. Drinkers would drop their footwear in a basket, which was then winched up to the ceiling out of reach.

Tasting notes: Lots of malty caramel, roasted nuts and a hint of spice make this perfect with a spicy kebab.
★ **Country:** Belgium ★ **Brewer:** Brouwerij Bosteels
★ **Style:** Belgian strong ale ★ **Appearance:** Amber
★ **Alcohol** 8% ★ **Serving temp:** 8–10°C

■■ La Chouffe

Strong, bubbly and thoroughly easy to drink, La Chouffe has been a firm favourite since its inception in 1982. Brewed in the green heartlands of the Belgian Ardennes, it's easy to spot a bottle as each one comes complete with a cheeky elf – a favourite character in many myths and legends of the Ardennes. La Chouffe is the flagship beer in the range, and like many Belgian ales, it's dangerously easy to drink despite its high alcohol content. Handle this one with care.

Tasting notes: Light fragrance of apple, orange and floral hops with an extremely bubbly yet soft finish.
★ **Country:** Belgium ★ **Brewer:** Brasserie d'Achouffe ★ **Style:** Belgian strong ale
★ **Appearance:** Light orange ★ **Alcohol** 8% ★ **Serving temp:** 4–7°C

▮▮ Leffe Brune

Leffe Abbey survived many disasters over the centuries, and was finally abandoned after the French Revolution. In the early 20th century the monks returned and restored the buildings, but suffered further setbacks during the two world wars. In the 1950s, in order to resolve the abbey's financial problems, the abbot decided to renew ancient brewing traditions and licensed a local brewery to make beer under the Leffe name.

Tasting notes: Delicate flavours of coffee, vanilla, cloves and heavy caramel malts. Great with caramelized onion soup.
* ★ **Country:** Belgium
* ★ **Brewer:** AB InBev
* ★ **Style:** Abbey dubbel
* ★ **Appearance:** Dark brown
* ★ **Alcohol** 6.5%
* ★ **Serving temp:** 5–6°C

▮▮ Liefmans Goudenband

Made in large open-topped vats, Liefmans Goudenband is then left to mature for up to 12 months before being blended with a younger version of itself to restart fermentation. This is a beer you can store for many years as in essence it's really already gone off! Sour beers are a special product: refreshing, complex, but something of an acquired taste.

Tasting notes: Sour rhubarb, cherries and brown sugar. Delicate palates may pick up on woody notes. Acidic finish.
* ★ **Country:** Belgium
* ★ **Brewer:** Liefmans
* ★ **Style:** Flemish Brown
* ★ **Appearance:** Dark brown
* ★ **Alcohol** 8%
* ★ **Serving temp:** 5–6°C

DID YOU KNOW?

Monastic brewers were prevented from using hops, which the church deemed the 'fruit of the devil', although the ban was most likely because the bishops had a monopoly over the 'gruyt' (herbs and spices) used instead.

Lindemans Pecheresse

All lambic beers ferment in shallow, open vats, to let natural yeasts enter and start fermentation. Fruit lambic beers are then boiled with fresh fruit – most commonly cherries. But here, peaches are used to give a refreshing, fruity taste you'll never forget.

Tasting notes: Vivid flavours of peach combined with a sour tang and a bubbly refreshing aftertaste. Serve in a champagne flute!
★ **Country:** Belgium
★ **Brewer:** Lindemans
★ **Style:** Fruit lambic
★ **Appearance:** Golden
★ **Alcohol** 2.5%
★ **Serving temp:** 4–5°C

DID YOU KNOW?

There are over 800 beers made in Belgium, so it's not surprising the world's first beer academy opened in Herk-de-Stad, in the Belgian province of Limburg, in 1999.

Malheur Bière Brut

Rarely seen outside Belgium, Malheur's champagne beer range is one some raise an eyebrow at. Using the same method as is used for Champagne, the beer is fermented and bottled; it undergoes a second fermentation in the bottle, after which the processes of *remuage* and *dégorgement* remove the residual yeasts before the beer is bottled in a thick glass bottle. This secondary fermentation in the bottle is what gives Champagne (and Malheur Bière Brut) its trademark sparkle and theatrical pop when the cork is removed.

Tasting notes: Light peach, orchard fruits and sour yeasts combine beautifully to mask a fairly high ABV.
★ **Country:** Belgium ★ **Brewer:** Malheur ★ **Style:** Champagne beer
★ **Appearance:** Golden ★ **Alcohol** 11% ★ **Serving temp:** 4–7°C

Mort Subite Gueuze

Gueuze is one of the most surprising tastes of Belgium. Made with a combination of young and old lambic beers, the yeast from the young lambics kickstarts a second fermentation which happens in the bottle. The hop presence is mainly for preservation rather than as a feature of the taste or aroma. This example from Mort Subite (sudden death) is nigh perfect.

Tasting notes: Vinegar, apples, cider and sour fruits dominate here. A great match for salmon with cream cheese.
★ **Country:** Belgium ★ **Brewer:** Alken-Maes ★ **Style:** Gueuze
★ **Appearance:** Hazy yellow ★ **Alcohol** 4.5% ★ **Serving temp:** 4–7°C

Orval

Orval Abbey is a Trappist monastery brewery, and its beer Orval is special in many ways. Its bottle is one of a kind, shaped like a skittle from a ten-pin bowling alley. Its cloudy colouring and large foamy head also mark it out. But the best part is the perfectly balanced dry, hoppy finish – a result of Orval's special yeasts combined with the use of dry-hopping techniques in the maturation process. Orval fully deserves its status as a world classic beer and one that only gets better with age… so keep some in the cellar!

Tasting notes: Long-lasting creamy head with citrus in the nose and banana in the taste. Try with honey-roast duck.
★ **Country:** Belgium ★ **Brewer:** Brasserie d'Orval ★ **Style:** Trappist
★ **Appearance:** Copper ★ **Alcohol** 6.9% ★ **Serving temp:** 8–10°C

DID YOU KNOW?

Dutch influence on Belgian beer persists in the use of spices, originally imported from the East Indies — Belgium was part of the Netherlands before a revolution in the 1830s, sparked partly by taxes on beer.

Rochefort 8

Sold in order to support the resident monks at the Abbey of Notre-Dame de Saint Rémy, Rochefort 8 makes up approximately 80 per cent of the brewery's output; it has an enthusiastic following around the world. To round off this beer, a small amount of demi-sec (medium dry wine) is added to give acidity. Serve in a champagne glass.

Tasting notes: Long-lasting aromas of plums and red berries pair nicely with gentle chocolate and raisins.
* **Country:** Belgium
* **Brewer:** Brasserie de Rochefort
* **Style:** Trappist
* **Appearance:** Deep brown
* **Alcohol** 9.2%
* **Serving temp:** 8–10°C

Rodenbach Grand Cru

The Rodenbach brewery is famous for its well-loved Flemish red-style beers. Usually barrel-aged for months at a time in oak barrels, this style of beer has a lot in common with wine or sherry. Once aged it can be blended with younger ales or bottle unblended – as is the case with Rodenbach's wonderful Grand Cru.

Tasting notes: Winey aromas, acidity and berry-like fruits make this a great match for fresh shrimp and other seafood.
* **Country:** Belgium * **Brewer:** Brauwerij Rodenbach * **Style:** Flemish red
* **Appearance:** Red-brown * **Alcohol** 6% * **Serving temp:** 8–10°C

St Bernardus Abt 12

The only thing stopping this beer from gaining the same mythical status as the famous Westvleteren is the term 'Trappist'. St Bernardus is not a Trappist brewery but its Abt 12 is surely one of the highest-regarded beers in the world. Based on an original Westvleteren recipe, it's brewed in the classic quadrupel style. Perfect with a wild game dish.

Tasting notes: Dark fruits, liquorice and sticky toffee malts. Serve with wild boar or roasted venison.
* **Country:** Belgium
* **Brewer:** St Bernardus
* **Style:** Quadrupel
* **Appearance:** Murky brown
* **Alcohol** 10.5%
* **Serving temp:** 8–10°C

St Feuillien Blonde

The St Feuillien brewery is built on the site of the Abbey of St Feuillien, named after an Irish monk, Feuillien, who passed through the forest in the 7th century. After he was martyred, his disciples built a chapel, which later became a prosperous abbey. The abbey was destroyed after the French Revolution, but St Feuillien's name lives on in this strong Belgian blonde.

Tasting notes: Candied oranges, spices and hops. A clever balance of sour, bitter and sweet.
* **Country:** Belgium * **Brewer:** Brasserie St Feuillien * **Style:** Belgian blonde * **Appearance:** Hazy gold * **Alcohol** 7.5% * **Serving temp:** 4–7°C

Tripel Karmeliet

Voted World's Best Ale in the 2008 World Beer Awards, Tripel Karmeliet owes its smooth body to a mixture of pale malt, wheat and a good percentage of oats. One of the most famous Belgian blonde ales for its full flavour, the addition of oats makes the body creamy and silky, while the limited use of hops allows yeast flavours to come through.

Tasting notes: Banana, vanilla with some citrus fruits. Perfect for robust seafood dishes like fish pie.

★ **Country:** Belgium ★ **Brewer:** Brouwerij Bosteels ★ **Style:** Belgian blonde
★ **Appearance:** Hazy gold ★ **Alcohol** 8.4% ★ **Serving temp:** 4–7°C

Tripel Van De Garre

Just off the main square of Bruges, a small, centuries-old beer café has been serving up this local brew for decades. Brewed exclusively for the Staminee de Garre, Tripel Van De Garre is made by the Van Steenberge brewery – the same people who brew Gulden Draak. At 11.5%, it's not really a session beer, more one to sip and savour.

Tasting notes: A hazy orange colour and swirling white cream foam. Flavours of orange, alcohol and yeast.
★ **Country:** Belgium ★ **Brewer:** Brouwerij Van Steenberge
★ **Style:** Tripel ★ **Appearance:** Hazy orange
★ **Alcohol** 11.5% ★ **Serving temp:** 4–7°C

DID YOU KNOW?

'Brussels lace' is a term for traces of foam left by the beer on the side of the glass, considered to be a sign of a well-made beer and an indicator of quality.

Vedett Extra Blond

It's no coincidence that Vedett Extra Blond comes in the same shape bottle as Duvel. The same brewer makes this easygoing 5.2% premium lager and it has gained a loyal cult following in the Antwerp-Brussels region since 1945. Made with a percentage of rice and extra hops, it has a very crisp and clean taste.

Tasting notes: Moderate amounts of hay, toast and grains in the aroma with a bubbly, carbonated character.
★ **Country:** Belgium
★ **Brewer:** Duvel Moortgat
★ **Style:** Pale lager
★ **Appearance:** Pale yellow
★ **Alcohol** 5.2% ★ **Serving temp:** 3–4°C

◼️◼️◼️ Westmalle Trappist Dubbel

Since 1856, the monks of the Trappist Abbey of Westmalle brewery have brewed a dark reddish-brown dubbel beer to go alongside their low-alcohol 'table beers'. The recipe has been modified over the years to make it stronger but the style remains the same. Skilfully blended malts, punchy sour yeast and soft, fruity, heartwarming flavour.

Tasting notes: Doughy, yeasty aromas of proving wholemeal bread. Sweet chocolatey body and a smooth caramel finish.
- ★ **Country:** Belgium
- ★ **Brewer:** Brouwerij der Trappisten van Westmalle
- ★ **Style:** Trappist dubbel
- ★ **Appearance:** Murky brown
- ★ **Alcohol** 7%
- ★ **Serving temp:** 8–10°C

◼️◼️◼️ Westvleteren 12

When the brewers of Westvleteren 12 first began brewing this beer, they limited buyers to ten crates at a time. But as the beer increased in popularity, buyers were permitted less and less until in 2009, they were allowed one crate only. Priced at €40 per crate of 24 bottles, the abbey prohibits any resale of the beer, meaning if you want to buy it then you must go to Belgium to the Abbey café. This scarcity of supply has only increased its popularity. In 2005 it was voted 'best beer in the world' and given worldwide press attention – much to the annoyance of the monks who brew it!

Tasting notes: A perfect balance of toffee, bitter, sweet, spice, vanilla, oak, berries and dried fruit. The best beer ever created.
- ★ **Country:** Belgium ★ **Brewer:** Westvleteren Abdij St Sixtus
- ★ **Style:** Trappist quadrupel ★ **Appearance:** Deep brown
- ★ **Alcohol** 10.2% ★ **Serving temp:** 8–10°C

KRAMAH
INDIA PALE ALE

Bevog Kramah IPA

This young Austrian microbrewer is hugely influenced by Britain and the traditional real ales, porters and IPAs that originated there. Kramah IPA takes the IPA style into the 21st century by using hops that are higher in alpha acids. These varieties are invariably fruitier and more aromatic than English hops and make for a vibrant citrus and tropical flavour.

Tasting notes: Fruity aromas of lychee, citrus and mango are carried on to the palate. Like biting into a juicy, boozy grapefruit!
★ **Country:** Austria ★ **Brewer:** Bevog Brewery ★ **Style:** IPA
★ **Appearance:** Clear amber ★ **Alcohol:** 7% ★ **Serving temp:** 4–7°C

Edelweiss Gamsbock

Wheat beer is a very common style of beer but *Weizenbocks* are a little different. Made with more malt than a standard wheat beer, *Weizenbock* is generally a little darker in colour and has a higher alcohol content, as seen in the Edelweiss Gamsbock. High in fruity aromas of ripe banana and caramel, try it with a banoffee pie.

Tasting notes: Banana, toffee, malted wheat and a yeasty, cloudy colour. Well-disguised alcohol.
★ **Country:** Austria ★ **Brewer:** Hofbräu Kaltenhausen
★ **Style:** Weizenbock ★ **Appearance:** Cloudy gold
★ **Alcohol** 7.1% ★ **Serving temp:** 8–10°C

Egger Märzenbier

Märzenbier derives from the German name for March and is thought to have originated in Bavaria. Beer was usually brewed in the autumn months and allowed to mature in the cellar through the icy cold months of winter. By March, the temperature begins to warm up and when the ice has melted, you know your Märzen is ready to drink.

Tasting notes: Malty, toasted bread flavours combine with a very light bitterness and slight spice. Great with roasted pork chops.
★ **Country:** Austria ★ **Brewer:** Privatbrauerei Fritz Egger
★ **Style:** Märzen ★ **Appearance:** Clear yellow
★ **Alcohol:** 5.2% ★ **Serving temp:** 4–7°C

Hirter Privat Pils

Much is made of the water source in Burton upon Trent in the UK and its importance in working well with hoppy beers. The same importance is placed on the Hanslbauer spring that provides Brauerei Hirt's water for this premium pilsner. As a result, hoppy flavours come through wonderfully, leaving a lasting impression of hops, bitterness and refreshment in the finish. Try pairing with light foods like tricolore salad, or with spicy chicken wings to douse the flames with hoppy, bitter fizz.

Tasting notes: Hoppy, bitter flavours come through strongly without much sweetness to balance it out.
★ **Country:** Austria ★ **Brewer:** Brauerei Hirt ★ **Style:** Pilsner
★ **Appearance:** Pale yellow ★ **Alcohol:** 5.2% ★ **Serving temp:** 3–5°C

Puntigamer Das Bierige Bier

Je größer die Flasche, desto besser die Stimmung – 'The bigger the bottle, the better the mood', is the motto of the Puntigamer brewery, which explains why Das Bierige is sold in 1.5 litre bottles. For sharing with friends, you can't ask for a better size. One of the most interesting pale lagers in the world, with pleasant grassy hop flavours coming through strongly.

Tasting notes: Grassy hop flavours with notes of dough, honey and lightly caramelized malts.
- ★ **Country:** Austria ★ **Brewer:** Brauerei Puntigam
- ★ **Style:** Pale lager ★ **Appearance:** Pale yellow
- ★ **Alcohol:** 5.1% ★ **Serving temp:** 3–5°C

DID YOU KNOW?

The Austrians have recently discovered the joys of the American drinking game Beer Pong, with the first team established in Innsbruck in 2009, and the first Viennese team in 2010.

Schladminger Märzen

The Schladminger brewery sits deep within the Schladminger Tauern mountains and has been brewing since 1909. It is fiercely proud of its range of beers, some of which are 100% organic. The brewery is inspected once a year for its Austria Bio Garantie certificate – confirming an adherence to organic produce.

Tasting notes: Sweet malt flavours with a very clean bubbly mouthfeel. Lots of bread-like flavours and grain too.
- ★ **Country:** Austria
- ★ **Brewer:** Schladminger Brau
- ★ **Style:** Märzen
- ★ **Appearance:** Clear gold
- ★ **Alcohol:** 5.1%
- ★ **Serving temp:** 4–6°C

Schloss Eggenberg Samichlaus

Once upon a time, before the new brewing methods and shamelessly controversial brewers of the early 21st century, Samichlaus was the strongest beer in the world at 14% ABV. Brewed once a year, Samichlaus (Santa Claus) is aged for 10 months before it is bottled, allowing the strong flavours to mellow and mature. Great with rich, hearty dishes or chocolate truffles.

Tasting notes: Alcohol and raisins dominate the aroma with toffee, wood and spice to follow in the flavour.
- ★ **Country:** Austria
- ★ **Brewer:** Schloss Eggenberg
- ★ **Style:** Doppelbock
- ★ **Appearance:** Dark copper
- ★ **Alcohol:** 14%
- ★ **Serving temp:** 8–10°C

Stiegl Bier

The Stiegl brewery in Salzburg is home to a huge array of beery curiosities and artefacts related to brewing. The real stars, though, are the beers it brews. Stiegl Goldbräu is their premium lager and is brewed in accordance with the purity laws passed in Germany in 1516. Made with pure Austrian mountain spring water and two-row barley, it's a classic taste of Austria.

Tasting notes: Lightly toasted bread, sweet corn flavours and a crisp, dry finish from the hops.
★ **Country:** Austria ★ **Brewer:** Stieglbrauerei ★ **Style:** Lager
★ **Appearance:** Dark gold ★ **Alcohol:** 4.9% ★ **Serving temp:** 4–6°C

Wieselburger Stammbräu

Sold in the traditional swing-top bottles – recently reintroduced to Austria – Wieselburger Stammbräu is packed with sweet-smelling caramel and toasted malt bread. It's a classic pilsner style that originated in the Czech Republic in 1842 and is now popular all over the world – but particularly in this region of central Europe. A very versatile beer due to its light flavour profile and crisp carbonated finish.

Tasting notes: Lightly vegetal, moderate grain flavours with a sweet and slightly thin finish.
★ **Country:** Austria ★ **Brewer:** Wieselburger Brauerei ★ **Style:** Pilsner
★ **Appearance:** Clear yellow ★ **Alcohol:** 5.4% ★ **Serving temp:** 7°C

Zipfer Urtyp

One of the many breweries to be severely affected by World War II, the Zipfer brewery is named after the small village of Zipf, north-east of Salzburg, Austria. Having been ravaged by bombs, the brewery was rebuilt and now exceeds a 500,000-hectolitre capacity. This pale lager packs a big flavoursome punch – more so than many of the same style.

Tasting notes: Light hoppy citrus hops in the aroma coupled with toasted grain and sweet malt.
★ **Country:** Austria ★ **Brewer:** Zipfer ★ **Style:** Pale lager
★ **Appearance:** Clear yellow ★ **Alcohol:** 5.4% ★ **Serving temp:** 4–6°C

🇨🇿 Bernard Celebration Lager

The Bernard brewery was bought by three investors in 1991. It is an operation that oversees the ingredients of its beer from start to finish and it produces around 6,700 tons of pilsner malt per year in its own malt house. Bernard Celebration Lager uses this excellent supply of malt and is one of the most-decorated beers in the country. The secret to its taste is the secondary fermentation it receives in the bottle so don't be surprised to find a light sediment in the bottom of your glass.

Tasting notes: Toasted grains, doughy bread-like note with a floral earthy hop aroma and dry bitter finish.
★ **Country:** Czech Republic ★ **Brewer:** Bernard
★ **Style:** Pilsner ★ **Appearance:** Golden
★ **Alcohol** 5% ★ **Serving temp:** 3–5°C

DID YOU KNOW?

A Czech saying claims that 'beer makes beautiful bodies', a proverb demonstrated by what Radio Prague calls the 'stunningly round physique' of Czech men – whether or not they are beautiful is a matter of taste!

🇨🇿 Bohemia Regent Prezident

There can surely be no better place to drink a pilsner than the Czech Republic and this classic example from Bohemia Regent will have any Czech-born beer lover weeping patriotically into his glass after one sip. Noted for its rich gold colour and extensive use of the locally grown Saaz hop, this crisp and bitter lager boasts a huge amount of flavour. The Regent brewery is one of the oldest in the world dating back to 1379, and now has a beerhouse in the courtyard, where you can drink the beers.

Tasting notes: Floral, earthy hop aromas from the Saaz hops and a freshly baked bread flavour on the palate.
★ **Country:** Czech Republic
★ **Brewer:** Bohemia Regent
★ **Style:** Pilsner ★ **Appearance:** Golden
★ **Alcohol** 6% ★ **Serving temp:** 3–5°C

🇨🇿 Budweiser Budvar

Not to be confused with the American Budweiser, this Czech pilsner has been the subject of a trademark dispute for many years. The term Budweiser describes something (or someone) from the city of Budweis in Bohemia, which the company believes cannot apply to an American beer. However, Anheuser-Busch created their beer in the late 19th century, after a visit to Budweis.

Tasting notes: A wonderful Saaz hop aroma with grass, flowers and a slightly peppery note. Dominated by hops.
★ **Country:** Czech Republic
★ **Brewer:** Budějovický Budvar
★ **Style:** Pilsner
★ **Appearance:** Golden
★ **Alcohol** 5%
★ **Serving temp:** 3–5°C

🇨🇿 Gambrinus Premium

Named after the legendary king of Flanders (present-day Belgium), who was famed for his magical brewing abilities, Gambrinus Premium is a well-known product in the Czech Republic. Founded in 1869, the brewery shares the site of Pilsner Urquell. Gambrinus's name is used in honour of the unofficial patron saint of brewing.

Tasting notes: Easy-drinking pilsner with flavours of malty bread, floral hops and a bitter aftertaste.
★ **Country:** Czech Republic
★ **Brewer:** Plzensky Prazdroj
★ **Style:** Pilsner ★ **Appearance:** Golden
★ **Alcohol** 5% ★ **Serving temp:** 3–5°C

🇨🇿 Koniček Grošák

Despite the threatening label, this isn't a 14% bottle of instant hangover! At a little over 6%, though, it still packs a serious punch. The Polotmavý style is a hybrid of Czech Pilsner and Dark Lager. With a richer malt character than the American style 'Vienna' lager but with a similarly satisfying hop profile, the flavour in all respects has been ramped up to 11 by this tiny microbrewery. A taste you'll never forget.

Tasting notes: Thick, sugary caramel malts with a surprisingly light and zesty lemon hop finish with long lasting duration.
★ **Country:** Czech Republic
★ **Brewer:** Minipivovar Koniček
★ **Style:** Polotmavý
★ **Appearance:** Amber
★ **ABV** 6.3%
★ **Serving temp:** 7–10°C

🇨🇿 Jihlavský Grand

Not all pilsners in the Czech Republic are light and easy. This 8% ABV monster from the Jihlava brewery is one of the more challenging beers in the pilsner style. Though it still tastes strongly of Saaz hops and freshly-baked brown bread, there is a definite note of ethanol that creeps in too. One of the most full-tasting beers in all of the country.

Tasting notes: Brown bread, honey and earth, floral hops. Pairs well with hot chicken wings and spicy shellfish.
★ **Country:** Czech Republic
★ **Brewer:** Jihlava Pivovar
★ **Style:** Imperial pilsner
★ **Appearance:** Deep gold
★ **Alcohol** 8.1%
★ **Serving temp:** 3–5°C

LAGER: THE WORLD BEER

Pilsner lager is the dominant beer type in the world, and it can all be traced back to 1842 and the town of Pilsen, or Plzen, in the Czech Republic. At the time, the region was part of the Kingdom of Bohemia. The city fathers established a brewery to counteract the variable quality of the dark local beers, and hired Bavarian Josef Groll as the head brewer.

Bohemian beers of that era were generally dark and cloudy. Groll's combination of Bavarian-style 'lagering', pale malts, local Saaz hops and the soft water of the region produced a clear golden beer that was an instant hit. It was first served on 11 November 1842 at the Feast of St Martin.

Sales of pilsner spread to Prague, Vienna and Paris within 20 years and soon other brewers were copying the styles. Pilsen's chamber of commerce registered the term 'Pilsner Bier' as a brand name in 1859, and in 1898 Pilsner Urquell –

meaning the 'source of pilsner' – was registered as a trademark for pilsner from the city.

It is estimated that around 90 per cent of beer consumed worldwide is pale lager, but the original Pilsner is still brewed in the city at the Pilsner Urquell brewery. An annual beer festival is held in October in and around the brewery. This includes a mass toast of the beers made here: Pilsner Urquell and Gambrinus.

Kocour 70 Quarterback

Named for the American football position, the Kocour Quarterback has its roots deep in American craft brewing. While IPAs were largely a British invention, the craft brewers in the USA reinvigorated the style towards the end of the 20th century. Kocour 70 Quarterback is a tribute to the brewers who gave this style of beer a much-needed shot in the arm.

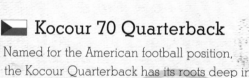

Tasting notes: Heavy hop flavours of grapefruit and lemon and sweeter malt flavours of toffee and caramel. Nicely balanced.
* **Country:** Czech Republic
* **Brewer:** Pivovar Kocour
* **Style:** Imperial IPA
* **Appearance:** Hazy gold
* **Alcohol** 8.7%
* **Serving temp:** 4–7°C

Kozel Světlý

Kozel is the Czech word for 'goat', and the brewery has been up and running since 1874, when Franz Ringhoffer opened a small brewery in a small town near Prague. The goat seen on the label was the result of a French painter passing through the brewery town and being inspired to create an emblem after a goat that lived there.

Tasting notes: Sweet, almost corn-like malts with a light hops aroma and a long bitter finish.
* **Country:** Czech Republic
* **Brewer:** Velkopopovický Kozel
* **Style:** Pilsner
* **Appearance:** Golden
* **Alcohol** 4%
* **Serving temp:** 4–7°C

Krušovice Černé

This pungent black beer has a great big hop bouquet, which it gets from the Saaz hops grown in the nearby Žatec region. The difference between this and a standard Czech pilsner is the deep brown body – a result of the dark malts used, in combination with the natural spring water from the Křivoklát Woods. Not too strong at 3.8%, this one is surprisingly sessionable.

Tasting notes: Roasted coffee aroma with hints of chocolate and doughy brown bread in the finish.
★ **Country:** Czech Republic ★ **Brewer:** Královský Pivovar Krušovice
★ **Style:** Schwarzbier ★ **Appearance:** Deep brown
★ **Alcohol** 3.8% ★ **Serving temp:** 4–7°C

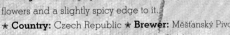

Lev Lion Lager

There are so many good-quality pilsners in the Czech Republic that it's almost impossible to choose a bad one. Here we have Lev Lion Lager – a classic full-bodied golden pilsner from Havlíčkův Brod, a city located right in the heart of Bohemia where the first pilsners were brewed by the Pilsner Urquell Brewery in 1842.

Tasting notes: Highly aromatic with earthy notes, flowers and a slightly spicy edge to it.
★ **Country:** Czech Republic ★ **Brewer:** Měšťanský Pivovar Havlíčkův Brod ★ **Style:** Pilsner ★ **Appearance:** Golden
★ **Alcohol** 4.4% ★ **Serving temp:** 2–4°C

Lobkowicz Premium 12

In the Czech Republic, many brewers name their beer with a 10° or 12° rating. This refers to the Plato scale of measuring the percentage of sugar in beer before fermentation. Thus a 12° beer starts with 12% fermentable sugar – giving an indication of how strong the beer will be when it is finished. Lobkowicz Premium is a perfect 12° beer with a full-bodied character.

Tasting notes: Lots of straw, hay and bitterness with rich, creamy-white foam and bready pale malts.
★ **Country:** Czech Republic
★ **Brewer:** Pivovar Protivin
★ **Style:** Pilsner ★ **Appearance:** Orange
★ **Alcohol** 4.7% ★ **Serving temp:** 3–5°C

🇨🇿 Matuška Hellcat Imperial India Pale Ale

Founded by Martin Matuška on Easter Monday 2009, the Matuška brewery is one of the more modern in the Czech Republic. The Hellcat Imperial IPA is a serious flavour bomb. With its use of American hops, big citrus flavours are achieved, including grapefruit, lemon peel and orange blossom. This heavy flavour profile is typical of the double IPA style, as is the refreshing green hoppy bitterness. This works fantastically well with jerk chicken to put out the fire.

Tasting notes: A range of tropical and citrus fruits, including tangerine, grapefruit, lemons and limes, with a toffee finish.
- ★ **Country:** Czech Republic
- ★ **Brewer:** Pivovar Matuška
- ★ **Style:** Double IPA
- ★ **Appearance:** Hazy orange
- ★ **Alcohol** 8.4%
- ★ **Serving temp:** 4–7°C

🇨🇿 Merlin Černý

A fantastically flavoursome dark lager, this beer is named after Merlin in the legends of King Arthur and the Knights of the Round Table. The legend tells of a sword called Excalibur that could be pulled from a stone, only by a worthy knight. Presumably the worthy knight, Arthur, had a pint of Merlin's black lager to give him the extra strength he needed!

Tasting notes: Heavy malt flavours of bread, roasted coffee and dark caramel with hints of chocolate.
- ★ **Country:** Czech Republic
- ★ **Brewer:** Pivovar Protivin
- ★ **Style:** Schwarzbier
- ★ **Appearance:** Black brown
- ★ **Alcohol** 4.7%
- ★ **Serving temp:** 8–10°C

🇨🇿 Pilsner Urquell

The name Urquell in German translates to 'the original source' and that's exactly what this beer is in the world of brewing. The first pilsner ever to be produced, approximately 90% of the beer drunk in the world today is inspired by this original recipe. The inventor, Josef Groll, used large amounts of Saaz hops and the palest malts possible (in those days dark and smoked malts were the norm). The golden lager beer that resulted went on to become the most popular style in the world. The original Pilsner Urquell is still going strong today.

Tasting notes: Lots of earthy aromatics from the Saaz hops and a long-lasting trademark bitter finish.
- ★ **Country:** Czech Republic ★ **Brewer:** Plzensky Prazdroj ★ **Style:** Pilsner
- ★ **Appearance:** Golden yellow ★ **Alcohol** 4.4% ★ **Serving temp:** 3–5°C

PilsnerUrquell ®

4.4% ABV

THE ORIGINAL PILSNER
GENUINE CZECH IMPORT

🇨🇿 Primátor Double 24

The higher the Plato rating, the fuller the body of the beer. Here, the Plato scale rating is 24 and this well-balanced doppelbock does not disappoint. Very smooth and dark, with a turbocharged 10.5% ABV, this beer is packed with flavours of prunes, caramel, brown bread and hints of honey. Sip it alongside a piece of barbecued meat to enjoy it at its best.

Tasting notes: Caramel, butter, prunes, hints of honey and a nice boozy hit of banana at the end.
★ **Country:** Czech Republic
★ **Brewer:** Pivovar Nachod
★ **Style:** Doppelbock
★ **Appearance:** Dark brown
★ **Alcohol** 10.5%
★ **Serving temp:** 8–10°C

🇨🇿 Rychtář Speciál

Celebrating its centenary in 2013, the Pivovar Rychtar in Hlinsko is not among the oldest or most distinguished breweries in the Czech Republic. However, soon after production began it became popular and in 1925 it was bought by wealthy investors. Unfortunately, they did not foresee the Nazi occupation, which limited the brewery's production severely. The brewery was nationalized in 1948 and soon became successful again. This Rychtář Speciál, labelled in Czech brewing convention as 15% Plato, is one of the brewery's stronger beers, with 6.5% ABV, a mild bitterness and well-hidden alcohol flavours.

Tasting notes: Toasted bread, hay and light toffee and buttery notes. Goes nicely with a barbecue.
★ **Country:** Czech Republic
★ **Brewer:** Pivovar Rychtář
★ **Style:** Imperial pilsner
★ **Appearance:** Yellow orange
★ **Alcohol** 6.5% ★ **Serving temp:** 3–5°C

🏴 Staropramen Premium Lager

The flagship product of the Staropramen brewery in Prague, this is one of the most famous beers to come out of the Czech Republic, being popular across much of Europe and the United Kingdom. The name Staropramen translates as 'old spring' and refers to the brewery's water source – an attribute it is fiercely proud of. Along with all the other Czech breweries, Staropramen was nationalized after World War II. It is now owned by brewing behemoth Molson Coors and has become the second most-popular beer in the Czech Republic.

Tasting notes: Delicately floral hops, light malt and a long bitter finish.
★ **Country:** Czech Republic
★ **Brewer:** Staropramen Breweries
★ **Style:** Pale lager
★ **Appearance:** Yellow
★ **Alcohol** 5%
★ **Serving temp:** 3–5°C

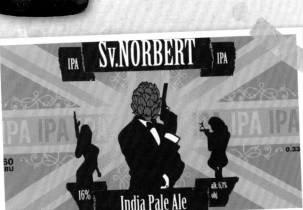

🏴 Svaty Norbert IPA

An excellent example of what a modern India Pale Ale should taste like. Using two of the most flavoursome American hops, Amarillo and Cascade, the historic Strahov brewery has shown how it can move with the times. Closed in 1907 after a 600-year history, in 2000 it was reopened and refurbished to accommodate 350 people in its restaurant and brewhouse.

Tasting notes: Relatively mild-mannered with strong hints of orange blossom, perfumed hops and a very bitter finish.
★ **Country:** Czech Republic ★ **Brewer:** Klášterní Pivovar Strahov
★ **Style:** IPA ★ **Appearance:** Hazy amber
★ **Alcohol** 6.3% ★ **Serving temp:** 4–7°C

DID YOU KNOW?

Before becoming President, the young Václav Havel was a dissident playwright. Finding himself short of money he worked in a brewery, rolling barrels and filtering beer, and based an absurdist play on his experiences.

■■ Baladin Xyauyù Barrel

A twee little brewpub in the sleepy Italian village of Piozzo is the setting for the Baladin brewery – opened by a local and a young French dancer. They brewed this superb barley wine in the spirit of experimentation to surprise their regulars with an unfamiliar taste and accidentally created one of the best – but least known – beers in all of Italy.

Tasting notes: Caramel, dates, banana, bread.
Goes superbly well with aged cheese.
★ **Country:** Italy ★ **Brewer:** Baladin ★ **Style:** Barley wine
★ **Appearance:** Deep red ★ **Alcohol:** 14% ★ **Serving temp:** 8–13°C

DID YOU KNOW?

A researcher from the Institute of Geriatrics at the University of Bari, Italy, has proved through extensive research that moderate consumption of beer is good for cognitive health and slows the ageing process.

■■ Birra Moretti

First introduced to the Italian public in 1859 and still going strong, Birra Moretti is a well-known and widely loved Italian lager. Originally owned by Luigi Moretti but now a Heineken brand, this pale lager can be found almost anywhere in the world, from Italian restaurants in the USA to the supermarket shelves of Denmark. An extremely popular and refreshing aperitif.

Tasting notes: Light malt, hay, straw and hints of honey. Great to serve alongside simple garlic bread.
★ **Country:** Italy
★ **Brewer:** Heineken
★ **Style:** Pale lager
★ **Appearance:** Pale yellow
★ **Alcohol:** 4.6%
★ **Serving temp:** 1–2°C

ITALY'S BEER BOOM

Beer has always been a popular drink in Italy, alongside the country's great wine heritage. However, like many countries, production in the 20th century was dominated by a small number of large, industrialized brewers.

That is now changing as Italy has developed its own home-grown craft beer scene. Just as the country's Slow Food movement emphasizes the importance of seasonality, local ingredients and tradition, Italy's craft brewers place quality before quantity.

The website Microbirrifici, which catalogues Italian beer, lists more than 600 small breweries, up from a mere handful 20 years ago. Because of the cost of importing malt and hops and the small scale of production, Italian beer can be expensive, but drinkers seem prepared to pay.

Examples include the Baladin range from Piedmont, presented in stylish wine bottles and featuring amber beers, IPAs and Belgian influenced brews. Birrificio Italiano was the first microbrewery in Lombardy, in 1996, and emphasizes natural ingredients and a traditional process for its range of beers.

Some breweries have collaborated with vineyards. LoverBeer uses Barbera grapes and wild yeast fermentation for its BeerBera. Birrificio Barley's BB10 imperial stout uses fresh grape juice, known as must, in its production.

The Italian beer story is still evolving. Birrificio Del Ducato (pictured), one of the most awarded Italian breweries, was formed in 2007. Its beers, including Sally Brown and Verdi Imperial Stout, are contributing to an annual growth rate of 80 per cent.

■■ Birrificio Del Ducato Sally Brown

This young and thriving microbrewery is located in a small village in Parma province – home to the famous Parma ham and sparkling wines like Lambrusco. Taking its name from a Laurel Aitken song, Sally Brown is a masterpiece, using a blend of 11 different malts all skilfully woven together into one smooth, complex beer.

Tasting notes: Comforting aromas of coffee, cocoa beans and campfires. Pair with dry smoked salmon or oysters.
* **Country:** Italy
* **Brewer:** Birrificio del Ducato
* **Style:** Stout
* **Appearance:** Ebony black
* **Alcohol:** 5.2%
* **Serving temp:** 8–13°C

■■ Birrificio Italiano Tipopils

Birrificio Italiano Tipopils is a simple, light and refreshing beer with no frills and no gimmicks. Sold as a pilsner, the beer isn't matured for nearly as long as a standard lager – being bottle-ready in a little over two weeks after its primary fermentation. The short maturation means the flavours are strong, but uncomplicated.

Tasting notes: Sweet caramel, citrus hops and a dry bitter finish. Exactly what you want from a lager.
* **Country:** Italy
* **Brewer:** Birrificio Italiano
* **Style:** Pilsner
* **Appearance:** Clear yellow
* **Alcohol:** 5.2%
* **Serving temp:** 4–7°C

■■ Birrificio Pausa Cafè Tosta

One of the most unusual breweries in the world. Operating within state prisons, the Pausa Cafè brewery is built to help rehabilitate as well as refresh. Inmates at the brewery learn their brewing skills while serving their time and every bottle sold helps their reintegration to society in this unique and progressive enterprise. Its Tosta barley wine is true to style with big hints of berry, cocoa, dried fruit and caramel. At 12.5% ABV, it's also full of heartwarming alcoholic flavour, so sip it slowly.

Tasting notes: Dates, spiced berries with caramel and chocolate in the body. Great with hearty stews and soups.
★ **Country:** Italy ★ **Brewer:** Birrificio Pausa Cafè
★ **Style:** Barley wine ★ **Appearance:** Dark amber
★ **Alcohol:** 12.5% ★ **Serving temp:** 8–13℃

■■ Brewfist 24k

A truly modern Italian brewery, Brewfist is rewriting the rules on beer within its home country. Founded in 2010, it has already built up a good core range: one of the most popular beers is this British-style golden ale, 24k. Rich in biscuit flavour and light citrus in the finish, it's one meant for drinking all evening.

Tasting notes: Biscuity malt, sweet and buttery with a note of honey. Pairs well with tempura prawns.
★ **Country:** Italy ★ **Brewer:** Brewfist
★ **Style:** Golden ale ★ **Appearance:** Golden
★ **Alcohol:** 4.6% ★ **Serving temp:** 4–7℃

DID YOU KNOW?

In the 4th century AD, the Roman Emperor Julian composed an epigram mocking the beer of the Celts and claiming that a wine-drinker smells of nectar while a beer-drinker smells like a goat!

■■ Menabrea 1846

Lots of beers pride themselves on using only four ingredients: barley, hops, yeast and water. Other grains like maize or rice can be added for extra sweetness or a lower cost and this is the case with Menabrea 1846. A fairly easygoing beer, its flavours do not dominate the palate, meaning it's good to drink as a session beer.

Tasting notes: Light flavours of malt, sweetcorn and a thin body. One to drink for refreshment rather than mindblowing flavour.
★ **Country:** Italy ★ **Brewer:** Menabrea
★ **Style:** Pale lager ★ **Appearance:** Golden yellow
★ **Alcohol:** 4.8% ★ **Serving temp:** 1–2°C

■■ Nastro Azzurro Peroni

Peroni is certainly the most recognizable brand in the country, having been dominant since the 1960s. The name Nastro Azzurro means 'blue ribbon' in honour of the Blue Riband won by the Italian ocean liner SS *Rex* in 1933. Nastro Azzurro is the company's flagship premium lager and extremely successful worldwide – not just in its native Italy.

Tasting notes: Aromas of grass, malt and earthy hops with a lightly sweet, slightly metallic flavour.
★ **Country:** Italy
★ **Brewer:** Birra Peroni
★ **Style:** Pale lager
★ **Appearance:** Golden yellow
★ **Alcohol:** 5.1%
★ **Serving temp:** 1–2°C

ITALIAN BEER BY DESIGN

In Italy, how things look is as important as what they do, and the new artisanal beers are no exception.

Italians choose their beers as carefully as they choose their wines, which is perhaps not surprising as craft beers can cost €15 and upwards for a 750ml bottle. Italians also have a love of cool design and products that look great.

Many Italian beers come in 750ml wine bottles, which partly explains the higher price and indicates that the beer is to be savoured, usually with food. Lengthy tasting notes are a feature of many breweries, such as Almond '22 in Pescara.

Treviso brewery 32 Via dei Birrai takes design to a new level with its colour-coordinated range of beers, all featuring the prominent '32' brand. The company claims that it wants to 'create objects that become collectors' items' as much as brew great beer and its approach is certainly detailed. Design touches flow through everything from the beer labels and beer mats to the unique bottle top and cork closure system.

Another brewery that has spent as much time on its image as its beer is Birra dell'Eremo in Assisi. Its bottles feature labels inspired by Umbrian folklore and are designed by a trendy creative consultancy.

Meanwhile, one of Italy's longest-established microbreweries, Baladin, bottles its range in embossed wine bottles. The funky labels feature a typeface resembling monastic script imagined by a graffiti artist. It almost makes the bottles too pretty to recycle.

Revelation Cat
Black Knight

Some of the most critically acclaimed beers in Italy come from the Revelation Cat brewery in Rome. With his evil-looking logo, Anglo-Italian head brewer Alex Liberati makes modern-style beers with big flavour and personality. This one is the first imperial stout from the brewery and was aged for one year before being bottled in 2012. The release is being staggered over three years as there are a limited number of this fantastically boozy creation. Be sure to age this one to mellow the flavours before drinking.

Tasting notes: Chocolate, cherries, bourbon and vanilla. Pours a thick, oily black with a dense, tan head.
- ✶ **Country:** Italy
- ✶ **Brewer:** Revelation Cat Craft Brewing
- ✶ **Style:** Imperial stout ✶ **Appearance:** Black
- ✶ **Alcohol:** 14% ✶ **Serving temp:** 12–16°C

Toccalmatto Russian Imperial Stout Wild Bretta

A very special seasonal beer from the Toccalmatto brewery in Emilia-Romagna. Barrel ageing is becoming more and more widespread in craft brewing, with high prices being paid for different ageing vessels. Whisky, bourbon and sherry casks have all become popular to impart flavour. The Wild Bretta Imperial Russian Stout is aged in barrels that previously contained a premium Italian wine made with 100% Sagrantino grapes from the province of Perugia. The barrel-ageing process gives the beer an unusual vinous quality – a wonderfully mischievous twist on the Imperial Russian Stout.

Tasting notes: Sherry, tannins, liquorice and vanilla. Superb with vanilla ice cream or as an all-evening beer. Serve just below room temperature.
- ✶ **Country:** Italy ✶ **Brewer:** Toccalmatto ✶ **Style:** Imperial stout
- ✶ **Appearance:** Black ✶ **Alcohol:** 12% ✶ **Serving temp:** 13–16°C

▪ ▪ 3 Monts

The bière de garde (literally a 'beer for keeping') style of beer was originally brewed in French farmhouses during the colder months and kept until summer, when farmworkers would drink it as payment or part payment. The reason for this long storage was because it was so difficult to brew in summer, when higher temperatures had an unpredictable effect on yeast. The long maturation period allows the beer to develop pronounced flavour and this is certainly the case with 3 Monts.

Tasting notes: Freshly baked white bread in both taste and aroma. Wonderfully simple and perfect with cheese and ham.
* ★ **Country:** France
* ★ **Brewer:** Brasserie de St. Sylvestre
* ★ **Style:** Bière de garde
* ★ **Appearance:** Clear gold
* ★ **Alcohol** 8.5% ★ **Serving temp:** 4–7°C

▪ ▪ Belzebuth Pur Malt

Named after the devil himself, this beer varies in alcohol content depending on which batch you are drinking but it never strays much below 12% – it is devilishly strong. Depending on which year it was brewed it may be labelled Pur Malt, Blonde or Extra Strong. The Grain d'Orge brewery just can't seem to make up its mind on this one.

Tasting notes: Devilish flavours of warming brandy, honey and faint traces of elderflower.
* ★ **Country:** France
* ★ **Brewer:** Brasserie Grain d'Orge
* ★ **Style:** Belgian strong ale
* ★ **Appearance:** Amber
* ★ **Alcohol** 13%
* ★ **Serving temp:** 8–13°C

DID YOU KNOW?

A recent archaeological excavation in Provence has uncovered one of the most ancient breweries in the world, and shows that brewing was done 2,500 years ago in much the same way as today.

▪ ▪ Castelain Ch'ti Ambrée

Another *bière de garde*, but Ch'ti Ambrée is a little different to the 3 Monts. Slightly lower in alcohol but still with bags of flavour, it demonstrates the variety in French farmhouse ales. This amber-coloured *bière de garde* bears a strong resemblance to the *saison* beers of Belgium but has a much more pronounced malt profile over the yeast.

Tasting notes: Strong flavours of toffee, caramel and brown bread. Good with a hard, mature cheese.
* ★ **Country:** France
* ★ **Brewer:** Brasserie Castelain
* ★ **Style:** Bière de garde ★ **Appearance:** Amber
* ★ **Alcohol** 5.9% ★ **Serving temp:** 7–9°C

Brasserie Fischer

▮▮ Fischer Tradition

The ever-popular pale lager style finds its way all over the world. This example is from the company that brought the world Desperados Tequila lager. Fischer Tradition is sold in large swing-top bottles and has all the refreshing characteristics of pale lager with the usual easygoing flavour profile. Very light in sweetness.

Tasting notes: Flavours of malt, grain toast and corn make themselves known over the thin texture and easy finish.
★ **Country:** France ★ **Brewer:** Heineken ★ **Style:** Pale lager
★ **Appearance:** Yellow ★ **Alcohol** 6% ★ **Serving temp:** 1–2°C

▮▮ Kronenbourg 1664

France's bestselling beer by a long way and the second-biggest premium lager across the channel in the UK. Kronenbourg 1664 is made from malted barley, malted wheat and maize for extra sweetness, and one of the few hops that grow in the Alsace region: Strisselspalt. This earthy hop gives the beer its distinct aroma. Caramel colouring is added for extra depth in the appearance. First brewed in 1952, this beer just seems to go from strength to strength.

Tasting notes: Moderate flavours of corn, malt and hints of toasted grain. Serve ice cold.
★ **Country:** France ★ **Brewer:** Kronenbourg ★ **Style:** Pale lager
★ **Appearance:** Yellow ★ **Alcohol** 5.5% ★ **Serving temp:** 1–2°C

■■ Le Brewery Odo

It would be fair to say the French and the English have had a slightly chequered history. In Le Brewery's Odo, though, the two countries meet to superb effect. The milk stout style made popular by the English in the years following World War I is done extremely well by the Normandy-based brewery founded by Englishman Steve Skews in 2001.

Tasting notes: Sweet, creamy chocolate with hints of coffee, milk and light liquorice.
- ★ **Country:** France
- ★ **Brewer:** Le Brewery
- ★ **Style:** Milk stout
- ★ **Appearance:** Dark ruby
- ★ **Alcohol** 6.6%
- ★ **Serving temp:** 8–13°C

DID YOU KNOW?

In his book *Studies on Fermentation* in 1876, French chemist Louis Pasteur revolutionized the scientific understanding of the beer-making process, changing the course of brewing and paving the way for modern brewers.

■■ Meteor Pils

With a nod to the aromatic and bitter qualities of Czech-style pilsners, the Brasserie Meteor has created a fitting tribute to those historic beers in its own version – Meteor Pils. Made with the same Saaz hops that the Czechs use, the earthy yet lightly floral aroma makes it flavoursome while still being wonderfully refreshing – as golden lagers should be.

Tasting notes: Slightly sweeter than most Czech pilsners but with the same bitter aftertaste and aroma.
- ★ **Country:** France ★ **Brewer:** Brasserie Meteor
- ★ **Style:** Pilsner ★ **Appearance:** Clear yellow
- ★ **Alcohol** 5% ★ **Serving temp:** 1–2°C

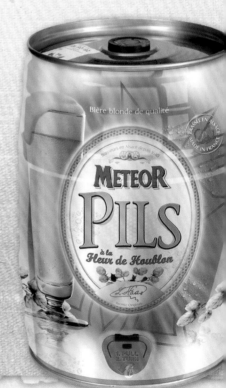

■■ Pelforth Blonde

The Pelforth brewery has a distinctly British sound to it. In fact, it uses an English strain of yeast to ferment its *bière de garde*. The brewery was originally called Pelican – an image it still uses on the bottles. The name was changed in the 1930s: part Pelican (Pel), part French (*forte*, meaning 'strong'), with a nod to the English adding 'th' at the end.

Tasting notes: Mildly malty with notes of toast, grain and straw and a very thin texture.
* ★ **Country:** France
* ★ **Brewer:** Pelforth
* ★ **Style:** Bière de garde
* ★ **Appearance:** Clear yellow
* ★ **Alcohol** 5.8%
* ★ **Serving temp:** 1–2°C

■■ Thiriez Vieille Brune

In a beer inspired by the traditional Belgian creations brewed just over the border from its brewhouse, the Brasserie Thiriez has created one of the finest beers in France. The beer is aged for three months in French oak wine barrels to impart woodiness and a vinous nature as the beer matures. The sour, acidic taste is very evident and a great example of the Flemish sour brown style.

Tasting notes: Cedar, oak, brandy and light wine flavours with a touch of vinegary acidity.
* ★ **Country:** France
* ★ **Brewer:** Brasserie Thiriez
* ★ **Style:** Flemish brown
* ★ **Appearance:** Ruby brown
* ★ **Alcohol** 5.8%
* ★ **Serving temp:** 8–13°C

FRENCH BEER FOR KEEPING

Bière de garde is a type of farmhouse ale from the beer-loving north of France. The name means 'beer for keeping' as it was originally brewed using the abundance of ingredients available in the autumn, to last throughout the year.

The brewing season was short as ingredients were seasonal and temperatures were best for brewing in early winter. Cold-conditioned into the spring, the beer kept for months and was used as refreshment, and to pay the farmhands.

Bière de garde is often likened to Belgian 'saison' farmhouse beers. However, it tends to be less hoppy and more malty than the Belgian beers. The lengthy ageing gives the beer its deep flavour and complex character.

Bière de garde may be blonde, amber or brown. The beer style relates more to the farmhouse breweries of northern France than a strict flavour profile. Each brewery makes a unique product, so there is a large range of flavours.

The style remains something of a cottage industry, and little known outside its native region. Examples to search out include La Bavaisienne from Brasserie Theillier, which claims to be France's oldest farmhouse brewery, Gavroche French Red Ale from Brasserie de St Sylvestre, and Brasserie Duyck's Jenlain Ambrée, which celebrated its 90th anniversary in 2012.

Like many old European styles, *bière de garde* has been rediscovered by US brewers, who are now crafting their own versions.

➕ 1936 Bière

Set in the spectacular surroundings of the Swiss Alps, 1936 is a family-run brewery with a close eye on its environmental impact. Taking water from a beautifully pure source in the Alps, malt grown at 1,650 metres above sea level and organic hops, this is pale lager with a touch of class.

Tasting notes: Lemony citrus hops, with a pale malt taste to match and a nice bitter finish.
★ **Country**: Switzerland ★ **Brewer:** 1936 Bière ★ **Style:** Premium lager
★ **Appearance:** Gold ★ **Alcohol** 4.7% ★ **Serving temp:** 2–5°C

➕ BFM √225 Saison

The Belgian 'saison' style is not necessarily the most popular in the world but when done properly it has a taste you'll never forget. BFM, the Brasserie des Franches-Montagnes, makes one of the most perfect examples you'll ever try. Extremely refreshing with tart apple, pear and grape flavours, it pairs well with almost any food but especially a simple loaf of bread and soft cheese.

Tasting notes: Slightly sour with yeasty, lemony and floral notes in the aroma.
★ **Country:** Switzerland ★ **Brewer:** BFM ★ **Style:** Saison
★ **Appearance:** Clear gold ★ **Alcohol** 5% ★ **Serving temp:** 4–7°C

➕ Brasserie Trois Dames
Grande Dame Oud Bruin

A perfect example of what you might call a happy accident. The Grande Dame is the result of a chance encounter between fermenting Valais apricots and a Belgian stout. A tribute to the sour brown beers of Flanders in Belgium, the name Oud Bruin literally translates to 'old brown', because the beer is aged before bottling. Complex flavours of red wine, juniper, acidic lemon and sour redcurrants emerge on first sip and there's a beautifully tart finish. Only 1,200 bottles were made of this gorgeous sour beer so be sure to cherish one if you find it.

Tasting notes: Pairs well with spring lamb, duck, mussels or soft cheeses.
★ **Country:** Switzerland ★ **Brewer:** Brasserie Trois Dames ★ **Style:** Sour brown
★ **Appearance:** Deep ruby red ★ **Alcohol** 7% ★ **Serving temp:** 4–7°C

🇨🇭 Eichhof Hubertus

A brewery that values tradition: its use of horse and cart to deliver beer is not just a marketing stunt but in fact a way of keeping the extremely rare horse breed Vladimir Heavy Draft alive. The horses pull wagons loaded with Eichhof beer to bars, pubs and restaurants all over the city of Lucerne where the brewery is situated.

Tasting notes: Caramel malts, sweet bready notes and a very low hop character.
- ★ **Country:** Switzerland
- ★ **Brewer:** Brauerei Eichhof
- ★ **Style:** Dunkel lager
- ★ **Appearance:** Dark copper
- ★ **Alcohol** 5.7%
- ★ **Serving temp:** 8–10°C

🇨🇭 Locher Appenzeller Hanfblüte

As well as hops, the brewers at Locher add a close relative of hops, hemp. Using both the flowers and leaves from this pungent plant imparts aromas of ginger, pepper and spice as well as the distinctive aroma of hemp.

Tasting notes: Hemp aromas, hemp flavours, with hints of chilli, ginger and other spices thrown in for good measure.
- ★ **Country:** Switzerland
- ★ **Brewer:** Brauerei Locher
- ★ **Style:** Hemp beer
- ★ **Appearance:** Yellow orange
- ★ **Alcohol** 5.2%
- ★ **Serving temp:** 8–10°C

DID YOU KNOW?

The Swiss have the highest concentration of breweries per capita in the world; however, they are moderate drinkers and consider it tacky to become drunk.

🇨🇭 Ittinger Amber

The Ittinger brewery creates the only Swiss beer with a real monastic history behind it. Its trademark Amber beer is made with a combination of four types of malted wheat and barley to create the brewery's signature taste. Pair this Vienna-style lager with a wide variety of food, from spicy chicken wings to pork goulash.

Tasting notes: Moderate flavours of caramel, molasses and lighter hop flavours with dried fruit in the finish.
- ★ **Country:** Switzerland
- ★ **Brewer:** Heineken Switzerland
- ★ **Style:** Vienna lager ★ **Appearance:** Amber
- ★ **Alcohol** 5.6% ★ **Serving temp:** 8–10°C

🇨🇭 Ticino Bad Attitude Dude

Dude is named after the main character in the 1998 cult film classic *The Big Lebowski*. A cartoon drawing of Jeff Bridges – 'The Dude' – even adorns the side of the can. Dude is a Californian-style double IPA with hops from the west coast of America that are added both during the boil and also during fermentation, in a process known as dry-hopping. This second hop addition imparts even more aroma and flavour without resulting in too much bitterness.

Tasting notes: High caramel malt flavours are matched nicely by aromatic citrus notes from the heavy hopping.
★ **Country:** Switzerland ★ **Brewer:** Ticino Brewing Company ★ **Style:** Double IPA
★ **Appearance:** Dark amber ★ **Alcohol** 7.51% ★ **Serving temp:** 4–7°C

DID YOU KNOW?

A 700-year-old Austrian castle boasts the world's only beer swimming pools, each containing 42,000 pints of beer. Rich in vitamins and calcium, beer is said to be good for the skin.

🇨🇭 Ticino Bad Attitude Two Penny Porter

Ticino Brewing Company's tribute to the first porters that were brewed in London, England, the two penny porter is so named because in the 19th century, twopence is what a quart of porter used to cost. Two Penny, at 8.15% ABV, would have been known as a stout porter back then, but the difference between a stout and porter is really just a name in the modern age.

Tasting notes: Classic flavours of chocolate, coffee with hints of decadent molasses and liquorice.
★ **Country:** Switzerland
★ **Brewer:** Ticino Brewing Company
★ **Style:** Imperial porter
★ **Appearance:** Dark brown
★ **Alcohol** 8.15%
★ **Serving temp:** 8–13°C

Okult No.1 Blanche

A tribute to the Belgian *witbier* style revived by Pierre Celis at Hoegaarden in the 1960s, Okult No.1 Blanche is laced with fragrances of orange peel and coriander and is brewed with pale wheat instead of barley. The beer uses 100% organically farmed ingredients. Look out for its hazy light-yellow appearance – there is yeast still in the bottle.

Tasting notes: Zesty citrus aromas, bitter orange blossom and a light spice towards the end.
★ **Country:** Luxembourg
★ **Brewer:** Brasserie Simon
★ **Style:** Witbier
★ **Appearance:** Hazy yellow
★ **Alcohol** 5.4% ★ **Serving temp:** 4–7°C

Diekirch Premium

The pale lager style has made it into pretty much every country in the world. Diekirch Premium is another example. A light-coloured, light-flavoured beer with a thin texture and a refreshing character. Perfect served as an aperitif or in hot weather to slake a thirst.

Tasting notes: Light malt, light hops and an easygoing grassy bitter finish.
★ **Country:** Luxembourg
★ **Brewer:** Brasserie de Luxembourg Mousel-Diekirch
★ **Style:** Pale lager
★ **Appearance:** Light yellow
★ **Alcohol** 4.8%
★ **Serving temp:** 2–5°C

Mousel Premium Pils

A beer with a loyal following, Mousel Premium Pils is a true taste of Luxembourg. With a more pronounced bitterness than other lagers around the small country, it has more in common with a Czech-style pilsner than a basic pale lager. The very recognizable long bitter finish comes from the Saaz hops.

Tasting notes: Sweet malts are crowded out by dry Saaz hops, culminating in the trademark Czech-style finish.
★ **Country:** Luxembourg
★ **Brewer:** Brasserie de Luxembourg Mousel-Diekirch
★ **Style:** Pilsner
★ **Appearance:** Pale yellow
★ **Alcohol** 4.8%
★ **Serving temp:** 2–5°C

Amstel Lager

One of the more famous brands of the Netherlands, Amstel lager was first brewed in Amsterdam in 1870 and is named after the Amstel river. As well as giving this beer its name, the Amstel river also provided refrigeration as brewers used the winter ice build-up to keep their purpose-built double-walled cellars cold enough for lagering.

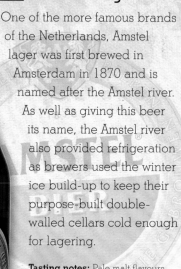

Tasting notes: Pale malt flavours with hints of canned sweetcorn and light crisp hops.
★ **Country:** The Netherlands
★ **Brewer:** Amstel Brouwerij
★ **Style:** Pale lager
★ **Appearance:** Pale yellow
★ **Alcohol** 5%
★ **Serving temp:** 2–3°C

Bavaria 8.6

Bavaria 8.6 is a premium-strength pilsner which is named after the ABV it's brewed to. Or at least it used to be. In 2013, Bavaria 8.6 was reduced in strength to 7.9% ABV. At either strength, a large quantity of malt is required to produce such a strong beer. In this case, a blend of five malts are sourced from France, Switzerland and the Netherlands.

Tasting notes: Deep malt flavours, sweetness with a hint of almond and marzipan. Perfect with a spicy bratwurst.
★ **Country:** The Netherlands ★ **Brewer:** Bavaria Brouwerij
★ **Style:** Imperial pilsner ★ **Appearance:** Clear yellow
★ **Alcohol** 7.9% ★ **Serving temp:** 2–3°C

THE GROLSCH SWING TOP

While most beers are closed with a metal cap, Dutch lager Grolsch is known for its distinctive swing-top cap, which eliminates the need for an opener. Introduced in 1897, the swing top is still going strong, producing a satisfying 'pop' whenever a bottle is opened.

The tops used to be porcelain, but are now usually made of plastic, although bottles with ceramic tops are still in circulation in the Netherlands. These are popular with home brewers, as they are very robust and can easily be sealed by hand. The swing tops also enjoyed brief popularity in the 1980s as shoe accessories following a fashion started by boy band Bros.

Bros are now long gone, but Grolsch is still going strong and will celebrate its 400th

anniversary in 2015. In 2012 the brewer held the first Grolsch Swing-top Challenge, where contestants from around the world gathered in Amsterdam to display the most creative ways of opening the 'de beugel' Grolsch bottles.

De Molen Hel & Verdoemenis

De Molen's Hel and Verdoemenis (literally translating to 'Hell and Damnation') is a Belgian-style imperial stout. Brewed to a strength similar to the stouts that were exported to Russia from London in the 18th and 19th centuries, this super flavoursome stout is one of the crown jewels of De Molen's highly rated selection. Like many artisanal breweries, the first brews were made in head brewer Menno Olivier's kitchen and then, after a year, in his garage. These humble beginnings soon gave way to a restaurant, a 500-litre brewing capacity and some of the best beers in all of Europe.

Tasting notes: Lots of sweet chocolate malt with spices, smoke and a hint of peat. Great with a berry dessert.
★ **Country:** The Netherlands ★ **Brewer:** Brouwerij de Molen ★ **Style:** Imperial stout
★ **Appearance:** Red/brown ★ **Alcohol** 10% ★ **Serving temp:** 8–13°C

DID YOU KNOW?

In 1983 brewery heir Alfred 'Freddy' Heineken was kidnapped for three weeks until a ransom of 35 million Dutch guilders was paid – a Hollywood film version of these events is being made starring Anthony Hopkins.

Grolsch Premium Lager

The Grolsch Brewery is the second largest in all of the Netherlands (after Heineken) with more than three million hectolitres brewed every year. The name Grolsch literally means 'of Grolle' – the name of the town where Grolsch was first brewed. Its premium lager is its flagship product and is often sold in the old-fashioned swing-top bottles.

Tasting notes: Toasted grains, brown bread with a sweet malt aftertaste. Crisp and clean on the palate.
★ **Country:** The Netherlands
★ **Brewer:** Grolsch Bierbrouwerij
★ **Style:** Premium lager
★ **Appearance:** Pale yellow
★ **Alcohol** 5%
★ **Serving temp:** 2–3°C

Heineken
ORIGINAL RECIPE
HEINEKEN LAGER BEER
TRADE MARK
Heineken
MEDAILLE D'OR PARIS 1875
GRAND PRIX PARIS 1889
HORS CONCOURS MEMBRE DU JURY PARIS 1900
PREMIUM

Heineken

A dominant worldwide brand, this is the bestselling beer in all of the Netherlands. When the papers announced the end of Prohibition in America, a shipload of Heineken was sent across the Atlantic to wait patiently off the East Coast until 5pm on 11 April 1933. After a 14-year wait, the Americans could finally taste Heineken again – just after they clocked off work for the day.

Tasting notes: Pale malt imparts a light white breadiness in the aroma. Low hop bitterness.
★ **Country:** The Netherlands ★ **Brewer:** Heineken Nederland
★ **Style:** Pale lager ★ **Appearance:** Golden
★ **Alcohol** 5% ★ **Serving temp:** 2–3°C

La Trappe Quadrupel

De Koningshoeven is one of only two Trappist breweries outside of Belgium. La Trappe Quadrupel is the strongest in its range at 10% ABV and gets its banana and almond-like aromas from its second fermentation, which happens after it is bottled. Consequently, the longer you keep this in the cellar the more it matures and the flavours develop. Serve this wonderful beer at cellar temperature with a dense sweet dessert like a plum pudding with crème anglaise.

Tasting notes: Ripe, boozy plums, with sweet spices, hints of cinnamon and big caramel malt backbone.
★ **Country:** The Netherlands ★ **Brewer:** De Koningshoeven
★ **Style:** Quadrupel ★ **Appearance:** Cloudy amber
★ **Alcohol** 10% ★ **Serving temp:** 8–10°C

DID YOU KNOW?

A beer called Kwispelbier, advertised as 'a beer for your best friend' and made with beef extract and malt, was created by pet-shop owner Gerrie Berendsen for her dogs to enjoy after hunting.

Alhambra Premium Lager

Situated in the south of Spain where the weather is hottest, the Alhambra brewery makes some of the most widely consumed beer in the region. This light, easy-to-drink lager is made with very little bitterness and only the lightest of malt character to ensure you focus purely on its refreshing qualities. Most often served as an aperitif in Spanish tapas bars.

Tasting notes: Light malt and light citrus with a thin, slightly watery texture and no aftertaste.
- ★ **Country:** Spain ★ **Brewer:** Cervezas Alhambra
- ★ **Style:** Pale lager ★ **Appearance:** Light yellow
- ★ **Alcohol** 4.6% ★ **Serving temp:** 2–3°C

Reina Oro

Not a beer often found in mainland Spain, Reina Oro is most often found in the Canary Islands where tourists and locals quaff it down for its refreshing and thirst-quenching qualities. A standard pale lager in every respect, it has a few characteristics of a German-style pilsner with slight bready overtones and little hop aroma.

Tasting notes: Light and slightly bready malt flavours with only a hint of bitterness at the end.
- ★ **Country:** Spain ★ **Brewer:** Cervezas Anaga ★ **Style:** Pale lager
- ★ **Appearance:** Pale yellow ★ **Alcohol** 5.5% ★ **Serving temp:** 2–3°C

Cruzcampo

Founded by Roberto and Agustín Osborne in 1904, the Cruzcampo brewery was named after La Cruz del Campo (The Cross of the Field), which still stands in a nearby field. It is the biggest beer producer in Spain and this 4.8% ABV lager is the flagship product of the brewery. Like many other brewers, it uses the legendary brewing king Gambrinus on its logo.

Tasting notes: Slightly metallic with hints of corn, peppery hops and a very slight fruity note.
- ★ **Country:** Spain
- ★ **Brewer:** Cruzcampo
- ★ **Style:** Pale lager
- ★ **Appearance:** Pale yellow
- ★ **Alcohol** 4.8%
- ★ **Serving temp:** 2–3°C

DouGall's 942 IPA

The craft beer revolution that swept America is still young in Spain. But nevertheless a growing proportion of the country's beer producers are taking influence from across the pond. DouGall's brewery is one such producer. This modern American-style IPA is hard to find in Spain unless you visit the brewery pub in Liérganes near Santander.

Tasting notes: Grapefruit aroma with a caramel note to match. Well balanced with a long and very bitter finish.
* **Country:** Spain
* **Brewer:** DouGall's
* **Style:** IPA
* **Appearance:** Deep gold
* **Alcohol** 7%
* **Serving temp:** 4–7°C

Estrella Damm

The oldest beer brand in Spain, if no longer the biggest, Estrella Damm is brewed in the city of Barcelona. The name Estrella means star in both Spanish and Catalan and the gold star has adorned the bottle ever since it was first produced in 1876. Not to be confused with Estrella Galicia from the north-western tip of Spain.

Tasting notes: Light and bubbly with easygoing flavours of malt, and very lightly bitter hops.
* **Country:** Spain
* **Brewer:** Estrella Damm
* **Style:** Pale lager
* **Appearance:** Pale yellow
* **Alcohol** 5.2%
* **Serving temp:** 1–2°C

Mahou Clásica

The Mahou logo is seen on a range of beer styles, from the lightest of pale lagers to the dark Mahou Negra. Mahou Clásica was the first beer produced when the brewery was founded in 1890; it remains very popular in Spain. The taste is typical of pale lagers and meant for refreshment and easy drinking.

Tasting notes: Slightly sour with subtle hints of cereal and a very bubbly, highly carbonated texture.
* **Country:** Spain
* **Brewer:** Mahou-San Miguel
* **Style:** Pale lager
* **Appearance:** Pale yellow
* **Alcohol** 4.8%
* **Serving temp:** 1–2°C

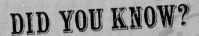 Nómada Royal Porter A La Taza

The most highly rated beer in all of Spain and without doubt the most flavoursome in the country, Nómada Royal Porter A La Taza is a must-try beer. A classic example of the Russian imperial porters and stouts that were exported to Russia from the UK in the 18th and 19th centuries, its thick, pitch-black texture is almost oily in the glass. Aromas of liquorice, dark chocolate and oak are followed by a boozy flavour of dried fruit, more chocolate and hints of fresh espresso on the palate. Pairs with an indulgent chocolate dessert and vanilla ice cream.

Tasting notes: Liquorice, chocolate, coffee, prunes, brandy, vanilla and more. A balanced and complex beer.
★ **Country:** Spain ★ **Brewer:** Nómada Brewing
★ **Style:** Imperial porter ★ **Appearance:** Black
★ **Alcohol** 10.5% ★ **Serving temp:** 11–15°C

DID YOU KNOW?

A survey found that however hard-pressed recession-hit Spaniards are, they won't give up their daily beer, claiming it is 'necessary' in getting them out of the house and helping them through the difficult economic times.

 San Miguel Especial

The bestselling beer brand in all of Spain, it's impossible to go into a European supermarket without running into 'Miguel'. The company produced its first bottle of San Miguel Especial in 1957. A very light and slightly malty pale lager that's as ubiquitous as it is refreshing.

Tasting notes: Sweet malt, light corn with almost zero hop profile. Drink ice cold.
★ **Country:** Spain
★ **Brewer:** Mahou-San Miguel
★ **Style:** Pale lager
★ **Appearance:** Gold
★ **Alcohol** 4.8%
★ **Serving temp:** 1–2°C

Coral

On the island of Madeira off the west coast of Portugal, there lies a town named Camara de Lobos or 'The Chamber of the Wolves'. This refers to the sea lions (*lobos marinhos* in Portuguese) that were common when the island was discovered in 1419. Coral is by far the most popular drink on the island after the famous sweet Madeira wine.

Tasting notes: Light, bubbly and easy to drink. There is some pale malt flavour and very little hop bitterness.
★ **Country:** Portugal ★ **Brewer:** Heineken
★ **Style:** Pale lager ★ **Appearance:** Clear yellow
★ **Alcohol** 5.3% ★ **Serving temp:** 1–2°C

Sagres Cerveja

In the most south-western point of mainland Europe there is a small village named Sagres, which is famous for teaching sailors about navigational science, after which the Sagres beer brand was named. It's a common aperitif all over Portugal and mainland Spain. Serve ice cold with some Spanish tapas.

Tasting notes: Light flavour profile of sweetcorn, mild grain and almost zero bitterness. Serve ice cold.
★ **Country:** Portugal ★ **Brewer:** Central de Cervejas
★ **Style:** Pale lager ★ **Appearance:** Clear yellow
★ **Alcohol** 5% ★ **Serving temp:** 1–2°C

Super Bock Stout

From the most popular brewery in Portugal – mainly because of its strong pale lager – the Super Bock brand goes from strength to strength. In this black beer – which is actually a dark lager, not a stout – Unicer has created something at the 5% ABV mark while simultaneously retaining a rich, thick body and a complex malt character. Served a little colder than most stouts.

Tasting notes: Caramel, berries with a slight earthy smokiness and a peat aroma. A very dry finish.
★ **Country:** Portugal ★ **Brewer:** Unicer Bebidas ★ **Style:** Black beer
★ **Appearance:** Dark red-brown ★ **Alcohol** 5% ★ **Serving temp:** 6–8°C

🇩🇰 Evil Twin Even More Jesus

Imperial stouts are a favourite among craft beer enthusiasts. Famous for their huge flavour profiles, their thick, viscous texture and high alcohol content, beers like Evil Twin's Even More Jesus can be intimidating. Beers like this should be treated more like fine wine. Sip slowly and make them last.

Tasting notes: Toffee, chocolate fudge and a hefty whack of coffee compete with alcohol and muscovado sugar.
★ **Country:** Denmark ★ **Brewer:** Westbrook Brewing
★ **Style:** Imperial stout ★ **Appearance:** Black
★ **Alcohol** 12% ★ **Serving temp:** 8–13°C

DID YOU KNOW?

After Niels Bohr won the Nobel Prize in Physics in 1922, Carlsberg gave him a house next to the brewery with a beer pipeline so he could have a free beer at any time.

🇩🇰 Fuglsang Hvid Bock

Bock is a style of beer that has long been associated with times of celebration – particularly religious festivals. During long periods of fasting, Bavarian monks would use this strong, flavoursome lager as a form of nourishment to stave off a rumbling belly. Though bocks are usually very dark, this one is brewed with light malt from Fuglsang's own maltings.

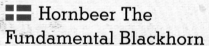

Tasting notes: Doughy flavours with aromas of proving bread and toasted grains. Great with Mexican cuisine.
★ **Country:** Denmark ★ **Brewer:** Bryggeriet S.C. Fuglsang
★ **Style:** Bock ★ **Appearance:** Hazy honey
★ **Alcohol** 7.6% ★ **Serving temp:** 4–7°C

🇩🇰 Hornbeer The Fundamental Blackhorn

Hornbeer brews every beer with artistry. This supercharged imperial stout has been given a heavier dose of hops than is usual for the style. It is then aged in walnut and oak casks. A powerful flavour profile of liquorice and dark chocolate, with hints of oak and honey, awaits you in every bottle.

Tasting notes: Try this one with rich chocolate desserts, vanilla ice cream or aged blue cheese.
★ **Country:** Denmark
★ **Brewer:** Westbrook Brewing
★ **Style:** Imperial stout
★ **Appearance:** Black
★ **Alcohol:** 11%
★ **Serving temp:** 8–13°C

🇩🇰 Mikkeller Beer Geek Breakfast

Mikkeller has two loves: beer and coffee. As well as its Koppi (coffee IPA) and its Beer Geek Brunch Weasel, the beer it is most famous for is the Beer Geek Breakfast. Brewed with oats for that silky smooth texture and a good helping of the brewer's favourite coffee, this one is guaranteed to wake you up with a bang. It uses a complex blend of malts – pilsner, oat, smoked, caramunich, brown, and two types of chocolate malt – and roasted barley and flaked oats also make an appearance in this masterpiece.

Tasting notes: Espresso aromas, lightly smoky with a pleasant and interesting pine resin hop flavour on the palate. Drink with (or for) breakfast.
- ✯ **Country:** Denmark ✯ **Brewer:** Mikkeller
- ✯ **Style:** Stout ✯ **Appearance:** Deep brown
- ✯ **Alcohol** 7.5% ✯ **Serving temp:** 8–13°C

🇩🇰 Ørbæk Fynsk Forår

On first taste, you could be forgiven for thinking that Ørbæk Fynsk Forår was a strange type of shandy. Brewed with elderflowers, a fragrant sweetness is revealed. Freshly pressed apple notes appear with hints of cider – you'll have to double check the label to make sure it's definitely a beer you just opened.

Tasting notes: Concentrated elderflower flavours in both the aroma and taste, with hints of fermented apple.
- ✯ **Country:** Denmark
- ✯ **Brewer:** Ørbæk Bryggeri
- ✯ **Style:** Blonde ale
- ✯ **Appearance:** Cloudy yellow
- ✯ **Alcohol** 5%
- ✯ **Serving temp:** 4–7°C

🇩🇰 Skovlyst BøgeBryg Brown Ale

If you ever get bored with the conventional beers of the world, remember to try BøgeBryg Brown Ale. Translating as 'Beech Brew', this American-style brown ale is unusual because of the addition of beech wood twigs from the nearby forest, which impart a woodsmoke aroma.

Tasting notes: Floral hops, smoky campfire and roasted toffee. Drink with a nutty aged Gouda cheese or smoky grilled lamb.
- ✯ **Country:** Denmark
- ✯ **Brewer:** Bryggeri Skovlyst
- ✯ **Style:** Brown ale
- ✯ **Appearance:** Deep brown
- ✯ **Alcohol** 5.2%
- ✯ **Serving temp:** 8–13°C

🇸🇪 CAP Endless Vacation Pale Ale

The flagship product of the CAP brewery, Endless Vacation is an American-style pale ale. Using four different hop varieties – Warrior, Centennial, Cascade and Chinook – mainly from the Yakima Valley region of Washington state, strong bold hop flavours of elderflower, grapefruit and passionfruit are rounded off nicely by a heady dose of caramel.

Tasting notes: Classically paired with seafood, the citrus fruitiness will act as that all-important squeeze of lemon you'd normally add.
★ **Country:** Sweden ★ **Brewer:** CAP ★ **Style:** Pale ale
★ **Appearance:** Clear orange ★ **Alcohol** 5.3% ★ **Serving temp:** 4–7°C

🇸🇪 Carnegie Stark Porter

Carnegie Porter was first brewed in 1836 and is officially the oldest registered trademark still in use today. There are two versions: one at 3.5% ABV and this Stark ('strong') version. It has true national status in the same way Guinness does in Ireland. Currently owned and brewed by Carlsberg Sverige, there are plans alongside Brooklyn Brewery in the USA to open a microbrewery in the Hammarby area in Sweden to make this beer.

Tasting notes: Chocolate, bitter coffee and toffee. The flavour mellows as it ages so try to cellar a bottle if possible.
★ **Country:** Sweden
★ **Brewer:** Carlsberg Sverige
★ **Style:** Porter ★ **Appearance:** Dark brown
★ **Alcohol** 5.5% ★ **Serving temp:** 8–13°C

🇸🇪 Jämtlands Hell

If you want to brew a truly great beer, ask the people who drink the most for some help. This premium lager was made in collaboration with two pubs – The Akkurat and the Oliver Twist – in the heart of Stockholm. Undoubtedly the crown jewel of the Jämtlands Brewery collection, it packs more flavour than all the other lagers in Sweden put together. Highly hopped for maximum bitterness without going overboard. Serve with flash-fried chilli-flecked squid or mild cheddar to get the full, crisp cleansing effect.

Tasting notes: Aromatic hops, dried fruit and bitter orange in the nose. Bitter hops, honey and citrus on the tongue. Perfect lager.
★ **Country:** Sweden ★ **Brewer:** Jämtlands Bryggeri ★ **Style:** Lager
★ **Appearance:** Medium orange ★ **Alcohol** 5.1% ★ **Serving temp:** 8–10°C

Nils Oscar God Lager

The Nils Oscar brewery is named after a young Swede who in the 19th century travelled to America four or five times to learn farming and agricultural skills. His Swedish farming empire is managed by his descendants today and they grow the oats, wheat and barley that go into this beautiful golden lager. A genuinely traditional Swedish product from grain to bottle.

Tasting notes: Pure, unadulterated liquid bread in a bottle. Goes nicely with any food you throw at it.
★ **Country:** Sweden
★ **Brewer:** Nils Oscar
★ **Style:** Helles
★ **Appearance:** Golden
★ **Alcohol** 5.3%
★ **Serving temp:** 4–7°C

Norrlands Guld Export

One of the most popular beers in Sweden and one instantly recognizable to any Swedish native, Norrlands Guld is advertised as the beer for the most laid-back people. The principal on-screen advocate since the early 1990s is the relaxed Ingemar, who comes from the peaceful Norrland province. A classic pale lager.

Tasting notes: Light malt, toasted grains and an easygoing crisp finish. A drink free from all pretension.
★ **Country:** Sweden
★ **Brewer:** Spendrups Bryggeri
★ **Style:** Pale lager
★ **Appearance:** Golden
★ **Alcohol** 5.3%
★ **Serving temp:** 4–7°C

Spendrups Julöl

Brewed as a special Christmas beer, the Spendrups brewery makes two versions of this seasonal beer – one at 2.1% ABV for those long Christmas lunches where you might fancy more beers than normal, and a stronger one at 5.3%. Nice balanced toffee flavours with hints of spice – traditional yuletide flavours dominate this one.

Tasting notes: Perfect at the Christmas dinner table. Spicy cloves, hints of coffee and a nutty, bread-like aftertaste.
★ **Country:** Sweden
★ **Brewer:** Spendrups Bryggeri
★ **Style:** Amber lager
★ **Appearance:** Golden
★ **Alcohol** 5.3%
★ **Serving temp:** 4–7°C

🇳🇴 Aass Bock

As one of the only breweries left in the region of Drammen, Norway, the Aass brewery takes its responsibility very seriously. In its humble beginnings in 1834, it sold beer with no packaging to people who brought along their own bins or buckets to fill up – much like today's growlers. Aass Bock is a dark strong lager and one of the closest things to a pint of liquid brown bread you can drink. Strong, doughy and versatile – it pairs well with a wide range of foods.

Tasting notes: Doughy brown bread and yeast aromas. Very comforting and warming to drink.
★ **Country:** Norway ★ **Brewer:** Aass Bryggeri
★ **Style:** Bock ★ **Appearance:** Deep red
★ **Alcohol** 6.5% ★ **Serving temp:** 4–7°C

🇳🇴 Berentsens Rogalands Pils

The Berentsens brewery is famous for producing all kinds of drinks, including apple juice and mineral water, alongside a wide range of beers. By far its most popular brew is this pilsner lager. Nice as a light aperitif, served very cold with a bowl of salty mixed nuts.

Tasting notes: Pale yellow in colour with very light, dusty malt notes and a carbonated finish.
★ **Country:** Norway
★ **Brewer:** Berentsens Brygghus
★ **Style:** Pilsner
★ **Appearance:** Light yellow
★ **Alcohol** 4.7%
★ **Serving temp:** 1–2°C

🇳🇴 Hansa Borg Bayer

Dunkel ('dark') is the term used to describe many types of dark German-style beers. They are typically brewed using dark Munich malts, a proportion of which may have been boiled to a higher temperature to extract more starch and impart a deeper malty flavour. This is a classic example of the style from the Hansa Borg brewery.

Tasting notes: Deep, sweet salty caramel and roasted malt. Liquorice flavours dominate the finish.
★ **Country:** Norway
★ **Brewer:** Hansa Borg Bryggerier
★ **Style:** Dunkel lager
★ **Appearance:** Dark amber
★ **Alcohol** 4.5%
★ **Serving temp:** 4–7°C

🇳🇴 Kinn Julefred

Christmas beers are especially common in Scandinavia and here we have a fine example. Julefred ('Christmas peace') is brewed every year and always to a slightly different recipe, ranging from 4.5 to 6.7% ABV. Often very spice-led, Kinn's Julefred is subtle in its use of spice, with dark fruit and caramel taking the lead. A consistently well-made Christmas seasonal.

Tasting notes: Raisins, plums and dried figs with hints of coffee, candy sugar and butterscotch.
- ✯ **Country:** Norway
- ✯ **Brewer:** Kinn Bryggeri
- ✯ **Style:** Christmas seasonal ale
- ✯ **Appearance:** Hazy brown
- ✯ **Alcohol** 6.5%
- ✯ **Serving temp:** 8–10°C

🇳🇴 Nøgne Ø India Pale Ale

One of the best-respected breweries in Norway, Nøgne Ø's mastery of brewing extends to brown ales, imperial stouts and beyond. This is their perfectly balanced IPA. A combination of American Cascade and Chinook hops lead to the pungent and resinous nose before the caramel malts take over on the palate.

Tasting notes: Strong pine resins, sweet grapefruit and hints of lime dominate this perfectly executed IPA. Try it with spicy jerk chicken..
- ✯ **Country:** Norway
- ✯ **Brewer:** Nøgne Ø
- ✯ **Style:** IPA
- ✯ **Appearance:** Orange
- ✯ **Alcohol** 7.5%
- ✯ **Serving temp:** 8–10°C

🇳🇴 Ringnes Extra Gold

The largest brewing group in Norway, Ringnes is based in the country's capital, Oslo. Now owned by Carlsberg, its extremely popular Extra Gold is a strong , full-flavoured lager. Extra malt is added to the brew for sweetness and levelled off with a touch of hoppy pine resin in the finish. A very flavoursome beer with bags of punch.

Tasting notes: Light fruitiness with sweet malt flavours and a hefty, boozy hit at the end.
- ✯ **Country:** Norway
- ✯ **Brewer:** Ringnes Bryggeri
- ✯ **Style:** Strong pale lager
- ✯ **Appearance:** Clear amber
- ✯ **Alcohol** 6.5%
- ✯ **Serving temp:** 4–7°C

DID YOU KNOW?

The Norse word 'berserk' means 'bear shirt' and comes from the Viking habit of stopping mid-battle for a beer break, drinking huge quantities, and then returning to fight like a bear without armour or a shirt!

🇮🇸 Einstök Icelandic Toasted Porter

The Einstök brewery makes much of its location – just 60 miles south of the Arctic Circle. The water is claimed to be perfect for brewing beer, having filtered down through ancient lava flows and mountain glaciers. This toasted porter is made with well-toasted and chocolate malts to give its deep, dark and silky black colour.

Tasting notes: Strong notes of espresso and dark chocolate. Perfect with well-charred meat.
★ **Country:** Iceland ★ **Brewer:** Einstök Ölger
★ **Style:** Porter ★ **Appearance:** Dark brown
★ **Alcohol** 6% ★ **Serving temp:** 8–13°C

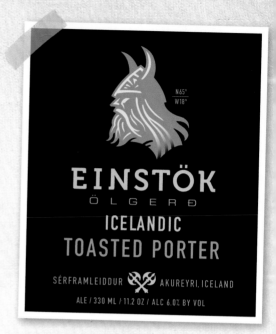

🇮🇸 Ölvisholt Lava

From the Ölvisholt brewhouse door, the active volcano Hekla is clearly visible, especially when its eruptions flow freely down the mountainside. The aptly named Lava is made with malt that has been smoked, imparting a unique burnt flavour and aroma to the beer alongside the usual flavours of a proper imperial stout. Great with smoky barbecued pork.

Tasting notes: Lots of smoke, chocolate and caramel make a great match for any chargrilled meats.
★ **Country:** Iceland
★ **Brewer:** Ölvisholt Brugghús
★ **Style:** Smoked imperial stout
★ **Appearance:** Black
★ **Alcohol** 9.4%
★ **Serving temp:** 8–13°C

DID YOU KNOW?

The Finnish national folk-epic Kalevala, based on centuries-old folklore and mythology, has 400 lines dealing with beer, but only 200 dealing with the origin of mankind.

✚ Hartwall Lapin Kulta

The brand name Lapin Kulta is used for a variety of different strength lagers, including a 2.7%, a 4.5% and a 5.2%. The bestseller is the 4.5% premium lager, which is one of the most popular bottled beers in Finland. Its extremely light flavour profile is easy to drink and can go with a wide variety of food.

Tasting notes: Very light maltiness with very little bitterness and a soft finish.
★ **Country:** Finland
★ **Brewer:** Hartwall
★ **Style:** Pale lager
★ **Appearance:** Pale yellow
★ **Alcohol** 4.5%
★ **Serving temp:** 1–2°C

✚ Laitilan Kievari Imperiaali

Brewed for the 15th anniversary of the brewery in Laitila, Finland, Laitilan Kievari Imperiaali is an imperial-style stout. In a celebration of the age of the brewery, it has a 15-month maturation process, which allows its strong alcohol flavours to mellow and broaden. Keep a bottle in the cellar to take this process further.

Tasting notes: Malty brown bread, roasted coffee and strong liquorice. Pairs excellently with coffee ice cream.
★ **Country:** Finland
★ **Brewer:** Laitilan Wirvoitusjuomatehdas
★ **Style:** Imperial stout
★ **Appearance:** Dark brown
★ **Alcohol** 9.2%
★ **Serving temp:** 8–13°C

✚ Sinebrychoff Koff Porter

Founded in 1819 in Helsinki by a Russian-born trader, the Sinebrychoff brewery is now one of the largest in Finland. Its most famous product is predictably its pale lager but this Baltic-style porter is by far its best product. Made with a slightly higher amount of hops than most Baltic porters for an added flavour dimension.

Tasting notes: Mild smoke, light alcohol, roasted malt and smooth bitter chocolate and coffee.
★ **Country:** Finland
★ **Brewer:** Sinebrychoff
★ **Style:** Baltic porter
★ **Appearance:** Clear black
★ **Alcohol** 7.2%
★ **Serving temp:** 8–13°C

THE WORLD'S TOP-SELLING BEERS

Although Europe sees itself as the home of beer, the list of the biggest beer brands is dominated by drinks from other countries.

China is the country with the largest number of brands. This should come as no surprise as China is the world's biggest market for beer. Although its people are relatively modest drinkers compared to more bibulous nations like Germany and the Czech Republic, its population is huge, at 1.35 billion. China produced more than 44 billion litres of beer in 2012. This was twice as much as the US, which is the second biggest brewing nation.

10
BRAHMA
18.1m barrels

Along with Skol, Brahma dominates the fast-growing Brazilian beer market. It is brewed by Companhia Cervejaria Brahma, which was founded in 1888. The company is now part of AB InBev and Brahma has been marketed globally since 2004.

9
COORS LIGHT
25.1m barrels

First brewed in 1978 as a lower-calorie beer for health-conscious baby boomers, Coors Light has grown globally under owner Molson Coors. It has targeted further growth in Asia, and in particular in China and Japan.

8
HEINEKEN
29.1m barrels

Although its parent company, Heineken International, has more than 170 brands worldwide, the pilsner lager that gives it its name remains the biggest seller. First brewed in the Netherlands in 1874, Heineken is still brewed at the massive Zoeterwoude brewery. A recent convert is James Bond, after a partnership between the beer and movie franchise.

7 SKOL
29.9m barrels

UK drinkers may remember Skol as a brand that was big in the 1970s but whose appeal has since faded. However, Skol has found favour in other markets, particularly in Africa and Brazil, where it is the biggest brand with around 30 per cent market share.

6 CORONA EXTRA
31.6m barrels

The original lime-decked Mexican beer is the leading beer brand in the country and is sold in more than 170 countries around the world. A pilsner lager, it was first produced in 1925. The brand is now wholly owned by AB InBev.

5 BUD LIGHT
36.7m barrels

Launched in 1982 as a lower-alcohol, lower-calorie beer, Bud Light is now the most popular beer in the US. The brand has continued to evolve from its original appearance as Budweiser Light and has recently spawned offshoot Bud Light Platinum, a 6% ABV beer that has signed up Justin Timberlake as its 'creative director'.

PROBABLY THE BEST BEERS IN THE WORLD?

Of course sales aren't everything. The World Beer Awards uses blind tastings around the world to choose the best beers in particular styles. These are the 2013 winners:

- ✸ **Best beer – Primator Weizenbier, Czech Republic**
- ✸ **Best dark beer – Malheur 12, Belgium**
- ✸ **Best flavoured beer – Tazawako Beer Rauch, Japan**
- ✸ **Best lager – Sharp's Cornish Pilsner, England**
- ✸ **Best pale beer – Maison de Brasseur Thou, France**
- ✸ **Best sour beer – Lindemans Old Kriek Cuvée René, Belgium**
- ✸ **Best speciality beer – Le Trou du Diable La Bretteuse Brassin Special, Canada**
- ✸ **Best stout and porter – Minoh Beer Imperial Stout, Japan**
- ✸ **Best wheat beer – Primator Weizenbier, Czech Republic**

(Source: The World Beer Awards)

4

YANJING
39.6m barrels

Also known as Beijing Beer, this pale lager has an almost 85 per cent market share in the city and was the official beer of the 2008 Beijing Olympics. Its brewery is one of the largest in Asia, with 20,000 employees. With a solid foothold in China it is increasingly focused on international sales.

3

BUDWEISER
40.4m barrels

Budweiser may be the quintessential American beer, but these days it is sold in more than 85 countries and its parent company AB InBev is Belgian. The brand has made particular inroads into the burgeoning markets of Brazil and China and has been ranked as the world's most valuable beer brand. It is a sponsor of the 2014 FIFA World Cup in Brazil.

TSINGTAO
57.9m barrels

2

Tsingtao was first brewed in 1903 in a brewery established by German and British settlers and it has around 15 per cent of the Chinese market. It has been successfully exported since 1954 and is the top-selling Chinese beer in the US. After being state-owned for a number of years the company was privatized in 1990.

(Source: The Drinks Business

SNOW BEER

1

74.8m barrels

This 3.9% ABV beer is China's fastest-growing and most valuable beer brand. Snow Beer is brewed through a joint venture between SABMiller and China Resources Enterprises. It was first produced in 1993, using hops imported from the Czech Republic. Further growth is likely as the brewery has added capacity for a further 20 million litres of beer every year.

Jablonowo Piwo na Miodzie Gryczanym

The Browar Jablonowo brewery in Poland is famous for its connoisseurs range and the Miodzie Gryczanym is one of them. Brewed with a late and potent addition of honey, this dark amber beer is extremely sweet and warming. Not for those looking for bitterness, but excellent to drink in wintery weather.

Tasting notes: Honey in both aroma and taste, but also with lighter hints of buckwheat and biscuit.
* **Country:** Poland
* **Brewer:** Browar Jablonowo
* **Style:** Honey beer
* **Appearance:** Dark amber
* **Alcohol** 5.2%
* **Serving temp:** 8–13°C

Lech Premium Lager

Not many breweries can boast a world record to their name but Lech certainly can. It is famed for a 2007 stunt at the newly opened part of their brewhouse in Poznań, when the world's biggest beer mug was created. It held 4,250 litres of beer and allowed 10,625 people to take a sip from it – the largest number drinking from one mug ever on record.

Tasting notes: Light malt, sweetcorn, crackerbread and a skunky low hop bitterness at the end.
* **Country:** Poland
* **Brewer:** Lech Browary Wielkopolski
* **Style:** Pale lager
* **Appearance:** Yellow
* **Alcohol** 5.2%
* **Serving temp:** 1–2°C

DID YOU KNOW?

Poles often enjoy their beer flavoured with raspberry or blackcurrant juice (*piwo z sokiem*) and drunk through a straw, while in winter they drink hot beer with cloves and cinnamon, sweetened with honey (*piwo grzane*).

Okocim Mocne

The word *Mocne* in Polish means 'strong', so the beer does exactly what it says on the tin. Higher than usual amounts of malt are added to the mash to create more sugar and eventually more alcohol in this imperial pilsner. Okocim Mocne is one of the most popular strong beers in Poland and has a loyal following.

Tasting notes: Fruity with notes of apple, toasted grain and light caramel flavours.
* **Country:** Poland
* **Brewer:** Carlsberg Polska
* **Style:** Imperial lager
* **Appearance:** Amber
* **Alcohol** 7%
* **Serving temp:** 1–2°C

Perła Chmielowa

Many of the beers brewed in central Europe take their lead from the Czech pilsner style of lager. Perła Chmielowa is an example from Lubin, Poland. With a marked aroma of noble hops and a slightly increased sweetness to match, this extra flavour helps differentiate it from standard pale lager. However, the goal here is still refreshment and the flavour is not enough to overwhelm on the palate. Good served in hot weather at a barbecue.

Tasting notes: Bready malts, earthy hops. A classic combination.
✱ **Country:** Poland ✱ **Brewer:** Browary Lubelskie ✱ **Style:** Pilsner
✱ **Appearance:** Light gold ✱ **Alcohol** 6% ✱ **Serving temp:** 3–5°C

Tyskie Gronie

Commanding nearly 20 per cent of the Polish beer market, Tyskie is one of the country's leading brands. Since the EU opened its doors to Poland, Tyskie has become more available in other countries, especially in the UK where many Polish people chose to settle in the mid 2000s. An easygoing yet flavoursome pale lager to knock back as a thirst quencher.

Tasting notes: Light citrus aromas from the hops and a sweet bready malt to match.
✱ **Country:** Poland ✱ **Brewer:** Tyskie Brewery
✱ **Style:** Pale lager ✱ **Appearance:** Yellow
✱ **Alcohol** 5.5% ✱ **Serving temp:** 3–5°C

Żywiec Porter

A mouthful in more ways than one, Żywiec (pronounced je-vi-ets) Porter is a strong, dark, Baltic-style porter designed to keep the spirits high and the heart warm in chilly weather – a common state of affairs in Poland. A nicely rounded beer with a delicate balance of sweet malt and light bitterness. Look out for its red-black colour and thick beige head.

Tasting notes: Chocolate, caramel and coffee with a warming, almost spicy sensation in the finish.
✱ **Country:** Poland ✱ **Brewer:** Bracki Browar Zamkowy
✱ **Style:** Baltic porter ✱ **Appearance:** Deep red-black
✱ **Alcohol** 9.5% ✱ **Serving temp:** 10–14°C

DID YOU KNOW?

'*Boza*' millet beer, from which the word 'booze' may originate, has been brewed for thousands of years, and is still in great demand in the Balkans and Turkey, partly due to a rumour that it enhances women's breasts!

Birra Tirana

This pale lager is named after the capital city of Albania, where the beers are brewed at the Birra Malto brewery. Albanians took a while to catch on to beer, their traditional drinks being wine and brandy. Today, the brewery produces 150,000 hectolitres per year.

Tasting notes: Light corn-like malts and very little bitterness. Extremely easy to drink as an aperitif.
* **Country:** Albania
* **Brewer:** Birra Malto
* **Style:** Pale lager
* **Appearance:** Light yellow
* **Alcohol** 4%
* **Serving temp:** 1–2°C

Shumensko Premium

Shumensko Premium is the slightly more upmarket version of Shumensko Light – it uses more malt in the mash to create extra sugar and a slightly higher alcohol content. It's only a few cents more than the lighter version and the extra cents go a long way. Pairs with a wide variety of foods, from steaks to salads, owing to its malty, bread-like nature.

Tasting notes: Malty grains, toasted wholemeal bread and a very subtle grassy hop aroma.
* **Country:** Bulgaria
* **Brewer:** Shumensko Pivo
* **Style:** Pale lager
* **Appearance:** Yellow orange
* **Alcohol** 4.6%
* **Serving temp:** 1–2°C

Stolichno Bock

Brewed in the capital of Bulgaria, the literal translation of *Stolichno* is 'of the capital city'. This German-style bock was first brewed in 2004. Bock is a very old style, originating in Germany in the 14th century; it is a strong and slightly sweet lager with very little hop bitterness.

Tasting notes: Malty, toasty with hints of alcohol and a nice caramel hit in the taste, with little hop presence.
* **Country:** Bulgaria
* **Brewer:** Zagorka
* **Style:** Bock
* **Appearance:** Dark brown
* **Alcohol** 6.5%
* **Serving temp:** 4–7°C

◼◼ Ursus Premium

Romania's very own 'King of Beer', Ursus Premium is a 5% pale lager and one of the bestselling beers in Romania. *Ursus* is Latin for bear; there are various versions of the beer, including black and pilsner – all feature a bear on the label.

Tasting notes: Grainy, corn-like aromas and taste. Soft carbonation and a dry bitter finish.
* ✴ **Country:** Romania
* ✴ **Brewer:** Ursus Breweries
* ✴ **Style:** Pale lager
* ✴ **Appearance:** Pale yellow
* ✴ **Alcohol** 5%
* ✴ **Serving temp:** 1–2°C

▬▬ Dreher Bak

The Dreher brewery is one of the most popular in Hungary and produces more premium-rated products than any other. It was founded by the Austrian brewer Anton Dreher, who developed technology to ferment at low temperatures, which helped him create a new type of lager called Vienna lager. This Dreher beer, however, is a *dunkel* bock or dark, strong lager.

Tasting notes: Heavy malt, roasted coffee and bitter chocolate. Pair with a smoky sausage.
* ✴ **Country:** Hungary
* ✴ **Brewer:** Dreher Brewery
* ✴ **Style:** Dunkel bock
* ✴ **Appearance:** Dark red
* ✴ **Alcohol** 7.3%
* ✴ **Serving temp:** 8–10°C

▬▬ Szalon Világos Sör

Founded by Leopold Hirschfeld in 1848, the Pécs Brewery in southern Hungary was taken on by his son Samuel. Samuel Hirschfeld drilled a spring in order to provide a good-quality water source, which is still in use to this day. The Szalon Sör brand was registered as a trademark in 1907 and the name lives on in this pale lager that is popular throughout the entire country.

Tasting notes: Notes of lemon hops and straw, with a lightly metallic feel. A dry, bitter and appley finish.
* ✴ **Country:** Hungary ✴ **Brewer:** Pécsi Sörfözde ✴ **Style:** Pale lager
* ✴ **Appearance:** Light yellow ✴ **Alcohol** 4.6% ✴ **Serving temp:** 1–2°C

🇭🇷 Ožujsko

Croatia's most popular beer brand dates back to 1893 and takes its lead from the Czech pilsners pioneered by Josef Groll half a century earlier. A decent aroma of hops can be detected, with a refreshing dose of pale malt and a long bitter finish. Pairs well with a wide variety of foods.

Tasting notes: Hay, straw and hints of toasted grain back up the earthy hop aroma.
* ★ **Country:** Croatia
* ★ **Brewer:** Zagrebačka Pivovara
* ★ **Style:** Pilsner
* ★ **Appearance:** Clear gold
* ★ **Alcohol** 5%
* ★ **Serving temp:** 3–5°C

🇭🇷 Tomislav Tamno

A warming and comforting Baltic-style porter, this beer is brewed with a high amount of sugar extracted from the double malted barley. This extra sugar content eventually ferments into the strongest beer in Croatia at 7.3% ABV. The alcohol is masked well by treacle, chocolate and rich hints of coffee and dates.

Tasting notes: Dried fruit, toast and caramel with chocolate and syrupy sugar notes.
* ★ **Country:** Croatia
* ★ **Brewer:** Zagrebačka Pivovara
* ★ **Style:** Baltic porter
* ★ **Appearance:** Dark brown
* ★ **Alcohol** 7.3%
* ★ **Serving temp:** 8–10°C

🇲🇪 Nikšićko Tamno

The one and only brewery in Montenegro, the Trebjesa brewery is based in Nikšić and was founded in 1908. Being the only brewery in the country means that its beers are pretty much the only ones consumed in Montenegro. This is its black lager, made with dark malts for a more pronounced, slightly burnt malt taste.

Tasting notes: Dark dried fruits, chocolate and medium sweetness with a dark chocolate finish.
* ★ **Country:** Montenegro
* ★ **Brewer:** Pivara Trebjesa
* ★ **Style:** Schwarzbier
* ★ **Appearance:** Very dark nut brown
* ★ **Alcohol** 6.2%
* ★ **Serving temp:** 4–7°C

🇷🇸 Jelen

On the gates of the Apatinska brewery hangs an old doorbell from the early days of its history. Sounding twice a day, the bell signified the start and end of the brewery working day and that it still rings to this day shows a work ethic and dedication to tradition that the Apatin brewery is proud of. Jelen is the bestselling beer in Serbia.

Tasting notes: Sweet corn flavours, slightly papery with a metallic edge in the finish.

* **Country:** Serbia
* **Brewer:** Apatinska Pivara
* **Style:** Pilsner
* **Appearance:** Clear yellow
* **Alcohol** 5%
* **Serving temp:** 2–3°C

🇷🇸 Lav

The Lav brand is one of the most recognizable names in Serbia thanks to its sponsorship of the Serbian national football team. The second-bestselling beer in the country, it has a loyal following and in 2006 was named the second-best brand in Serbia behind Gorki brandy. A classic premium lager.

Tasting notes: Mild corn flavours with a slightly grassy hop aroma and a sweet, almost syrupy finish.

* **Country:** Serbia
* **Brewer:** Carlsberg Serbia
* **Style:** Pale lager
* **Appearance:** Dark yellow
* **Alcohol** 5%
* **Serving temp:** 2–3°C

DID YOU KNOW?

The Independent newspaper named the six-day Belgrade Beer Fest, held in Ušće park on the river Danube and featuring live music and hundreds of beers, as one of the worldwide events to visit in 2006.

🇷🇸 Zaječarsko Svetlo

Serbian beer is not known for its wide variety. The dominant style of beer is pale lager, with a few darker lagers being produced in small quantities. This is a pilsner-style beer with its roots more in the mellow pilsners of Germany than in those of the Czech Republic. Serve ice cold as an aperitif.

Tasting notes: Bready and full bodied yet light in the finish and very drinkable.

* **Country:** Serbia
* **Brewer:** Efes Zaječar Pivara
* **Style:** Pilsner
* **Appearance:** Pale golden
* **Alcohol** 4.7%
* **Serving temp:** 2–3°C

▬ Gubernijos Ekstra

Not just the oldest brewery in Lithuania, Gubernija is one of the oldest businesses in the world, having been founded in 1665. Ekstra is the flagship product, a pale lager sold in most pubs in Lithuania. A very easygoing drink and nicely balanced with just the right amount of light hoppy bitterness to contest with the light malt.

Tasting notes: An easy-drinking balance of sweet malt and earth, floral hops. Drink ice-cold.
* ✻ **Country:** Lithuania
* ✻ **Brewer:** Gubernija
* ✻ **Style:** Pale lager
* ✻ **Appearance:** Clear yellow
* ✻ **Alcohol** 5.5%
* ✻ **Serving temp:** 1–2°C

▬ Švyturys Baltas

Taking strong influence from many of the flavoursome yeasty wheat beers of Germany, Švyturys has brewed a classic *Hefeweizen*. As the beer is unfiltered, the yeast left in the bottle imparts a lot of aroma, including banana, cloves, orange peel and other exotic fruits. It is served in its own tall German-style *Hefeweizen* glass and should be served with a slice of lemon.

Tasting notes: Try pairing this one with spicy seafood, Chinese dim sum or soft creamy cheese.
* ✻ **Country:** Lithuania
* ✻ **Brewer:** Švyturys
* ✻ **Style:** Hefeweizen
* ✻ **Appearance:** Hazy yellow
* ✻ **Alcohol** 5%
* ✻ **Serving temp:** 4–7°C

▬ Utenos Porteris

Using water from a 207-metre deep well in the Aukštaitija National Park in Lithuania, the Utenos brewery is one of the largest in the Baltic States. With more than 100 million litres of beer brewed every year, it also brews on behalf of other breweries around Scandinavia. Its own products are as good as anything you'll try from the region and this porter is no exception. No lightweight at 6.8% ABV, it pours a lovely deep red with a bubbly beige head. More refreshing than you'd imagine for such a dark, viscous beer.

Tasting notes: Notes of sweetened coffee, liquorice and a little chocolate with a very dry finish – almost like an Irish stout.
* ✻ **Country:** Lithuania
* ✻ **Brewer:** Utenos
* ✻ **Style:** Baltic porter
* ✻ **Appearance:** Deep red
* ✻ **Alcohol** 6.8%
* ✻ **Serving temp:** 8–13°C

Aldaris Porteris

Now owned by Scandinavian brewing giants Carlsberg, Aldaris has been able to continue brewing this Baltic-style porter, thanks to its great popularity. The biggest brewery in Latvia, its central location in the Baltic States means Carlsberg can distribute beer with ease, so happily you're likely to find Aldaris products wherever you go.

Tasting notes: Roasted coffee, caramel and heavy brown sugar flavours. Deliciously warming in cold weather.
* **Country:** Latvia
* **Brewer:** Aldaris
* **Style:** Baltic porter
* **Appearance:** Dark brown
* **Alcohol** 6.8%
* **Serving temp:** 8–10°C

DID YOU KNOW?

Brewer Andrius Perevičius stars in a Lithuanian reality television show called 'Find the Brewer a Wife', where potential mates pull pints, shovel grain and taste-test beer to impress him.

A. Le Coq Porter

When a brewer's mission statement is to 'be the most attractive and respected' brewery in Estonia it's bound to make you sit up and take notice. Lighter than most Baltic-style porters, A. Le Coq's version is surprisingly easy drinking, with flavours of smooth caramel and some spice in the finish.

Tasting notes: Try this one with charred, barbecued belly pork with a sweet sauce.
* **Country:** Estonia
* **Brewer:** A. Le Coq
* **Style:** Baltic porter
* **Appearance:** Nut brown
* **Alcohol** 6.5%
* **Serving temp:** 8–13°C

Saku Porter

Like many beers brewed in this region, Saku Porter is designed not necessarily for refreshment but for warming you up on a chilly day – a scenario quite common in the Baltic States. Ideal served with wintery foods like stews, slow-roast game or decadent chocolate desserts, this beer fulfils all warming criteria while being utterly delicious at the same time.

Tasting notes: Slightly burnt aromas of coffee, alcohol and sugar combine to great effect. An oily texture and long boozy finish.
* **Country:** Estonia
* **Brewer:** Aldaris
* **Style:** Baltic porter
* **Appearance:** Dark brown
* **Alcohol** 6.9%
* **Serving temp:** 8–13°C

🏴 Kaltenecker Brokát 13° Dark Lager

Many beers from large breweries are pasteurized – a process that prolongs the life of beer and makes it easier to transport because of its extended shelf life. Unfortunately, even gentle pasteurization kills off much of the beer's original flavour. The Kaltenecker brewery does not pasteurize this dark lager – meaning that its flavour profile is kept to its maximum.

Tasting notes: Nutty aromas with caramel, yeast and some sugary molasses.
* **Country:** Slovakia
* **Brewer:** Pivovar Kaltenecker
* **Style:** Dunkel
* **Appearance:** Dark brown
* **Alcohol** 5%
* **Serving temp:** 8–10°C

🏴 Zlatý Bažant 12%

Distributed in the USA and Canada as 'Golden Pheasant' (its English translation), Zlatý Bažant 12% is one of the few beers that make it out of Slovakia. Don't be fooled by the 12% on the label, it actually refers to the sugar level before fermentation and eventually ends up at 5% ABV – so feel free to drink more than one.

Tasting notes: Hoppy with hints of earth, flowers and lightly toasted grains.
* **Country:** Slovakia
* **Brewer:** Heineken Slovakia
* **Style:** Pilsner
* **Appearance:** Golden
* **Alcohol** 5%
* **Serving temp:** 3–5°C

DID YOU KNOW?

Slovakia's Topvar brewery holds an annual competition to find the most beautiful waitress or bartender. The winner receives beer and appears in Topvar advertising campaigns – and has the chance to feature in the Topvar calendar.

🏴 Laško Zlatorog

Founded in 1825 by a gingerbread maker and a mead producer, the Laško brewery is named after the small town of Laško where it is located. It is now the largest in Slovenia. The Zlatorog Pilsner is its flagship product – a pale refreshing lager with easygoing sweet malts and low hop bitterness. Great served as an aperitif.

Tasting notes: Grassy hops with little bitterness balance out crackerbread malts nicely.
* **Country:** Slovenia
* **Brewer:** Pivovarna Laško
* **Style:** Pilsner
* **Appearance:** Yellow
* **Alcohol** 4.9%
* **Serving temp:** 1–2°C

SLOVAK BEER

While the Czech Republic gets plenty of plaudits for its brewing heritage, its former partner Slovakia is often sidelined. This is unfortunate as Slovak beers have plenty to recommend them, and the capital Bratislava is emerging as an alternative destination for beer tourists.

Slovak beers mainly fall into two types: *svetle* (light) or *tmave* (dark). Svetle beers tend to be bitter and hoppy. Zlatý Bažant (Golden Pheasant) is the most common svetle on draught. This golden beer is well balanced and quite refreshing. Another to search out is Urpiner Premium 12%. In 2012 it won a silver medal in the European Beer Star competition in the Bohemian pilsner category – the only Slovak beer to bring home a medal.

Tmave beers are a little sweeter, with less of an aftertaste. Urpiner Dark is another award-winner for the brewer, picking up a gold medal at the České Budějovice Beer Festival in 2012. Saris Tmave can also be found in many Slovak pubs and bars.

When it comes to choosing Slovak beers, it pays to know a bit about the labelling system. Beers are required by law to show their specific gravity in Plato units. This appears as degrees or a per cent symbol on the label. A beer of 10 degrees Plato is about 4% ABV and 12 degrees is roughly 5%.

Union Temno

This is a dark and smooth German-style *dunkel* beer with a slightly elevated sweetness. For this reason it makes a great end-of-the evening beer and pairs well with a sticky caramel or chocolate dessert. Lots of distinctive aromas and flavours come through as the beer gets a little warmer, so don't have it too cold.

Tasting notes: Liquorice, smoky bacon and chocolate in the aroma with a sweet prune and date profile.
★ **Country:** Slovenia
★ **Brewer:** Pivovarna Union
★ **Style:** Dunkel
★ **Appearance:** Black
★ **Alcohol** 5.2%
★ **Serving temp:** 8–13°C

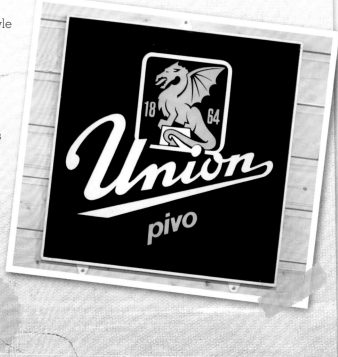

Lvivske Porter

It would be tempting to think that one Baltic porter is much the same as the next. How different can they really be from one another? The answer is Lvivske Porter. Unlike many beers in this strong, dark style, the brewers of Lvivske Porter aim for a more wine-like flavour, rather than the usual coffee/chocolate combination.

Tasting notes: Sweet, sticky caramel with a rich winey aroma. Lots of wine comes back in the finish, too.
- ✷ **Country:** Ukraine
- ✷ **Brewer:** Lvivske Pivovarnya
- ✷ **Style:** Baltic porter
- ✷ **Appearance:** Ruby
- ✷ **Alcohol** 8%
- ✷ **Serving temp:** 8–13°C

Alivaria Zolotoe

The country of Belarus is not known for its hot climate so most of the beers brewed in this region are dark, warming and hearty. On occasion the sun does come out though, and there is a need for the simple, refreshing yet bready taste of a Dortmund-style lager. Cue Alivaria Zolotoe – light, herbal and thoroughly enjoyable.

Tasting notes: A good balance of bready malts and crisp, bitter hops – neither in too high a measure.
- ✷ **Country:** Belarus
- ✷ **Brewer:** Pivzavod Alivaria
- ✷ **Style:** Helles
- ✷ **Appearance:** Light yellow
- ✷ **Alcohol** 4.8%
- ✷ **Serving temp:** 2–5°C

DID YOU KNOW?

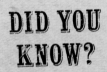

In Russia before 2011, beer containing less than 10% alcohol was categorized as food and was readily available 24 hours a day, until president Medvedev officially classified beer as alcoholic in an attempt to control alcoholism.

Krinitsa Porter

The similarities between certain beer styles can often be confusing. This is the case with Krinitsa Porter, which, despite its name, is really more of a doppelbock – a strong, dark lager. Using nearly twice the amount of malt to create extra strong flavours, the extra sugar is also responsible for ramping up the alcohol content. Whatever you want to label it, this is beer with real character.

Tasting notes: Doughy sweetness, caramel with notes of vanilla sugar and fainter notes of fruit.
- ✷ **Country:** Belarus
- ✷ **Brewer:** OAO Krinitsa
- ✷ **Style:** Doppelbock
- ✷ **Appearance:** Deep red
- ✷ **Alcohol** 8%
- ✷ **Serving temp:** 8–10°C

▬ Baltika No.4

Based in St Petersburg, Russia, the Baltika brewery is the largest in Eastern Europe. Its No. 4 *Dunkel* was first brewed in 1994 and uses maltose syrup and rye alongside other brewing ingredients, and has a fairly low hop profile.

Tasting notes: Burnt caramel, nutty and metallic flavours come through with a slightly artificial sugar taste.

- ★ **Country:** Russia
- ★ **Brewer:** Baltika Brewery
- ★ **Style:** Dunkel
- ★ **Appearance:** Dark amber
- ★ **Alcohol** 5.6%
- ★ **Serving temp:** 8–13°C

▬ Nevskoe Imperskoe

When a beer is referred to as 'imperial', it usually means strong – as in the Russian imperial stout for example. In this case, though, the 'imperial' tag is just to lend credence to the beer as a product for the noble – perhaps referring to Russia's imperialistic past! At 4.6% this pale lager might not be as imperial as beer drinkers would like it but it's a good session lager.

Tasting notes: Very light with notes of crackerbread and honey and almost no bitter aftertaste.

- ★ **Country:** Russia
- ★ **Brewer:** Baltika Brewery
- ★ **Style:** Pale lager
- ★ **Appearance:** Pale gold
- ★ **Alcohol** 4.6%
- ★ **Serving temp:** 1–2°C

▬ Siberian Crown

Marketed as a premium lager, Siberian Crown is one of the most popular pale lagers on the Russian market. First brewed in 1996, it was so successful that after only three years its producer, Omsk Brewery, was bought by SUN, part of AB InBev, the biggest brewing group in the world.

Tasting notes: Sweet grains, hints of sweetcorn and toasted white bread. One for the summertime of Russia.

- ★ **Country:** Russia
- ★ **Brewer:** SUN InBev
- ★ **Style:** Pale lager
- ★ **Appearance:** Light yellow
- ★ **Alcohol** 5%
- ★ **Serving temp:** 1–2°C

ASIA

As beer consumption has slowed in the West, beer producers have looked east for new markets as Asian drinkers have developed a thirst for beer.

China is now the biggest market for beer in the world by volume. The country is also the world's biggest brewer, producing more than 44 billion litres of beer.

This growth has led to interesting times as global brewery giants AB InBev, SAB Miller and Heineken have positioned themselves to collaborate with Asian brewers or buy up local brands in this fast-developing region.

Rough and ready traditional 'beer' made with rice or millet was first brewed in India several thousand years ago. Beer as we know it today has been around in Asia since the mid-19th century, when the colonial powers began to set up breweries to cater for the

> China is now the biggest market for beer in the world by volume; it also produces more than 44 billion litres of beer.

Europeans who had moved to the region. Prior to this, most beer had to be imported from Europe at great expense. The lengthy nature of the journey led to the development of the British India Pale Ale style. Today, pale lager is the predominant style throughout Asia, with some dark beers such as San Miguel Dark in the Philippines.

Until 1994 choice was fairly limited in Japan, because legislation prevented microbreweries being established unless they could produce two million litres a year. When this limit was dropped to just 60,000 litres, the doors opened to a group of new brewers producing local beers, known as Ji Bīru.

Among the new names that have sprung up are Hitachino Nest, an exciting range of beers produced by Kiuchi Brewery, a traditional *sake* producer. Baird Brewing is another operator that is offering Japanese drinkers an alternative to bone-dry pilsners.

Despite India's relatively low consumption of beer, brewpubs are springing up in some cities to cater for the new middle class. There are even microbreweries in China, sometimes using local ingredients such as Sichuan peppers, Chinese tea and date honey.

With a population of more than 1.3 billion, turning even a fraction of China on to different beers presents a huge opportunity.

● Asahi Super Dry

A brewery that takes its environmental responsibilities very seriously, the Asahi brewery recycles everything it uses – the waste yeast product is sent to pharmaceutical companies, and spent malt is used for cattle feed. This is the beer that kick-started a love of lager in Japan. The use of rice in the brewing mash is also something a little different and the beer's makers might tell you it results in less of a hangover the morning after. Whether that is true or not, Asahi commands more than 40 per cent of the Japanese brewing market for a good reason.

Tasting notes: As the name would suggest, incredibly dry at the end. Corn malts and bitter hops.
* ✴ **Country:** Japan
* ✴ **Brewer:** Asahi Breweries
* ✴ **Style:** Pale lager
* ✴ **Appearance:** Golden yellow
* ✴ **Alcohol** 5%
* ✴ **Serving temp:** 3–5°C

DID YOU KNOW?

A Guinness World Record for the largest aluminium can sculpture was set when a model of Yoshida Castle was constructed from 104,840 empty beer cans, in a project emphasizing the importance of recyclable materials.

● Baird Dark Sky Imperial Stout

Craft brewing has really taken off in Japan. Since its inception in 2000, Baird Brewing has been responsible for some of the country's best beer. Brewed in the tiny backroom brewery at their Numazu taproom, Dark Sky is about as serious as stout gets. Huge, hoppy flavours betray the brewery's American inspiration, while a blend of eight different malts balances the beer out.

Tasting notes: Floral and almost tropical hop aromas work well with the big chocolate and coffee flavours.
* ✴ **Country:** Japan
* ✴ **Brewer:** Baird Brewing Co.
* ✴ **Style:** Imperial stout
* ✴ **Appearance:** Dark brown
* ✴ **Alcohol** 7.6%
* ✴ **Serving temp:** 8–13°C

Echigo Pilsner

The Czech style of pilsner lager appears all over the world. With the use of Saaz hops for their floral, slightly peppery quality and an increased malt presence, Echigo Pilsner is very much true to the old style. Brewed in the Niigata region on the north-west coast of Honshu, Japan's largest island, look out for this beer in its golden can.

Tasting notes: Bready malt flavours with a pronounced hop character from the Saaz hops. Pairs well with Monterey Jack cheese.

* **Country:** Japan
* **Brewer:** Echigo Beer Co.
* **Style:** Pilsner
* **Appearance:** Clear yellow
* **Alcohol** 5%
* **Serving temp:** 3–5°C

Hitachino Nest Japanese Classic

The Hitachino Nest brand is brewed by the Kiuchi Brewery in Ibaraki, and this is its interesting take on the IPA style. Vibrant hop character is present in spades. What makes this beer really stand out, though, is its maturation process – in cedar casks commonly used in the maturation of Japanese *sake*.

Tasting notes: Lots of woody notes in the aroma combine with citrusy hops and a peppery malt profile.

* **Country:** Japan
* **Brewer:** Kiuchi Brewery
* **Style:** IPA
* **Appearance:** Amber
* **Alcohol** 7.5%
* **Serving temp:** 4–7°C

IS IT A BEER OR IS IT A BUBBLING SPIRIT?

When is beer not beer? In Japan it is not always clear. Many stores sell drinks that superficially resemble beer, but which are actually lower-priced alternatives.

These drinks, called *happōshu*, are often brewed by the same companies that make beer, but have a lower malt content. Because of this they incur less tax for the brewers and are consequently cheaper to the consumer.

To confuse things further, *happōshu* packaging makes them look very similar to beer, and they can be alcoholic, although non-alcoholic versions are also available. The difference relates to the level of malt used in the brewing process. Since 1994, in order to be called beer, brews need to be made with at least 67 per cent malt.

Happōshu, which translates as 'bubbling spirits', is brewed with as little as 25 per cent malt, with the bulk of the fermentable material being made up of soybeans, corn or peas. Some *happōshu* is marketed as a lower-calorie alternative to beer. Well-known brands include Asahi Cool Draft, Kirin Tanrei-nama and Sapporo Dosan Sozai.

A third category of 'near beer' also exists called *happousei*. This is for even lower taxed, non-malt brews made from soybeans and other ingredients that do not fit the classifications for beer or *happōshu*.

When drinking in Japan, it pays to read the small print – if you can!

● Hitachino Nest Beer Amber Ale

Brewed with a combination of two pale and two dark malts for a distinctive colour and toffee-like flavour, and two types of American hops for the fruity aroma essential in this type of beer, Hitachino Nest Amber Ale is a perfect example of the American amber style. Pairs well with a wide variety of foods but especially chargrilled meats.

Tasting notes: Plenty of toffee, caramel and spicy bitter hops in the aroma with a very similar taste on the palate.
✯ **Country:** Japan ✯ **Brewer:** Kiuchi Brewery
✯ **Style:** Amber ale ✯ **Appearance:** Amber
✯ **Alcohol** 5.5% ✯ **Serving temp:** 4–7°C

● Kirin Ichiban

The Kirin brewery is just one arm of a much larger company that has interests in restaurants, logistics, nutrition and real estate, to name but a few. Its brewing business boasts one of the most popular beers in Japan in Kirin Ichiban. This pale lager is extremely light, with almost no aftertaste or bitterness.

Tasting notes: Serve as an aperitif or as a refreshing palate cleanser between dishes.
✯ **Country:** Japan ✯ **Brewer:** Kirin Brewery Co. ✯ **Style:** Pale lager
✯ **Appearance:** Pale yellow ✯ **Alcohol** 4.9% ✯ **Serving temp:** 1–2°C

● Sapporo Premium Beer

The Sapporo brewery is perhaps most famous for brewing Space Barley, a beer made from barley that had spent five months aboard the International Space Station as part of an experiment. The resultant beer tasted no different from the flagship premium light lager – despite the hefty price tag of 10,000 yen per six pack. Thankfully, you can buy Sapporo Premium for much less.

Tasting notes: Light malt, light hops and a crisp dry aftertaste. Very refreshing alongside barbecued food.
✯ **Country:** Japan ✯ **Brewer:** Sapporo Breweries ✯ **Style:** Pale lager
✯ **Appearance:** Pale yellow ✯ **Alcohol** 4.7% ✯ **Serving temp:** 1–2°C

● Suntory The Premium Malt's

Formed in 1899, the Suntory brand is more closely associated with the whisky made famous by the 2003 film, *Lost in Translation*. The Premium Malt's beer is most commonly found in a can. As the name suggests, it has a very pronounced malty taste, which is all at once caramel, buttery and sweet. Pairs nicely with a wide range of foods.

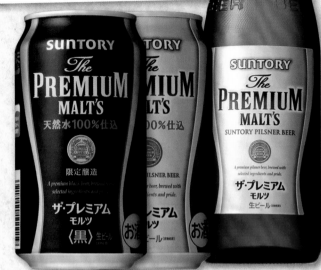

Tasting notes: Heavy on malt, toffee and caramel with a very smooth buttery texture and short dry finish.
★ **Country:** Japan ★ **Brewer:** Suntory ★ **Style:** Lager
★ **Appearance:** Golden ★ **Alcohol** 5.5% ★ **Serving temp:** 3–5°C

● Yo-Ho Tokyo Black

Up until 1994 it was illegal in Japan to brew beer unless you could produce more than two million litres per year. Once this law was relaxed, dozens of microbreweries were set up and the Yo-Ho Brewing Company was one of them. This beautifully silky black porter is one of their more popular brews, with a relatively low alcohol content and rich mahogany colour.

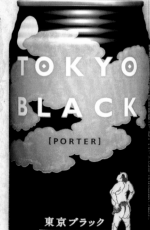

Tasting notes: Roasted malt, dried fruit and the hugely desirable chocolate/coffee combination typical of porter.
★ **Country:** Japan
★ **Brewer:** Yo-Ho Brewing Co.
★ **Style:** Porter
★ **Appearance:** Deep brown
★ **Alcohol** 5%
★ **Serving temp:** 8–13°C

● Yo-Ho Yona Yona Ale

The phrase *Yona Yona* translated from the Japanese means 'every night'. At 5.5% ABV, this American-style pale ale is not a beer that will have you on the floor after two cans, yet it packs in masses of flavour. If the sign of a great brewer is the ability to make beer flavoursome without going overboard on strength, Yo-Ho Brewing Company is surely one of the greatest.

Tasting notes: Lots of melon, pineapple and other tropical fruits in the aroma. Great with a lightly spiced Thai curry.
★ **Country:** Japan
★ **Brewer:** Yo-Ho Brewing Co.
★ **Style:** Pale ale
★ **Appearance:** Clear amber
★ **Alcohol** 5.5%
★ **Serving temp:** 4–7°C

Harbin

China is is not known as a country with a long beer-drinking history. Even the oldest brewery in the country, the Harbin Brewery, was only founded in 1900. This lager is made with Chinese-grown Qindao Dahua hops and a small quantity of rice to add extra sugar before fermentation.

Tasting notes: Lightly fruity, toasted malts and a grassy hop flavour with an easygoing bitter finish.
✴ **Country:** China ✴ **Brewer:** Harbin Brewery Co. ✴ **Style:** Pale lager
✴ **Appearance:** Yellow ✴ **Alcohol** 4.8% ✴ **Serving temp:** 3–5°C

Snow Beer

Believe it or not, the country of China brews the world's top-selling brand of beer. In 2008, Snow had an annual output of 61 million hectolitres – sold mainly in China. To put this in perspective, the combined sales of Bud Light and Bud Ice beers weighed in at just over 55 million hectolitres. Snow is jointly owned by SABMiller and China Resources Enterprises.

Tasting notes: Standard issue pale lager. Light malt, light hops and a hint of bitterness in the finish.
✴ **Country:** China
✴ **Brewer:** Snow Breweries
✴ **Style:** Pale lager
✴ **Appearance:** Yellow
✴ **Alcohol** 3.9%
✴ **Serving temp:** 1–2°C

Tsingtao

Tsingtao is bittered with domestically grown hops and uses water from the Laoshan mountain range – an area of China renowned for the purity of its water. When the brewery was founded in 1903, the beer was brewed in accordance with the German Purity Law of 1516; rice was introduced later, to cut costs.

Tasting notes: Light malt aroma with a very light malt flavour and a thin texture. Refreshing.
✴ **Country:** China
✴ **Brewer:** Tsingtao Brewery Co.
✴ **Style:** Pale lager
✴ **Appearance:** Golden
✴ **Alcohol** 4.8%
✴ **Serving temp:** 1–2°C

Wind Flower Snow and Moon

The water used in this light and refreshing beer is taken from the snowy mountaintops in Dali, Yunnan – more than 4,000 metres above sea level. The purity of the water is allowed to shine through with minimal malt flavours and a very low hop bitterness, making it extremely easy to drink, especially in hot weather.

Tasting notes: Lightly malty with faint hints of lemon zest and hops.
* **Country:** China
* **Brewer:** Dali Brewery
* **Style:** Pale lager
* **Appearance:** Pale golden
* **Alcohol** 4%
* **Serving temp:** 1–2°C

Yanjing Beer

Although relatively unknown in the west, the Beijing Yanjing Brewery is so vast that the site it sits on covers nearly two and half square kilometres (550 acres). This makes it the largest brewery in China. It produces a range of pale lagers but its main brand is Yanjing Beer, a 3.6% ABV session lager.

Tasting notes: Slightly sour, this beer has a very light all-round flavour profile with hints of potato and corn.
* **Country:** China
* **Brewer:** Beijing Yanjing Brewery
* **Style:** Pale lager
* **Appearance:** Pale straw
* **Alcohol** 3.6%
* **Serving temp:** 1–2°C

DID YOU KNOW?

The Guinness World Record for driving over beer bottles was set by army driver Li Guiwen from Beijing when he took 8 minutes and 28 seconds to steer 60.19 metres along 1,789 bottles.

Zhujiang Beer

Pronounced 'joo jung', the name translates as Pearl River beer, but in China, Zhujiang is known widely as 'the beer of the south'. It is brewed in Guangzhou in the Pearl River Delta – an area more known for the Cantonese cooking style than for brewing. However, Zhujiang is now one of the most popular beers in all of China.

Tasting notes: Faint hints of rice and corn, with a very light and refreshing texture.
* **Country:** China
* **Brewer:** Guangzhou Zhujiang Brewery Co.
* **Style:** Pale lager
* **Appearance:** Pale yellow
* **Alcohol** 5.3%
* **Serving temp:** 1–2°C

🇮🇳 Cobra

Cobra was originally brewed in India for export to the UK. It's now contract-brewed in Britain. In 1989 Karan Bilimoria thought that Britain needed a less gassy lager and he founded the Cobra Brewery. The brand is now owned by Molson Coors and brewed in Burton upon Trent.

Tasting notes: Very light in colour, aroma and taste. Works well to put out the fire started by a spicy Indian curry.
* ★ **Country:** India
* ★ **Brewer:** Molson Coors
* ★ **Style:** Pale lager
* ★ **Appearance:** Pale gold
* ★ **Alcohol** 4.8%
* ★ **Serving temp:** 1–2°C

🇮🇳 Haywards 5000

India's population has historically preferred stronger types of alcohol, such as whisky or brandy, because they are cheaper and do the job of getting you drunk a bit faster! When they do drink beer, many Indians tend to go for the stronger stuff, such as Haywards 5000 – a very malty and strongly scented beer with 7% ABV.

Tasting notes: Aromas of corn and grain with a hint of pungent hops in the background.
* ★ **Country:** India ★ **Brewer:** Shaw Wallace
* ★ **Style:** Malt liquor ★ **Appearance:** Pale gold
* ★ **Alcohol** 7% ★ **Serving temp:** 3–5°C

🇮🇳 Indus Pride Citrusy Cardamom

A smart concept from the brewing giants SABMiller saw the release of four different flavoured beers, collectively known as Indus Pride. Coming in Cardamom, Coriander, Fiery Cinnamon and Spicy Fennel, these are a real taste of Indian spices for those looking for something a little different in their beer. The cardamom is blended with the hops and added at the boil stage to impart aroma.

Tasting notes: Cardamom, green herbs and a faint trace of lemon infuse this otherwise standard lager.
* ★ **Country:** India ★ **Brewer:** Mysore Breweries / SABMiller ★ **Style:** Spiced lager
* ★ **Appearance:** Clear golden ★ **Alcohol** 5% ★ **Serving temp:** 4–7°C

🇮🇳 Kingfisher Premium

The Kingfisher brand of premium lager takes a whopping 36 per cent of the beer market in India. It is also widely available in many countries all around the world and is possibly the most famous of India's beer exports. Very hoppy for its style, the hops not only impart a great aroma but also lead to a satisfying bitter finish.

Tasting notes: A very grassy hop aroma is followed by a light malt taste with a finish dominated by the hops.

* **Country:** India
* **Brewer:** United Breweries
* **Style:** Pale lager
* **Appearance:** Clear golden
* **Alcohol** 5%
* **Serving temp:** 2–3°C

🇮🇳 Royal Challenge Premium Lager

Since its launch in 1997, Royal Challenge has quickly become the second biggest-selling beer in India, thanks largely to its loyal customer base. Some 2.5 million cases are made every year and the beer is mostly sold in the domestic market rather than to export. A simple, easygoing pale lager that works well as an aperitif.

Tasting notes: A light beer with very low malt and hop profile.

* **Country:** India
* **Brewer:** Shaw Wallace
* **Style:** Pale lager
* **Appearance:** Clear golden
* **Alcohol** 5%
* **Serving temp:** 2–3°C

▬ Bintang

Bintang, 'star beer', was made as a response to the popularity of pale lagers in other parts of the world. It is often compared to Heineken, not only because of its taste but also because the green bottle and the use of the red star as a logo are remarkably similar. Perfect refreshment in Indonesia's hot climates.

Tasting notes: Malty, toasted grain with hints of pepper and a citrus hoppy finish.

* **Country:** Indonesia
* **Brewer:** Multi Bintang
* **Style:** Pale lager
* **Appearance:** Clear yellow
* **Alcohol** 4.8%
* **Serving temp:** 2–3°C

DID YOU KNOW?

Beer-swilling Indian elephants have been rampaging through villages in the north-eastern state of Assam in search of a brew after developing a taste for *laopani*, a rice beer locally brewed and stored in underground vats.

:o: Hite Ice Point

The bestselling beer in South
Korea is, unsurprisingly, styled
upon American pale lagers such as
Budweiser and Miller. Along with
barley malt, rice is added to the
mash to reduce the amount of malt
needed, which cuts the cost to the
brewer. Rice is often used in this
way by Asian brewers, and indeed
is used to make Anheuser Busch's
Budweiser.

Tasting notes: Rice cereal, sweet malt and a
light sweetcorn aroma. The finish has a slightly
metallic edge to it.
* ✱ **Country:** South Korea
* ✱ **Brewer:** The Hite Company
* ✱ **Style:** Pale lager ✱ **Appearance:** Pale yellow
* ✱ **Alcohol** 4.5% ✱ **Serving temp:** 1–2°C

:o: Hite Max

There are only two beers in South
Korea that are brewed with 100%
malted barley – Hite's Prime
Max is one of them. This makes
Max a little more expensive
than its rivals in South Korea
but that hasn't stopped it from
becoming the third most-
popular beer in the country.

Tasting notes: Notes of brewing
cereal and slightly acidic corn
aromas are present in aroma
and taste.
* ✱ **Country:** South Korea
* ✱ **Brewer:** The Hite Company
* ✱ **Style:** Pale lager
* ✱ **Appearance:** Pale yellow
* ✱ **Alcohol** 4.5%
* ✱ **Serving temp:** 3–5°C

:o: Tiger

Tiger was the first beer to be brewed in Singapore, in 1932.
It soon became much-decorated beer, winning awards for
quality in London, Paris and Geneva. The recipe hasn't
changed much since those days and it remains the flagship
beer of the Asia Pacific Brewery. Tiger is widely available in
more than 60 countries and is very popular in the UK.

Tasting notes: Light malt, light aroma and excellent for thirst-quenching.
* ✱ **Country:** Singapore ✱ **Brewer:** Asia Pacific Breweries
* ✱ **Style:** Pale lager ✱ **Appearance:** Pale gold
* ✱ **Alcohol** 5% ✱ **Serving temp:** 3–5°C

An urban legend
relating to the
Philippines' Red Horse
beer claims that one
bottle in every case
has a 'Happy Red
Horse' logo rather
than the usual poker-
faced version, and is
stronger and sweeter
than the others.

Lion Stout

Here we have something of an anomaly in Asian brewing. A high-strength, flavoursome, dark and super-charged foreign export stout. While most of Asia's beers are brewed for refreshment and easy drinking, Lion Stout roars loudly with a combination of British, Czech and Danish malts fermented with a strain of British ale yeast.

Tasting notes: Sweet chocolate, burnt coffee and rich liquorice. Try it alongside (or in) a thick lamb stew.
* ★ **Country:** Sri Lanka
* ★ **Brewer:** Lion Brewery
* ★ **Style:** Export stout
* ★ **Appearance:** Black
* ★ **Alcohol** 8.8%
* ★ **Serving temp:** 10–13°C

San Miguel Cerveza Negra

Cerveza Negra is a full-bodied dark lager. Its colour and richness are largely down to the roasted malts used. The San Miguel brewery was founded in the Philippines in 1890; the largest beer producer in the Philippines, it has a market share of over 90 per cent.

Tasting notes: Brown caramelized sugar, brown bread and a deep overall maltiness. Very low in hops.
* ★ **Country:** Philippines
* ★ **Brewer:** San Miguel Brewery
* ★ **Style:** Dark lager
* ★ **Appearance:** Dark brown
* ★ **Alcohol** 5%
* ★ **Serving temp:** 4–7°C

San Miguel Pale Pilsen

Brewed with a combination of German and American hops, San Miguel Pale Pilsen is the Philippines' most popular beer and the company's flagship brand. Often known as San Miguel Draft or simply San Miguel Beer, it is exported to the United States as well as 40 other countries worldwide. A great beer to have ice cold alongside a stunning Philippine sunset.

Tasting notes: Sweet malt notes with hints of hop bitterness towards the end. Pairs well with barbecued meat.
* ★ **Country:** Philippines
* ★ **Brewer:** San Miguel Brewery
* ★ **Style:** Pale lager
* ★ **Appearance:** Yellow
* ★ **Alcohol** 5%
* ★ **Serving temp:** 2–3°C

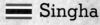 Chang

Chang is the Thai word for 'elephant' and this beer features two Asian elephants on its label, in reference to the animal's huge cultural significance in Thailand. Two versions of Chang are brewed – one at 6.4% ABV, which is made with rice to keep costs low, and one at 5% ABV, which is made with 100% malted barley for the export market. This is because the use of rice is often viewed as undesirable in western markets.

Tasting notes: Sweet molasses, malt and a softly carbonated finish. Great with spicy Thai food.
- **Country:** Thailand
- **Brewer:** ThaiBev
- **Style:** Pale lager
- **Appearance:** Yellow
- **Alcohol** 5%
- **Serving temp:** 3–5°C

Singha

Known to the western world as 'Singer', this classy-looking pale lager should actually be pronounced 'sing'. The Singha is a mythical lion, a powerful character in many old Hindu and Thai legends. Now popular in many overseas countries, Singha is also the most popular beer in Thailand – closely followed by Chang.

Tasting notes: Aromas of honey, dry grass and sweet candied lemons.
- **Country:** Thailand
- **Brewer:** Boon Rawd
- **Style:** Pale lager
- **Appearance:** Golden
- **Alcohol** 5%
- **Serving temp:** 3–5°C

DID YOU KNOW?

Thais were ahead of the 'ice in cider' trend, as it is their habit to add ice to beer. With temperatures in the 40s and beers more than 6% ABV, it's not a bad idea.

 Beerlao

Brewed with locally grown jasmine rice, with hops and yeast imported from Germany, France and Belgium, Beerlao is the most popular brand in Laos, with a market share of 99 per cent. While some of the beer is exported worldwide, most of it remains in Asia, where increased tourism is playing a massive part in its continuing success.

Tasting notes: Fragrant with notes of sticky rice, light anise and a faint toasted barley flavour.
- **Country:** Laos
- **Brewer:** The Lao Brewery Company
- **Style:** Pale lager
- **Appearance:** Pale yellow
- **Alcohol** 5%
- **Serving temp:** 1–2°C

★ Halida

The Halida brand was created in 1993, with the formation of South East Asia Brewery, a joint venture project with Danish brewing giants Carlsberg. The name was created by combining letters from Vietnam's capital city 'Hanoi', the word *'lien'* (which means joint venture) and *'Danmach'* (Denmark in Vietnamese).

Tasting notes: Light flavours of malt, corn and vegetable.
★ **Country:** Vietnam ★ **Brewer:** South East Asia Brewery ★ **Style:** Pale lager
★ **Appearance:** Light yellow ★ **Alcohol** 4.5% ★ **Serving temp:** 3–5°C

★ Huda

A beer from the original capital of Vietnam, Hué City. Hué is famous for its cuisine, with incredible spicy food being served in delicate portions. To counteract all that spicy chilli, you could do a lot worse than Huda beer. Incredibly refreshing, it's great for putting out fires in the mouth and belly!

Tasting notes: Ultra-thin texture with very light flavours of malt, corn and hops.
★ **Country:** Vietnam ★ **Brewer:** Carlsberg ★ **Style:** Pale lager
★ **Appearance:** Pale yellow ★ **Alcohol** 4.7% ★ **Serving temp:** 1–2°C

★ Angkor

Named after the capital of the ancient Khmer Empire, not far from the modern-day city of Siem Reap, Angkor beers are the most widely consumed in all of Cambodia. The beer is similar to other Asian pale lagers, with only the daintiest of bitter finishes after the initial refreshment factor of this thirst-quenching brew.

Tasting notes: Very easy to drink with almost zero hop bitterness and little aftertaste.
★ **Country:** Cambodia ★ **Brewer:** Cambrew
★ **Style:** Pale lager ★ **Appearance:** Pale yellow
★ **Alcohol** 5% ★ **Serving temp:** 1–2°C

AUSTRALASIA

Beer is the most popular drink in both Australia and New Zealand, although international attention has been focused on their successful wine industries.

Beer has been a feature of Australian life since the country was colonized by the British in the 18th century. Captain Cook brewed beer aboard his ship *Endeavour* because beer was safer to drink than water, and his crew was drinking beer in 1770 when he landed on the east coast of the country. Cook also brewed beer from spruce needles when he first visited New Zealand in 1773.

Early administrations promoted the drinking of beer, as it was considered a healthier alternative to the preferred drink of rum. The first Australian beers were top-fermented, quick-maturing ales. The first lager was brewed in 1885 in Melbourne.

The sheer size of the country, combined with the cost of transporting bulk cargoes and different local laws, led to the emergence of strong regional brands, including Coopers in South Australia, Tooheys in New South Wales and Swan in Western Australia.

Beer was considered a healthier alternative to the preferred drink of rum.

A new generation of brewers have created a thriving industry that is producing a range of exciting new beers. There are now more

than 100 craft breweries, which produce beers as varied as Little Creatures Pale Ale, Southwark Old Stout and Feral Brewing's Razorback Barley Wine.

New Zealand has undergone a similar brewing revolution in the past 20 years. Lager remains the dominant style, as befits the home of scientist Morton Coutts, who developed the continuous fermentation process that makes large-scale production possible. However, a range of flavoursome beers is now emerging from a host of small breweries and brewpubs.

New Zealand's temperate climate makes it ideal for growing barley and hops. New hop varieties have been developed, particularly in the Nelson region. Varieties such as Nelson Sauvin, Motueka and Southern Cross have become popular with boutique brewers around the world. Drinkers can taste these hops in beers from Auckland's Epic and Liberty brewers, or Wellington's Tuatara, among others. The capital city, Wellington, has branded itself New Zealand's Craft Beer Capital, and visitors can follow a beer trail that takes in bars, off licences and breweries.

Bridge Road B2 Bomber Mach 2.0

Black IPAs are the result of taking dark-roasted, chocolate malts – mostly used in stouts and porters – and hitting them with extra hops. In B2 Bomber Mach 2.0, huge amounts of malt and hops balance each other out, combined with a strong-flavoured Belgian yeast, resulting in a massive flavour hit.

Tasting notes: Big chocolate, coffee, tropical fruits and a long peppery background.
★ **Country:** Australia
★ **Brewer:** Bridge Road Brewers
★ **Style:** Black IPA ★ **Appearance:** Black
★ **Alcohol:** 8% ★ **Serving temp:** 8–12°C

Castlemaine XXXX Gold

Hugely popular in its home state of Queensland, 'fourex' was a well-known brand in the UK for many years in its canned form Castlemaine Export XXXX, until it became unavailable after InBev's licensing agreement expired. The XXXX refers to an age-old grading system for strong beers – although by today's standards, even the 4.8% export version is not particularly strong.

Tasting notes: Very light straw, corn notes and slightly sweet aftertaste.
★ **Country:** Australia
★ **Brewer:** Castlemaine Perkins
★ **Style:** Pale lager
★ **Appearance:** Pale yellow
★ **Alcohol:** 3.5% ★ **Serving temp:** 1–2°C

Coopers Original Pale Ale

Thomas Cooper brewed his first batch of beer in 1862 as a remedy for his sick wife. Since then, five generations of his family have carried on the business. Currently, Dr Tim Cooper and electronics entrepreneur Glenn Cooper are at the helm. This is a bottle-fermented pale ale, brewed in the style of the old English pale ales from Burton upon Trent. The yeast left in the bottle can be added to the decanted beer to taste.

Tasting notes: Citrus fruits, sweet malts and smooth, soft carbonation. Great with a burger and very refreshing.
★ **Country:** Australia ★ **Brewer:** Coopers Brewery ★ **Style:** Pale ale
★ **Appearance:** Cloudy yellow ★ **Alcohol:** 4.5% ★ **Serving temp:** 6–10°C

Crown Lager

Known affectionately as 'Crownie' in Queensland, this is one of the most popular beers in Australia. It was originally brewed in 1919, although it is widely believed that it was released to mark the visit of Queen Elizabeth II in 1954. Another familiar pale lager designed for the mass market.

Tasting notes: Very light, sweet malts with an easygoing flavour.
★ **Country:** Australia
★ **Brewer:** Carlton & United Breweries
★ **Style:** Pale lager ★ **Appearance:** Pale yellow
★ **Alcohol:** 4.9% ★ **Serving temp:** 1–2°C

DID YOU KNOW?

Aussies know exactly what makes a great leader. Former prime minister Bob Hawke features in the Guinness World Records for drinking 2.5 pints of beer in 11 seconds, thus securing the beer community's vote!

THE SIX O'CLOCK SWILL

Enjoying a beer in Australia hasn't always been the laid-back exercise it is these days. In the early part of the 20th century the temperance movement in Australia and New Zealand was particularly strong. As was the case in other countries, it campaigned against the evils of drinking.

During World War I the aims of the movement briefly dovetailed with those of the nation, and various Australian states brought in shortened opening hours for licensed premises, with pubs closing at six o'clock. The idea was to help the war effort while still allowing working men to walk to a bar and enjoy a quiet beer before driving safely home.

The reality was that the move encouraged the infamous 'six o'clock swill', as workers attempted to drink as much as they possibly could before closing time. Bars sometimes served beer from a tapped hosepipe as they sought to keep up with demand, and drinking venues were rowdy and hostile to women.

This remained the state of affairs for decades. New South Wales extended licensing hours in 1955, but New Zealand and some Australian states retained them until 1967.

Today's Australian bars are a world away from the beer barns of the past. The surroundings are more salubrious, women are welcome, food is paired with great beer, and the customers are better behaved. Most importantly, you can take your time now.

In fact, the concept of the Aussie bar is now as well-travelled as that of the Irish pub, and you can find Aussie bars in cities from Sydney to Seattle.

Fat Yak Pale Ale

Fat Yak is an American-style pale ale with all the hops you could want plus a quaffable alcohol content to make it both easy on the palate and one to drink for a session rather than swirl around the glass and pontificate over.

Tasting notes: Smooth and easy to drink, with a huge beige head and a balance of citrus hop and caramel.
* ★ **Country:** Australia ★ **Brewer:** Matilda Bay Brewing Co.
* ★ **Style:** American pale ale ★ **Appearance:** Amber
* ★ **Alcohol:** 4.7% ★ **Serving temp:** 4–7°C

Feral Hop Hog

American-style India Pale Ale, heavily dosed with Yakima Valley hops and with a secondary dry-hopping during fermentation, this beer has a resinous pine aroma and mouth-puckering bitterness. For hopheads only but, at only 5.8% ABV, one they can drink all evening.

Tasting notes: Very strong acidic and pine notes on the palate, with a long, dry bitter finish.
* ★ **Country:** Australia
* ★ **Brewer:** Feral Brewing Co.
* ★ **Style:** American IPA
* ★ **Appearance:** Cloudy orange
* ★ **Alcohol:** 5.8%
* ★ **Serving temp:** 4–7°C

Foster's Lager

Ostensibly an Australian favourite, you'd be hard pressed to find any in Australia – the 'amber nectar' has not been advertised since the early 2000s. Foster's is brewed in the UK and is popular because of its low price and easy-drinking nature; it is the UK's second most popular lager.

Tasting notes: A very light flavour profile with just a small hint of malt and very little bitterness. Drink ice-cold.
* ★ **Country:** Australia
* ★ **Brewer:** Heineken
* ★ **Style:** Pale lager
* ★ **Appearance:** Pale yellow
* ★ **Alcohol:** 4%
* ★ **Serving temp:** 1–2°C

DID YOU KNOW?

More land in Australia is devoted to pubs than to mines, even though mining accounts for 15 per cent of Australian GDP. Pubs were often the first buildings on the goldfields and new towns grew around them.

🇦🇺 Grand Ridge Moonshine

Named after the shady bathtub booze made famous in the 1920s in Prohibition America, Grand Ridge's Moonshine is classified by its brewers as a dessert beer owing to its high alcohol content and sweet, dark, fruity flavours. Almost like a sticky plum pudding in a bottle. Stylistically, it's known as a Scotch ale, a style that originated in Edinburgh in the 19th century. A perfect end-of-the-evening beer and one you'll need to sip slowly and savour to get the intended effect.

Tasting notes: Fresh, crisp, with a mellow but floral hoppy aftertaste. Good with strong cheese or a fruity, boozy dessert like Christmas pudding.
* ★ **Country:** Australia ★ **Brewer:** Grand Ridge Brewery
* ★ **Style:** Scotch ale ★ **Appearance:** Dark brown
* ★ **Alcohol:** 8.5% ★ **Serving temp:** 10–14°C

🇦🇺 James Boag's Premium Lager

Brewed in Tasmania, James Boag is a premium lager made with a long maturation, as all lager should be. Crisp, slightly lemony and very refreshing, it has a lot more to offer in the taste department than many other pale lagers.

Tasting notes: Toasted bread, lemon peel and a very soft smooth finish. Very good to drink on a hot day.
* ★ **Country:** Australia
* ★ **Brewer:** J. Boag & Son
* ★ **Style:** Pale lager
* ★ **Appearance:** Pale yellow
* ★ **Alcohol:** 5%
* ★ **Serving temp:** 3–6°C

🇦🇺 James Squire The Chancer Golden Ale

Born in England in 1754, James Squire was transported to Australia where he was, according to local legend, the first person to cultivate hops. The Malt Shovel Brewery named a brand of beer in his honour and this British-style golden ale was one of the first beers off the line. Made with a combination of malted wheat, barley and Amarillo hops for a smooth, fruity flavour.

Tasting notes: Fresh, crisp with a mellow but floral hoppy aftertaste.
* ★ **Country:** Australia
* ★ **Brewer:** Malt Shovel Brewery
* ★ **Style:** Golden ale
* ★ **Appearance:** Pale yellow
* ★ **Alcohol:** 4.5% ★ **Serving temp:** 4–7°C

Little Creatures Pale Ale

Described by many as American-style pale ale, but its clever balance between malt sweetness and hop bitterness is more akin to the styles of beer originally brewed in Burton upon Trent in the UK when the first hoppy pale ales had to make the long voyage to India and their hoppiness diminished as they matured. The result is a more rounded drink that's easy on the taste buds. This new Aussie classic is laced with locally grown whole cone (rather than the easier to control pellet form) Galaxy hops and American Cascade hops and is bottle-conditioned.

Tasting notes: Fresh, crisp with a mellow but floral hoppy aftertaste.
★ **Country:** Australia ★ **Brewer:** Little Creatures Brewing ★ **Style:** Pale ale
★ **Appearance:** Clear orange ★ **Alcohol:** 5.2% ★ **Serving temp:** 4–7°C

Murray's Wild Thing Imperial Stout

Stouts don't come much more exciting than this. Pouring a pitch black with a thick tan head, at 10% ABV you'll detect some rum-like alcohol in the aroma as well as rich dark chocolate. Only 1,100 bottles of this were brewed, so if you find one, then save it for a rainy day: this beer ages as well as any fine wine.

Tasting notes: Chocolate, rum, coffee. Try it with vanilla ice cream or a warm chocolate brownie. Or both.
★ **Country:** Australia ★ **Brewer:** Murray's Craft Brewing Co.
★ **Style:** Imperial stout ★ **Appearance:** Black
★ **Alcohol:** 10% ★ **Serving temp:** 12–15°C

Southwark Old Stout

Imperial 'Russian' stouts were first brewed in London for export to the cold climes of Russia. They are thick, strong, and glass-staining rich enough to warm the blood of the Tsar. Southwark Old Stout was voted champion stout at the 2001 Australian International Beer Awards, having also been voted best beer in 1988 and 1991.

Tasting notes: Dark roast coffee, light liquorice and a smooth, silky chocolate finish.
★ **Country:** Australia
★ **Brewer:** South Australian Brewing
★ **Style:** Imperial stout
★ **Appearance:** Dark brown
★ **Alcohol:** 7.4%
★ **Serving temp:** 12–15°C

🇦🇺 Redoak Organic Pale Ale

A beer influenced by the British pale ales first brewed in Burton upon Trent in the 19th century. This beer is made using only organically grown malts and hops, and a select strain of London ale yeast for a distinctively fruity taste. A superbly balanced homage to pale ales in their most traditional form.

Tasting notes: Soft stone fruits, sweet toffee malts and a nice bitterness in the finish. Great with roast chicken or British-style fish and chips.
★ **Country:** Australia
★ **Brewer:** Redoak Boutique Beer Cafe
★ **Style:** Pale ale
★ **Appearance:** Clear golden
★ **Alcohol:** 4.5%
★ **Serving temp:** 7–10°C

🇦🇺 Tooheys New

Irish immigrant John Thomas Toohey began running pubs with his brother in the late 1860s. Their first beer was Tooheys Black Old Ale. Their company went public in 1902 and they began brewing what was then known as Tooheys Lager in 1930. Today it's called Tooheys New and is still one of the country's most popular pale lagers.

Tasting notes: Lightly hoppy with hints of pale malt.
★ **Country:** Australia ★ **Brewer:** Tooheys
★ **Style:** Pale lager ★ **Appearance:** Clear yellow
★ **Alcohol:** 4.6% ★ **Serving temp:** 2–4°C

🇦🇺 VB

Victoria Bitter (VB) is not a bitter at all, but a pale lager. Often touted as a working man's reward, VB is sold in variously sized cans and bottles, such as 'tinnies', 'stubbies', 'tallies', or 'twisties'. A 1-litre can known as a 'killer' made a brief appearance. The bestselling beer in Australia before XXXX Gold took the lead in 2012.

Tasting notes: Toasted light malt aromas with a sweet and light bitter taste.
★ **Country:** Australia ★ **Brewer:** Carlton & United Breweries
★ **Style:** Pale lager ★ **Appearance:** Medium orange
★ **Alcohol:** 4.6% ★ **Serving temp:** 2–4°C

NEW ZEALAND HOPS

Hops are essential to the flavouring process in brewing and different varieties have their own unique properties. New Zealand is increasingly recognized as a source of fine hops.

Not only is the climate ideal for hop production, with long days and abundant rain, but the country's geographical location and biosecurity policy makes pests and diseases less of a problem than in other hop-producing countries. Many hops are grown organically, making them ideal for the increasing numbers of organic beers. The world's largest organic hop garden is located at Tapawera in the Nelson region of South Island.

New Zealand has developed new types of hops to make different flavours and aromas available to brewers. Producers such as NZ Hops have moved away from high alpha acid hops, which produce more bitterness, and developed speciality varieties such as Nelson Sauvin, which was released in 2000. Its aroma of crushed gooseberries is reminiscent of a New Zealand sauvignon blanc wine and the hop has gained widespread use across Australia and New Zealand. It is a dual-purpose hop which can be used to impart bitterness and aroma.

New Zealand has been selling hops in the international marketplace for many years. Marston's in the UK is one of the breweries that has used the hops. Its 2013 Single Hop cask ales included Pacific Gem and Wakatu varieties. Hawkshead, BrewDog and Thornbridge have also followed suit.

New Zealand hops have come a long way, in more ways than one.

🇳🇿 8 Wired
Saison Sauvin

First brewed in the farmhouses of France and Belgium, *saisons* were meant to be refreshing and safe to drink (water often wasn't) and were often well hopped. *Saison* beers can now be made with sackfuls of Nelson Sauvin hops. Earthy, pungent but very refreshing, this is definitely a beer worth savouring on a hot day.

Tasting notes: Cooked vegetables, earth, black pepper and citrus fruits. So versatile you can drink it with pretty much anything you like.
* ★ **Country:** New Zealand
* ★ **Brewer:** 8 Wired Brewing Co.
* ★ **Style:** Saison
* ★ **Appearance:** Hazy yellow
* ★ **Alcohol:** 7%
* ★ **Serving temp:** 4–7°C

Emerson's Pilsner

This is a full-bodied and extremely palatable beer. Pilsner is a type of hoppy pale lager first developed in Bohemia using pale pilsner malt and fresh Saaz hops. The addition of locally grown fruity Riwaka hops – noted for their similarity to fruity sauvignon blanc grapes – makes this a true New Zealand pilsner.

Tasting notes: Toasted malt, bread and tropical hop flavours. Drink with barbecue meat or creamy cheese such as Brie.
★ **Country:** New Zealand
★ **Brewer:** Emerson's Brewing Co.
★ **Style:** Pilsner
★ **Appearance:** Golden
★ **Alcohol:** 4.9%
★ **Serving temp:** 5–7°C

Epic Mayhem IPA

According to its brewery, Epic Mayhem sets out 'to wilfully maim and cripple the palate of the most extreme hop head'. Lots of fresh whole cone hops are added to the fermentation tank as the beer is maturing – a process called dry hopping – resulting in an aromatic beer in the modern style of India Pale Ales as pioneered by American brewers.

Tasting notes: Ripe citrus, orange and grapefruit, with a strong malty body in the background. Great with anything spicy.
★ **Country:** New Zealand
★ **Brewer:** Epic Brewing Co.
★ **Style:** IPA
★ **Appearance:** Cloudy amber
★ **Alcohol:** 6.2%
★ **Serving temp:** 7–10°C

DID YOU KNOW?

The annual Great Kiwi Beer Festival celebrates New Zealand's brewing world. Held at Hagley Park, Christchurch, in 2013 it covered 35,000 square metres: that's the equivalent of five football fields!

Hopsmacker Pale Ale

A New World style pale ale, typical in its use of aromatic hops, this beer combines New Zealand-grown Riwaka hops and the more spicy, grapefruit flavour of fresh American Cascade hops. The combination makes for a citrus flavour you'll definitely remember.

Tasting notes: Spicy pine resin in the nose and a nice amount of grapefruit, lychee and elderflower on the palate. Great with spicy dishes.
★ **Country:** New Zealand
★ **Brewer:** Bach Brewing Co.
★ **Style:** Pale ale
★ **Appearance:** Clear amber
★ **Alcohol:** 5.8%
★ **Serving temp:** 4–7°C

Liberty Citra

Liberty's Citra is a lesson in how Citra hops are supposed to taste. This is a double IPA, meaning that almost twice the usual amount of malt is used, which releases extra sugars, and accounts for its 9% ABV. To balance this out a mountain of Citra hops are added, followed by a second dry hopping to complete this masterclass.

Tasting notes: Dusty lemon aroma, sweet caramel malt base followed by a tropical fruit hoppy flavour explosion.
* ★ **Country:** New Zealand
* ★ **Brewer:** Liberty Brewing Co.
* ★ **Style:** Double IPA
* ★ **Appearance:** Clear gold
* ★ **Alcohol:** 9%
* ★ **Serving temp:** 8–13℃

Lion Red

Produced by brewing giant Lion, this is a 4% ABV session lager and a favourite among university students. In the mid-1980s, the brewery officially changed the name to Lion Red. Its amber colour, derived from the malts, relates it to the Vienna lagers created in the 1840s.

Tasting notes: A very malt-forward lager, rich in caramel sweetness as well as a definite bitterness in the finish.
* ★ **Country:** New Zealand
* ★ **Brewer:** Lion Breweries
* ★ **Style:** Vienna lager
* ★ **Appearance:** Amber
* ★ **Alcohol:** 4%
* ★ **Serving temp:** 4–7℃

McCashin's Stoke Bomber Smoky Ale

The flavour of this beer comes from smoke used when drying the malt. McCashin's version isn't nearly as smoky as its German ancestors, which makes it a great entry-level smoked beer for those who aren't quite sold on the idea.

Tasting notes: Peaty, beechwood smoke, floral hops and a long, lingering finish. Great with any smoked meat or fish.
* ★ **Country:** New Zealand
* ★ **Brewer:** McCashin's Family Brewery
* ★ **Style:** Smoked beer
* ★ **Appearance:** Golden
* ★ **Alcohol:** 5.7%
* ★ **Serving temp:** 7–11℃

Mike's IPA

Allegedly inspired by English pale ales of the past, this 9% ABV double IPA has far more in common with the supercharged, highly hopped versions of IPA pioneered by American craft brewers. All the usual tropical fruit flavours you'd expect from very hoppy pale ale, with a fiery hop kick in the aftertaste.

Tasting notes: Passionfruit, lychee and pineapple balanced with a toffee malt base and a long, dry, eye-watering bitterness in the finish.
* ★ **Country:** New Zealand ★ **Brewer:** Mike's Brewery ★ **Style:** Double IPA
* ★ **Appearance:** Gold/amber ★ **Alcohol:** 9% ★ **Serving temp:** 8–13℃

Moa Blanc

Moa Blanc is New Zealand's homage to the Belgian *witbier* style originally brought back to life by Pierre Celis in the late 1960s in the small village of Hoegaarden. But it has plenty in common with German wheat beer, too. Made with a blend of 50% wheat and 50% barley, a good dose of sediment remains in the bottom of the bottle to give its signature cloudy appearance. With banana, bubble gum and citrus in the nose, this is a refreshing summery beer.

Tasting notes: Banana, coriander and citrus followed by a smooth wheaty finish. Great with fish and Chinese dishes.
★ **Country:** New Zealand ★ **Brewer:** Moa Brewing Co.
★ **Style:** Witbier ★ **Appearance:** Hazy gold
★ **Alcohol:** 5.5% ★ **Serving temp:** 3–5°C

Monteith's Golden Lager

Although it uses a Munich malt, renowned for bringing extra depth of flavour and a deep amber colour, Monteith's Golden Lager is really best categorized as a pale lager, with a nutty richness and warm gold colour.

Tasting notes: Cashew nuts, sticky toffee, with only a hint of hoppy bitterness. Perfect with barbecue fodder.
★ **Country:** New Zealand
★ **Brewer:** Monteith's Brewing Co.
★ **Style:** Pale lager
★ **Appearance:** Clear gold
★ **Alcohol:** 5%
★ **Serving temp:** 3–5°C

DID YOU KNOW?

'Ice brewed beers' are popular in New Zealand: the beer is chilled until the water freezes but the alcohol, with a lower freezing point, doesn't – so after removing the ice you get a more alcoholic beer.

Pink Elephant
Imperious Rushin Stowt

A real heavy-hitting beer. Roger Pink started his brewery back in 1990, at a time when microbrewing in New Zealand had barely begun to take off. Since then, Mr Pink has become one of the most decorated brewers in New Zealand, with a string of awards to his name. Using malts and grains from around the world, a variety of carefully cultivated yeasts and exclusive New Zealand hops, Pink Elephant is a brewery that knows its stuff. Need proof? Just taste this 11% ABV Russian-style flavour bomb! Thick, black and teeming with chocolate, liquorice, vanilla and a hint of anise, it's one of the most memorable beers in the world.

Tasting notes: Heavy chocolate, liquorice and vanilla with overtones of rich coffee. Perfect with a vanilla ice cream sundae.
★ **Country:** New Zealand ★ **Brewer:** Pink Elephant Brewery
★ **Style:** Imperial stout ★ **Appearance:** Black
★ **Alcohol:** 11% ★ **Serving temp:** 10–14°C

Renaissance
Elemental Porter

Located in a region of Marlborough more famous for its sauvignon blanc grapes than for its craft brewing, Renaissance prides itself on making beer for the sophisticated palate. This is one of New Zealand's highest rated beers, unusual for a porter, but no surprise when you taste the beautiful balance of chocolatey malts and crisp hops.

Tasting notes: Rich and full-bodied with a long roasty malt flavour and crisp hoppy finish. Drink with barbecue meats, coffee-based desserts and blue cheese.
★ **Country:** New Zealand
★ **Brewer:** Renaissance Brewing Co.
★ **Style:** Porter ★ **Appearance:** Dark brown
★ **Alcohol:** 6% ★ **Serving temp:** 8–12°C

DID YOU KNOW?

In 1770 Captain James Cook brewed the first beer in New Zealand as a cure for scurvy aboard his ship. He used the needles of an indigenous spruce tree 'with the addition of inspissated juice of wort' and molasses.

🇳🇿 Speight's 5 Malt Old Dark

As the name suggests, Speight's 5 Malt Old Dark is made with a blend of five different malts: lager, caramalt, crystal, chocolate and roasted. This old-school porter develops a creamy texture as well as the flavour of a coffee fudge sundae.

Tasting notes: Coffee, raisin, chocolate and caramel. Try it with a thick, warming meat stew.
* ★ **Country:** New Zealand
* ★ **Brewer:** Speight's Brewery
* ★ **Style:** Porter
* ★ **Appearance:** Dark red
* ★ **Alcohol:** 4%
* ★ **Serving temp:** 8–13°C

🇳🇿 Steinlager Classic

First brewed in 1957, Steinlager Classic is without doubt New Zealand's biggest export, mainly to the US, which embraced the pale lager style wholeheartedly with beers like Budweiser and Miller Light. Steinlager Classic tastes crisp, clean, hoppy and refreshing.

Tasting notes: Light corn, fresh hop and mild citrus make for a very easygoing flavour you could drink all day.
* ★ **Country:** New Zealand
* ★ **Brewer:** Lion
* ★ **Style:** Pale lager
* ★ **Appearance:** Pale yellow
* ★ **Alcohol:** 5%
* ★ **Serving temp:** 2–5°C

🇳🇿 Tuatara APA

This American-style pale ale has been through two incarnations, and since 2012 it uses homegrown hops due to a short supply of American produce. This is a smartly made beer from a slickly marketed brewery – pronounced 'Too-Ah-Tah-Rah' – one that is fast becoming one of the most popular and trendy brands in the country.

Tasting notes: Biscuit malts, grapefruit aromas and big pine resin flavour. Classic with a hot dog or a burger.
* ★ **Country:** New Zealand
* ★ **Brewer:** Tuatara Brewing Co.
* ★ **Style:** American pale ale
* ★ **Appearance:** Cloudy yellow
* ★ **Alcohol:** 5.8%
* ★ **Serving temp:** 4–7°C

🇳🇿 Yeastie Boys Digital IPA

The Yeastie Boys have created this Digital IPA that is screaming with hoppy flavour from a blend of New Zealand's hop varieties and it's no surprise it won a gold medal from the Brewers Guild of New Zealand in 2012. The epitome of a modern, well-made and exciting hoppy pale ale.

Tasting notes: Passion fruit, lychee and caramel. Perfect with spicy barbecues and Indian curry.
* ★ **Country:** New Zealand
* ★ **Brewer:** Yeastie Boys
* ★ **Style:** IPA
* ★ **Appearance:** Medium orange
* ★ **Alcohol:** 7%
* ★ **Serving temp:** 4–7°C

AFRICA

Africa is one of the smaller markets for beer in the world, accounting for only 6.6% of production in 2012.

However that relatively small figure disguises huge growth of 11.3% from 2011, the 12th consecutive year of increase.

It is little wonder that brewers see Africa as something of a new frontier. It isn't that Africans don't drink beer, more often it's a case that they can't afford western-style clear beer.

Africa's thirst for beer is most commonly slaked by resorting to local homebrew. This rough and ready beer is estimated to make up to four times the size of the bought beer market. Brewers hope that as more Africans achieve affluence they will trade up to more commercial options.

Brewing in South Africa dates back to 1658, when the first Dutch governor, Jan van Riebeeck, established a brewery at the Fort of Good Hope.

Multinational brewing companies such as SAB Miller adopt a portfolio approach in which they produce beers that are more affordable for poorer Africans. The most obvious example of this is sorghum beer,

a commercialized version of homebrew. SAB Miller has also launched an initiative to halve the price of beer by using ingredients cheaper than malt, such as cassava and sorghum.

Brewing in South Africa dates back to 1658, when the first Dutch governor, Jan van Riebeeck, established a brewery at the Fort of Good Hope. Brewing gradually spread through the Cape and South African Breweries (SAB) came into being in 1895 (as Castle Breweries), serving thirsty miners and prospectors. Although lager is the most popular drink in this hot continent, it doesn't have it all its own way. Stouts, such as Guinness Export, have an enthusiastic customer base. Guinness brewer Diageo sells more Guinness in Nigeria than anywhere else in the world, including Ireland.

Inevitably, Africa also has its own emerging craft beer scene, mostly focused on South Africa. Breweries like Jack Black's, Darling Brew and Boston Breweries are bringing some much-needed variety into the beer sector in South Africa.

🇿🇦 Boston Breweries
Black River Coffee Stout

The Boston brewery is situated in the heart of Cape Town and is one of the craft beer landmarks of the city. Its tasting room at the Cape Quarter has become legendary, both as a place to drink beer from Boston Breweries and as one of the few places you'll find this Black River Coffee Stout on tap. Made with Ethiopian Yirgacheffe coffee extract.

Tasting notes: Big coffee, toffee and smaller hints of chocolate and brown sugar. A great way to wake up!
✴ **Country:** South Africa ✴ **Brewer:** Boston Breweries ✴ **Style:** Coffee stout
✴ **Appearance:** Pitch black ✴ **Alcohol:** 6% ✴ **Serving temp:** 8–13°C

SORGHUM BEER

Africans started brewing beer thousands of years ago and you can get a pretty good idea of what those early beers were like in many African states.

Beer brewed from sorghum or millet, and known as *chibuku* or 'shake shake', is still a big part of local life at many social or religious occasions. The beer was originally brewed by village women for local consumption and goes under various names, *dolo* in Burkina Faso, *pito* in Nigeria, *bili bili* in Cameroon, and *merissa* in Sudan.

These days it is more likely to be produced on an industrial scale, with big players such as SABMiller or South Africa's United National Breweries getting in on the action.

The beer itself bears little resemblance to the clear beers we are familiar with in the West. It is cloudy and more like a soup or porridge. It is also live (like yogurt) in the carton it is served in. When it leaves the brewery the alcohol content is about 2% ABV, but with a few days of fermentation it is up to 5% ABV. The taste changes from what some describe as 'lemony' to increasingly bitter, and after five days it is undrinkable.

This is changing, however, as SABMiller has introduced a pasteurized version, Chibuku Super. This has a shelf life of closer to 21 days, opening up the market for this new take on African homebrew.

🇿🇦 Castle Lager

Castle Lager is drunk almost everywhere in South Africa. It was first brewed in 1895 and uses both barley and maize (corn) in the brewing process, adding a corn-like taste and sweetness. Serve this one ice cold to enjoy the crisp, dry and lightly acidic finish at its best.

Tasting notes: Light grains, canned sweetcorn and mild floral hops. One to have in the fridge in times of thirst.
* **Country:** South Africa ✸ **Brewer:** South African Breweries
* **Style:** Pale lager ✸ **Appearance:** Light yellow
* **Alcohol:** 5% ✸ **Serving temp:** 1–2°C

🇿🇦 Devil's Peak The King's Blockhouse IPA

Here is a brewer that combines the best from modern American brewing with the traditional approach of Belgium to create beers with depth, character and flavour. Devil's Peak is looking to educate South Africa in how truly great beer can be and it is starting right here with this hop-charged American-style IPA. The King's Blockhouse is a perfect match for any spicy curries from Thailand, India or indeed South Africa thanks to its highly hopped bitterness and strong citrus flavours that cut through spice with ease.

Tasting notes: Lychee, passionfruit and general citrus fruits are balanced nicely with bitterness and biscuit malts.
* **Country:** South Africa
* **Brewer:** Devil's Peak Brewing Co.
* **Style:** IPA ✸ **Appearance:** Bronze
* **Alcohol:** 6% ✸ **Serving temp:** 4–7°C

🇿🇦 Hansa Pilsener

Proudly proclaimed as 'the kiss of the Saaz hop', Hansa uses the traditional Czech hop to add its bitterness and light aroma. Originally launched in 1975, drinkers did not immediately appreciate this refreshingly different alternative to the sweeter pale lagers they were used to. However, a shift in drinking trends saw this light pilsner become one of the most popular beers in all of South Africa.

Tasting notes: Very light bitterness, pale corn-like malts and a dry refreshing finish.
* **Country:** South Africa
* **Brewer:** South African Breweries
* **Style:** Pilsner
* **Appearance:** Yellow
* **Alcohol:** 4.5%
* **Serving temp:** 1–2°C

🏴 Primus Bière

Not to be confused with the Belgian Pilsner-style lager named Primus for the Duke of Brabant, Jan Primus. This Primus Bière is brewed in the capital city of Burundi, Bujumbura, in Central Africa.

Tasting notes: White bread, floury with a little touch of mint. A very refreshing lager.
* **Country:** Burundi
* **Brewer:** Brarudi
* **Style:** Pale lager
* **Appearance:** Clear gold
* **Alcohol:** 5%
* **Serving temp:** 2–5°C

DID YOU KNOW?

The average African drinks only eight litres of commercially produced beer per year – they prefer their own brews of sorghum, millet or pretty much anything fermentable, in a strong homebrewing tradition dating back thousands of years.

🏴 Mützig

Named after a French town in the historically contested province of Alsace, Mützig is brewed in three African states: Rwanda, Cameroon and the Democratic Republic of Congo. Mützig is still brewed in northern France, but it has been embraced in Africa to a far greater extent, in both its 5.5% and its 6.9% ABV versions.

Tasting notes: Malted grain with notes of sweetcorn, dusty hops and a light bitter finish.
* **Country:** Democratic Republic of Congo
* **Brewer:** Bralima Brewery
* **Style:** Pale lager
* **Appearance:** Pale gold
* **Alcohol:** 5.5%
* **Serving temp:** 2–5°C

🏴 Laurentina Preta

Translating from the Portuguese as 'Laurentina Black' owing to its distinctive colour, this is one of the most acclaimed beers on the continent. Well balanced with dark roasted-malt flavours, bready undertones and a lasting sweet coffee finish, it's a very well-made example of the dunkel style and one that can put many original dark lagers to shame.

Tasting notes: Pairs nicely with rich, smoky enchiladas.
* **Country:** Mozambique ★ **Brewer:** Cervejas De Moçambique
* **Style:** Dunkel ★ **Appearance:** Dark brown
* **Alcohol:** 5% ★ **Serving temp:** 8–10°C

Nile Special

The Nile Brewery could not be situated in a more picturesque location on the banks of the Nile river as it flows out of Lake Victoria. Using water tapped directly from north-eastern Africa's primary water source, the brewer produces more beer than anyone else in Uganda. Its flagship brand, Nile Special, is the most popular of the range.

Tasting notes: Balanced but very light in flavour with caramel, hop bitterness and a slight hint of fruit.
* **Country:** Uganda
* **Brewer:** Nile Breweries
* **Style:** Pale lager
* **Appearance:** Pale yellow
* **Alcohol:** 5.6%
* **Serving temp:** 3–5°C

Mosi Lager

The Mosi-oa-Tunya National Park in Zambia is the iconic location that gives this pale lager its name. 'The Smoke that Thunders' is the literal translation, referring to the raging torrent of Victoria Falls – the largest waterfall in the world. Mosi Lager is as recognizable as the falls, being by far the bestselling lager in Zambia.

Tasting notes: A long-lasting creamy white head tops grassy aromas and dry corn flavours.
* **Country:** Zambia
* **Brewer:** Zambian Breweries
* **Style:** Pale lager
* **Appearance:** Clear yellow
* **Alcohol:** 4%
* **Serving temp:** 3–5°C

Trophy Black Lager

The best-known beer brand in Nigeria is Trophy, a classic pale lager brewed by International Breweries. Their black lager is a little different: it uses darker malts with corn and other local grains to produce something closer to the German strong lagers, or bocks. A refreshing change from the usual lagers brewed in much of Africa.

Tasting notes: Light caramel, burnt coffee and a bready finish. Great with barbecued meat and game.
* **Country:** Nigeria * **Brewer:** International Breweries
* **Style:** Dark lager * **Appearance:** Black
* **Alcohol:** 5% * **Serving temp:** 3–5°C

GLOSSARY OF TERMS

Abbey beers – generic term for beers produced by Trappist monks, beers brewed at other monasteries, or beers that are brewed in the style of these beers.

ABV – alcohol by volume; a measure of the alcoholic portion of the total volume of liquid, determined during brewing by the use of a hydrometer.

Ale – ale is produced by top-fermenting yeasts at warmer temperatures, namely around 40° to 5–13°C. Types include amber, pale, Belgian blonde, golden, brown, mild.

Alpha acids – the chemical component of hops that determine the bitterness of the beer.

Altbier – German traditional ale. *Alt* means 'old', and an Altbier uses an old style of brewing, and is identified with the Rhineland, especially Düsseldorf.

Barley wine – a style dating from the 18th and 19th centuries, created for English patriots to drink in preference to French claret at a time when the two countries were often at war. A strong brew which is stored for many months.

Bière de garde – meaning 'beer for keeping', originates from the French/Belgian farmhouse ale brewing tradition of the late 19th century, centred in the Flanders region. Beers were brewed in the winter months for the summer farm workers to be paid with.

Bitter – originally real ale, served fresh at cellar temperatures under no pressure. Now refers to a type of pale ale.

Bock – a type of German strong lager with a relatively high alcohol content (more than 6.25% ABV), malty with low hops bitterness, and often dark in colour. *Bock* means 'goat' in German. Types include helles bock, doppelbock and eisbock.

Bottom-fermented – the use at low temperatures of yeasts in the brew – which sink to the bottom of the tank and thus have minimal contact with the air outside – produces lagers and pilsners.

Bottle conditioning – a secondary fermentation process where yeast is allowed to carbonate the beer naturally in the bottle.

Brewpub – a brewery that sells 25% or more of its beer on site, often directly from its storage tanks, brewing it primarily for sale in the restaurant or bar.

Cask conditioned ale – ale which is fermented and carbonated naturally in the cask from which it is served, with no additional treatments. Often known as 'real ale'.

Champagne beer – a delicate, highly alcoholic and highly carbonated style of beer, primarily brewed in Belgium with a lengthy maturation period. Some are cave-aged in the Champagne region of France and then undergo the remuage and dégorgement process whereby the yeast is removed from the bottle.

Continually hopped – the practice of adding hops at regular intervals throughout the boil process.

Craft brewery – small, independent brewery, using traditional ingredients (see *Microbrewery*).

Doppel – German for 'double'.

Dry-hopping – the process where hops are added to the fermentation tank as the beer is maturing as well as during the boil process, where the oils may be lost.

Dubbel, tripel and quadrupel (single, double, triple and quadruple) – the system of brewing strengths established by the Trappist monks.

Export – beers with a reputation for being superior since the expense of exportation requires a higher price tag. Stronger beers traditionally survived long sea journeys better, thus 'export' became a term for higher-strength brews.

Fermentation – the process whereby yeast consumes the sugars in the wort, producing alcohol and CO_2 as waste; the CO_2 is lost during this process.

Gateway beer – a beer which is drunk as an introduction to other types of craft beers.

Gravity – the relative density of wort at various stages during brewing. Usually expressed with the Plato scale.

Growlers – reusable beer transportation device, such as a large glass jug; originally even a bucket would have been used.

Hefeweizen – see *Wheat beer*.

Ice brewed beers – a process where beer is chilled until the water freezes but the alcohol, with a lower freezing point, doesn't – after removing the ice you get a more alcoholic beer.

IBU – International Bitterness Unit. The international standard for measuring the amount of bitterness in a beer. A highly-hopped beer such as an IPA will often have a higher IBU, while a stout or a light beer will usually have a low rating.

Imperial – style of pilsner or stout. Originally referred to a distinctive type of beer brewed in the 1800s in England for export to Imperial Russia. Now used to indicate a big and bold type of beer with double or even triple quantities of hops and malts, and a high alcohol content.

IPA – India Pale Ale. A style of beer originating in the UK and sold for export. A higher hop content in these beers helped preserve them for the long journey to India.

Keg – Keg beers are served cold; they are brewery conditioned and undergo only the primary fermentation, they are then cold stabilised in the brewery and then pasteurised or sterile filtered; they therefore have no yeast and have gas added.

Kilning – the final stage of the malting process, where the malt is heated with hot air to stop its growth and give it stability. The time and temperature variation produces pale or darker malts.

Kölsch – a local speciality beer from Cologne, Germany, defined by an agreement of the Cologne Brewery Association known as the Kölsch Konvention. Kölsch is warm-fermented and then lagered, a style which links it to the Altbiers of western Germany.

Kriek – a style of lambic beer from Belgium, using sour Morello cherries to ferment the beer. Traditionally the 'Schaarbeekse krieken' style of cherry is used, from where the beer gets its name.

Lager – a lager is produced by bottom-fermenting yeasts at cooler temperatures, namely around 0–7°C. Types include pale, helles, dark/dunkel, Vienna, Dortmund.

Lagering – storing at low temperatures, from the German word *lager* meaning 'storeroom'.

Lambic – a dry, sour beer created through spontaneous fermentation. No yeast is added and the beer is exposed to natural ambient yeasts.

Malt liquor – a North American term for high alcohol beers (not less than 5% ABV) made with malted barley. In practice the term refers to beer made with inexpensive ingredients, eg corn, rice, dextrose, very little hops and a special enzyme to give greater alcohol content.

Märzen/Oktoberfestbier – before the days of refrigeration *Märzen*, or 'March' beer was brewed in the spring and kept in cold storage to be ready for consumption in the autumn. In October the brewers needed to empty their Märzen kegs before brewing again in the cooler months, hence the tradition of Oktoberfest began.

Mashing-in – the stage where the malt is cracked by being run through a malt mill. This eases the release of the sugars which are converted from starch in the malt as it is mixed with hot water.

Mash tun – the vessel used for mashing-in.

Microbrewery – defined as a craft beer brewery producing less than 17,600 hectolitres of beer each year with 75% or more of its beer sold off-site.

Mild – see *Ale*.

Mouthfeel – a tasting term, used to describe beer in terms not covered by taste and smell, for example body, texture and carbonation.

Pilsner – also known as pilsener or pils. A type of pale lager taking its name from the Czech Republic city of Pilsen where it was first brewed in 1842, using the Bavarian techniques of brewing. Types include German, Czech and European.

Plato rating – a scale of measuring the specific gravity of beer in degrees (denoted as eg 10P, 15P), common in central and eastern Europe.

Porter – an 18th century London style, named for its popularity among London's street-market workers. A strong dark brown beer made from a blend of brown, pale and 'stale' or well-matured ales. The dark colour comes from the use of dark malts (unlike stouts which use roasted malted barley). A stronger version Baltic Porter was made for export across the North Sea to support Baltic trade.

Saison – a complex fruity Belgian farmhouse-style pale ale traditionally brewed in the winter for summer consumption; until recently this was described as an 'endangered' style although there has now been a revival, especially in the US.

Schwarzbier – 'black beer' in German, usually means very dark lager.

Secondary fermentation – the process whereby the fermentation in the beer is restarted, usually in a different vessel from the initial fermentation.

Session beer – mild, easygoing beer with alcoholic content of usually less than 4% so that several can be consumed over an evening.

Sour ale – this phrase covers non-traditional sour ales which are typically brewed with an ale yeast and then inoculated with souring bacteria and yeasts to produce a tart and unusual taste.

Stout – traditionally the generic term for the strongest porters. See *Porter*. Types include dry, milk, oatmeal, oyster, coffee, imperial, Russian.

Top-fermenting – ale yeasts are top-fermenting as they work at the top of the fermentation vessel at higher temperatures than lager yeast.

Wheat beer – beer with a large proportion of wheat as well as malted barley, usually top-fermented, creating a light, summery beer. Types include weissbier (including hefeweizen, dunkelweizen, weizenbock), witbier, and sour varieties such as lambic, Berliner Weisse and gose.

Witbier – see *Wheat beer*.

Wort – unfermented beer, i.e. the liquid produced by mashing the grains, containing the sugars which will turn to alcohol during fermentation.

INDEX OF BEERS

We would like thank all the featured breweries for supplying the bulk of the photographs used in this book and in particular Joanna Dring at Carlsberg, Alycia Macaskill at SABMiller, David Jones at Heineken, Oliver Bartelt at AB InBev, Ulf Trolle, Henrietta Drane and Maggie Ramsay for going the extra mile.